Stress Mastery

Stress Mastery

The Art of Coping Gracefully

JUAN R. ABASCAL, Ph.D.

Associate Dean
School of Natural and Social Sciences
Miami-Dade Community College
MindWorks, Int., Inc.

DOMINIC BRUCATO, Ph.D.

Assistant Professor
Psychology Department
Miami-Dade Community College
MindWorks, Int., Inc.

LAUREL BRUCATO, Ph.D.

Adjunct Professor
Miami-Date Community College
MindWorks, Int., Inc.

Job Skills NetEffect Series

Prentice
Hall

Upper Saddle River, NJ 07458

Library of Congress Cataloging-in-Publication Data

Abascal, Juan R.
  Stress mastery : the art of coping gracefully / Juan R. Abascal, Dominic Brucato, Laurel Brucato
    p. cm.
  Includes index.
  ISBN 0-13-634727-4
  1. Stress management.   I. Brucato, Dominic.   II. Brucato, Laurel.   III. Title.
  RA785 .A23 2001
  155.9′042—dc21

                                                                                    00-061973

Executive Editor: Elizabeth Sugg
Production Editor: Linda Zuk
Production Liaison: Eileen O'Sullivan
Director of Manufacturing and Production: Bruce Johnson
Managing Editor: Mary Carnis
Manufacuring Buyer: Ed O'Dougherty
Art Director: Marianne Frasco
Cover Design Coordinator: Miguel Ortiz
Cover Design: Lafortezza Design Group
Cover Illustration: Tom White
Editorial Assistant: Anita Rhodes
Composition: BookMasters, Inc.
Printing and Binding: R. R. Donnelley & Sons., Inc.

Prentice-Hall International (UK) Limited, *London*
Prentice-Hall of Australia Pty. Limited, *Sydney*
Prentice-Hall Canada Inc., *Toronto*
Prentice-Hall Hispanoamericana, S.A., *Mexico*
Prentice-Hall of India Private Limited, *New Delhi*
Prentice-Hall of Japan, Inc., *Tokyo*
Prentice-Hall Singapore Pte. Ltd.
Editora Prentice-Hall do Brasil, Ltda., *Rio de Janeiro*

Prentice
Hall

10 9 8 7 6 5 4 3 2 1
ISBN 0-13-634727-4

Contents

Preface

The idea for this book grew out of the numerous stress mastery seminars and workshops we have conducted with executives, employees, students, faculty, police officers, health professionals—people from all walks of life. The participants in our workshops often requested written materials to accompany our presentations and encouraged us to provide all materials within one volume. Initially, we created a short pamphlet entitled "A Manual for Less Stress." After constantly revising and adding to this work, it became clear that what was really needed was a complete yet succinct volume incorporating all of the relevant materials. This fact was further reinforced by the participation of one of the authors in the DACUM (Developing a Curriculum) process at Miami–Dade Community College and in multiple focus groups conducted with college and university professors, representatives from business and industry, students, and alumni. Again and again they reiterated the need for students to be able to handle the multitude of stresses they would face as they entered the workforce. They emphasized the need for coursework to address issues of coping with stress and to teach skills to maximize effectiveness on the job and elsewhere.

We have attempted to engage learners directly. To accomplish this end, our book is written in a rather unconventional style for a textbook: conversational rather than didactic, peppered with jokes and amusing anecdotes. Since most of the material in this book was derived from the information we present in our stress mastery seminars, we have endeavored to make the book read as if it is being presented or delivered to each learner personally—to literally encourage the reader to engage in a dialogue with the book.

Involve yourself with the exercises, techniques, and suggestions included in this book. The value of this book is in the doing, not simply in reading and/or memorizing facts. We have found that keeping a stress mastery journal provides an excellent foundation for processing the lessons and techniques presented in these chapters.

The Master Strategy summaries at the end of each section are much more than study guides, although they will serve that purpose quite well. They are shorthand cookbooks or recipes for coping with stress. Refer to them often, both for review and in preparation for dealing with life's vicissitudes.

Finally, we encourage you to have fun with this book. The book was designed to be humorous to reinforce the fact that humor is one of the great stress reducers. We hope you find yourself coping gracefully with the challenges of life, and that our book is of assistance in that process.

Acknowledgments

We would like to thank all of our students and the participants in our stress mastery workshops and seminars for their encouragement, feedback, and willingness to share their histories and personal experiences on the road to becoming masters of stress.

We offer our gratitude to the professors who reviewed this book for Prentice Hall for their invaluable suggestions and insights for improving this work. And we offer special thanks to Barbara Abascal and Kathy Stanton for their willingness to take the time to read our many drafts and offer constructive criticism and feedback from the lay perspective. Finally, many thank-you's to Libby Perez and Sandy Dowdee for helping to keep us organized and on task as we coped with the stress of writing this book.

Section 1

Understanding Stress

Introduction

What You Will Learn in this Chapter

- To compare and contrast the differences between *stress mastery* and *stress management*.

- To adopt the strategies for using this book effectively.

Welcome! We're pleased you have chosen to read this book. No doubt, the reasons behind your choice differ with each of you. To make the most out of this book, we suggest you take a moment to think about what motivated you to pick it up. Why are you reading it? Even if your initial response is that it was required for a course, think: Is there something else you want to get, other than a good grade, from reading this book? If you were able to change something as a result of your experience with this book, what would that be? What would be different about you? How would you look, feel, and act differently? Take a moment now to think about these questions.

There is a story about a group of scientists who were walking along the country-side when they saw a field of fruit-bearing trees. A local inhabitant told them that the fruit was called a *mango* by the natives of this land. This kind of fruit was unknown to the scientists, and they wanted to learn all they could about it. Half of the scientists went into one side of the field and began measuring the mangoes' weight and their size. They noted the color and the shape and recorded their findings. These scientists now *knew about* mangoes. The other half of the scientists went into the field, and each took down a mango from a tree and tasted it. These scientists *knew* mangoes.

Did you do what we suggested in the first paragraph? Did you take a moment to think about what you wanted to get from using this book? If you did, you are like the scientists who ate the mangoes. Continue tasting what we have to offer and we promise that you will notice a significant positive difference in your life and in your capacity for stress mastery. But if you didn't, your tendency might be to read this book much like the scientists who measured and weighed the mangoes. With that approach, this book might provide you with some interesting facts and general knowledge, but it is doubtful that it would create any significant changes in your life. The material discussed in this book will work for you only if you use it—only if you *do it*. Merely knowing about it is not enough. So if you have not considered the questions posed earlier, we invite you to go back and think about what you want to get, how you want to be different, and notice the results *after* you've tasted the mangoes. This way, you will not just know a lot *about* stress mastery when you are done. Instead, you will know *how* to master stress.

A Changing Marketplace

Knowing how to master stress has clearly become increasingly important in today's marketplace. To quote Bob Dylan, one of the premier songwriters and poets of the 1960s and 1970s, "The times they are a-changin'." Just a generation ago it was reasonable for young people to assume that if they were responsible, dependable, and loyal to a company, the company would take care of them. They could expect to rise through the ranks to a management position and this would be their lifelong occupation. Now, in the era of downsizing, a company will employ you only for as long as you, or your position, are useful to it. And usefulness is typically defined in terms of the bottom line: Are you profitable?

On the other hand, rather than expecting perpetual loyalty, it is understood that you will stay with the company only for as long as it meets your needs in terms of salary, working conditions, and other fringe benefits. Those of you who follow sports might remember a time not so long ago when a player was drafted and stayed with that team throughout his playing years. This was, of course, changed by the advent of free agency. Now a player goes to the highest bidder or to the city that might afford him better business opportunities or living conditions. Well, the fact is that we are all now becoming free agents. In his 1996 State of the Union address to Congress, President Clinton stated that in the changing marketplace all Americans should consider themselves entrepreneurs who are clearly selling a product: themselves.

Nor is the notion of picking one single career that lasts your lifetime considered the norm any more. Most people change careers, not just jobs, four to five times during their lifetime. This is primarily because we have left the Industrial Age and have entered the Information Age. It is staggering to consider that the information we are each exposed to in one year is the same as our grandparents were exposed to over their entire lifetimes! Change is occurring at increasing speed. In order to succeed in the Information Age, you need to be flexible and able to adapt to new situations and changing conditions. The ability to master your stress allows you to cope gracefully with novelty and be aware of and ready to take advantage of opportunities as they present themselves.

Stress Mastery versus Stress Management

You may have noticed that we have called our book *Stress Mastery* rather than using the more common term, *stress management.* This is not just a semantic difference. We really see a difference between the ability to achieve mastery over stress and the ability to merely manage your stress. The key is not just *surviving* stress, but *thriving from* stress. The term *stress management* is suggestive of "one more thing to do." As if you didn't have enough things to do already! Stress mastery is more a part of the fabric of your life. It is not *work,* not *another thing to do.* It is a *craft.* It is a way of taking the raw material of the stresses of life and creating a reality in which you can live. With the passage of time, your craft improves. It does not take time away from your schedule. It actually adds time to your life. Often people see stress management as having to do specific exercises to lower stress. But stress mastery is really about cultivating wisdom. It is not mechanical or rote. It is becoming increasingly aware of your situations and, perhaps even more so, of your reactions to these situations. The

Table 1.1 Stress Management versus Stress Mastery

Stress Management	Stress Mastery
One more "thing" to do	Part of the fabric of your life
Work	Craft
Takes time	Adds time
Do exercises	Cultivate wisdom, increase awareness
Mechanical	Organic

truth is, life is not always a calm sea of tranquility. Life throws waves at you, and these waves do not appear to be of your choosing. You do have a choice, though, of how you ride these waves. Do you choose to surf them gracefully, making use of the opportunities presented, or do you choose to go under, feeling as if you can't breathe and might drown at any moment? Stress mastery is organic. It changes and it is flexible while always remaining consistent with certain core skills and habits. Stress mastery is planting a garden that is enriched year after year. Stress management is opening another can of worms.

A Three-Week Commitment

The core skills and habits presented in the following chapters form the foundation on which stress mastery is based. They are absolutely necessary if you are to be able to cope gracefully with the demands placed on you by life. To acquire them will require an initial investment of time and focus. We ask that for the next three weeks, you dedicate yourself to stress mastery training. There are only two requirements to do this. The first is that you commit fifteen minutes a day to practice, so that you may learn to quiet your body. The second is that you commit to remember that you are in training as you go about your daily routines. These are your three weeks of stress mastery training! Make thinking about and applying what you read a priority during this time. We promise that you will ultimately gain time as a result of the increased energy and improved concentration you will experience. As you learn to master your stress, other priorities in your life will become clearer. You might find that not only are you climbing the ladder of success, but also that you know for sure that the ladder is against the right wall. As a result, the quality of your time will improve.

In order to support your efforts in achieving these outcomes, we strongly suggest that you write a journal about your experiences. While daily journal writing is certainly commendable, two entries per week for three weeks will suffice. The act of writing down your experiences and reflecting on them is an exquisite vehicle for remaining conscious and aware of all their different aspects. This in turn allows you to remember the many choices you have when confronting any situation.

The Mechanics of Reading this Book

We suggest that you follow a set of specific steps as you read this book. First, make sure to study the table of contents to get an overview of the terrain you will be covering. Spending a little time wondering about the different concepts and ideas you will encounter will ready you to make use of them. Surveying material before you read it has been found to be an effective means of really learning it. An appropriate analogy is that of a computer. Imagine you save new data to the hard drive without using directories or subdirectories. After a short time, although the information is stored in your computer, you can no longer find it! There is so much disorganized data that it's hard to find what you are looking for. Our memory works much the same. When you survey data to be learned, it is as if you are creating a directory in which the data will be organized to facilitate retrieval of the information. For the same reason, it is important that prior to each section, you contemplate the brief outline for that section.

Something else we know about learning is that reviewing what you have just learned is a powerful way to ensure that the neural pathway to the information is active and open. To use another analogy, think of your memory as a dense forest where your thoughts reside. When you review the information, you ensure that the path through the forest remains clear. For this reason, we strongly suggest that you review the chapter summaries and the master strategy outlines. These sections recapitulate the Master Strategy you are working toward. They outline a series of steps that, if practiced, will surely lead toward stress mastery.

This book is organized to present you with a framework for understanding how stress affects your life and your functioning, combined with teaching you a wide variety of physiological and cognitive strategies for coping with stress in the workplace and in your life in general. You will learn how to control your breathing and level of muscular tension as a way of calming yourself. You will learn the characteristics of individuals who are *stress hardy* (that is, resistant to stress) and how to adopt those qualities for yourself. You will be exposed to ways of interpreting situations that decrease stress, and you will learn how to counteract anger and upset by modifying your thoughts. You will be educated about how diet and exercise affect your stress level and your ability to cope. Assumptions that heighten workplace stress will be reviewed, along with ways to substitute healthier strategies. If procrastination or poor time management plagues you, this book offers effective guidelines for meaningful behavioral change. You will also learn about high-tech tools for coping with stress and how to use them in your daily life. You will be familiarized with a helpful framework for asserting yourself successfully. And this book will help you put all of these perspectives and tools together into a coherent strategy.

Remember, Don't Just Read the Book—Taste It

One of our favorite sayings from the Sufi masters is, "We eat at all tables that serve good food." We invite you to eat at our table and sample the different dishes we have to offer. Resist the temptation to decide you don't like any particular one until you try it. Taste them first and notice the results. Others before you have discovered that learning the skills of stress mastery has made a powerful impact on their ability to succeed and thrive in both their work and personal life. We suggest you give yourself a chance to do the same.

Are you willing to take this on? Take a moment to decide. If you are, and willingly do the things that we suggest, we guarantee that you will notice a significant positive difference in your life as you learn and apply the art of coping gracefully. The first step is to begin noticing the rhythm of your body as expressed through your breathing. But before you begin, let's take a look at this thing called stress and how it can play such havoc with your life.

Chapter Summary

Learn how to master stress, not just manage it. The key is not just to survive stress, but to thrive from it. We offer you many strategies and techniques, which we urge you to experience and not just learn about. Remember: taste the mangoes. We further ask you for a three-week commitment to this process. If you make this commitment to really try out and practice the techniques and strategies presented in this book, we guarantee that you will notice a significant positive difference in your life.

All About Stress

What You Will Learn in this Chapter

- To define stress.

- To discriminate between *eustress* and *distress*.

- To describe the effects of stress on physical, psychological, and occupational functioning.

- To understand the relationship between stress and illness.

- To assess your own level of stress with the Life Readjustment Scale.

- To recognize the fight-or-flight reaction.

- To list the symptoms and signs of fight-or-flight activation.

- To describe the General Adaptation Syndrome (GAS).

- To understand the mind–body connection.

- To identify how the mind–body connection relates to placebo effects.

Stress Defined

What is stress? When we ask students, employees, employers, and workshop participants this question, they typically respond that it is tension, nervousness, headaches, having deadlines to meet, and so on. Basically what we hear is a list outlining the effects of stress, or specific causes of stress. The official definition of stress is anything that requires an adaptive response on the part of the organism. But what does that mean? It means that anything that requires you to respond, to make a change or an adjustment, is stressful. So when people say they want to get rid of stress, the reality is that this is impossible. That is not to say that you cannot reduce the amount of change or responsibilities you have in your life. Indeed, this is at times recommended as a way of minimizing your stress level. But we want you to understand that even if you hid out on a mountaintop in order to escape the rat race, you would probably eventually get bored—and boredom itself is stressful. The fact is that stress is an inescapable part of modern life.

That is not necessarily as bad as it may sound. One of the best-known experts on stress, a Canadian scientist named Hans Selye, was once quoted as saying that *"stress is the spice of life."* Just as spice can make your food tasteful and come alive, stress can give your life meaning and excitement. This depends, of course, on the amount and type of spice you use. We all know that the wrong spice, or too much spice, can make you sick to your stomach (with a possible visit to the porcelain throne). Selye (1956) differentiates between these two types of stress, referring to positive stress as *eustress* and negative stress as *distress*. So stress is not all bad. In fact, in one study adult volunteers who were placed in a completely stress-free environment (a sightless, soundless, weightless, motionless liquid heated to body temperature) soon began to manifest disturbances of mood, thought, and action. Most asked to be quickly released. We all need an optimal level of change and stress in our life to keep things interesting—and that level varies from person to person.

Given the pejorative connotations given to stress, it is easy to forget that an appropriate level of stress in your life is often helpful. Stress can help motivate you to perform and meet the challenges you will face (Selye, 1974). The physiological and psychological aspects of the arousal produced by stress can be useful, and unless you are routinely overloaded and aroused, stress may not necessarily harm you (Kobasa, 1982). It may surprise you to find out that you need an optimal level of stress and arousal in order to perform at your best. This fact was established many years ago by pioneering psychologists Yerkes and Dodson (1908), who demonstrated that performance on a given task improves as physiological arousal increases until some optimal point, after which performance declines as arousal continues to climb. This optimal level of arousal varies with the type of task. The more complex the task for an individual, the less arousal can be tolerated before performance suffers. In everyday terms, when you are totally cool, calm, and collected in a performance situation, you may not have the requisite motivation or edge necessary to perform at your best. If, on the other hand, you are panic-stricken or a nervous wreck, your high arousal will interfere with your performance. Many tasks are best performed with moderate levels of arousal. This relationship, known as the

Yerkes-Dodson Law, is useful to remember next time you have to speak before a group, or are in any type of performance situation. There is a misconception that you should be "cool as a cucumber." This is not necessarily true, for you will actually perform better if you are moderately aroused (that is, stressed). What does this have to do with stress mastery? If you are underaroused, you will experience the stress of boredom; if overaroused, you will experience anxiety. If you can find your optimal level, where you are stimulated and performing at your best, you can experience satisfaction and master stress.

Stress and Illness

Do you believe that stress can make you sick? If you are like most people, you would answer with a resounding "YES!" When we ask people this question in our workshops and classes, all of them believe that stress can affect their emotional well-being, and the majority realize that it can lead to physical illness. Unless you have been living off the planet for the last few years, you have had some exposure to the fact that stress can and does have deleterious effects. However, had we asked this question just twenty-five or thirty years ago of people in general or even a group of health professionals, the majority would probably have denied the relationship between stress and our health. Back then we were just emerging from the era of infectious diseases, when we believed that illnesses were caused by exposure to germs and bacteria, and that the way to keep healthy was to create vaccines and medicines to combat these external agents. At that time, to have considered the notion that stress could lead to illness would have been avant-garde thinking.

Then Thomas Holmes, M.D., a professor at the University of Washington School of Medicine, began doing research on the effect of changes (that is, stress) on our physical and emotional well-being. Together with Richard Rahe, Dr. Holmes developed a questionnaire measuring life changes and set out to study whether there was a relationship between the number, seriousness, and pervasiveness of changes, and our frequency of illness (Holmes & Rahe, 1967). Using army personnel, because they were a captive audience and their progress could be followed easily, Holmes and Rahe demonstrated that the questionnaire could help them predict with remarkable accuracy those soldiers who would get ill within the next two years and those who would remain healthy. We suggest that you complete and score the Holmes-Rahe Life Readjustment Scale to determine your own level of stress as measured by this inventory.

But the Holmes-Rahe questionnaire has a major flaw. Do you know what it is? It fails to take into account individual differences in our abilities to cope with the changes and demands of our lives. In the years since the Holmes-Rahe scale was developed, a number of other inventories have been designed attempting to measure a variety of factors associated with stress. One that we have found particularly useful is the computerized *Brief Stress Inventory*, which pinpoints your particular sources of stress and the current effects these are having in your life. In addition, it identifies your present resources for dealing with stress, along with specific suggestions for enhancing your ability to cope.

Holmes-Rahe Life Readjustment Scale

Part A

Instructions: Think back on each possible life event listed, and decide whether it happened to you within the last year. If the event did happen, place a checkmark in the first column.

	Check Here If Event Happened to You	Mean Value (Use for Scoring Later)
1. A lot more or a lot less trouble with your boss	_____	_____
2. A major change in sleeping habits (sleeping a lot more or a lot less, or change in part of day when asleep)	_____	_____
3. A major change in eating habits (a lot more or a lot less food intake, or very different meal hours or surroundings)	_____	_____
4. A revision of personal habits (dress, manners, associations, etc.)	_____	_____
5. Major change in your social activities (clubs, dancing, movies, visiting, etc.)	_____	_____
6. A major change in your usual type and/or amount of recreation	_____	_____
7. A major change in church activities (a lot more or a lot less than usual)	_____	_____
8. A major change in number of family get-togethers	_____	_____
9. A major change in financial state (for better or worse)	_____	_____
10. In-law troubles	_____	_____
11. A major change in number of arguments with your spouse	_____	_____
12. Sexual difficulties	_____	_____

Part B

Instructions: In the first column, indicate the number of times that each applicable event happened to you within the last two years.

	Number of Times	Mean Value	Your Score
13. Major personal injury or illness	_____	_____	_____
14. Death of close family member (other than spouse)	_____	_____	_____
15. Death of a spouse	_____	_____	_____
16. Death of a close friend	_____	_____	_____
17. Gaining a new family member (through birth, adoption, oldster moving in, etc.)	_____	_____	_____
18. Major change in the health or behavior of a family member	_____	_____	_____
19. Change in residence	_____	_____	_____
20. Detention in jail or other institution	_____	_____	_____
21. Minor violations of the law (traffic tickets, jaywalking, disturbing the peace, etc.)	_____	_____	_____
22. Major business readjustment (merger, reorganization, bankruptcy, etc.)	_____	_____	_____
23. Marriage	_____	_____	_____
24. Divorce	_____	_____	_____
25. Marital separation from spouse	_____	_____	_____
26. Outstanding personal achievement	_____	_____	_____
27. Son or daughter leaving home (marriage, attending college, etc.)	_____	_____	_____
28. Retirement from work	_____	_____	_____

29. Major change in working
    hours or conditions _____ _____ _____

30. Major change in responsi-
    bilities at work (promotion,
    demotion, lateral transfer) _____ _____ _____

31. Being fired from work _____ _____ _____

32. Major change in living
    conditions (building a new
    home, remodeling, deteriora-
    tion of home or neighborhood) _____ _____ _____

33. Spouse beginning or ceasing
    work outside the home _____ _____ _____

34. Taking on a mortgage or loan
    of less than $25,000 (purchas-
    ing a home, business, etc.) _____ _____ _____

35. Taking on a mortgage or loan
    of more than $ 25,000 (making a
    large purchase) _____ _____ _____

36. Foreclosure on a mortgage or
    loan _____ _____ _____

37. Vacation _____ _____ _____

38. Changing to a new school _____ _____ _____

39. Changing to a different line
    of work _____ _____ _____

40. Beginning or ceasing formal
    schooling _____ _____ _____

41. Marital reconciliation with
    mate _____ _____ _____

42. Pregnancy _____ _____ _____

       YOUR TOTAL SCORE _____ _____ _____

Scoring

The "mean values" for each life event are listed. Go back to Part A and Part B and write in the mean values for those events that happened to you. For items in Part B, multiply the mean value by the number of times an event happened, and enter the result in the "Your Score" column. Add up the mean values in Part A and the scores in Part B to get your total score.

Life Event	Mean Value	Life Event	Mean Value
1	23	22	39
2	16	23	50
3	15	24	73
4	24	25	65
5	19	26	28
6	18	27	29
7	19	28	45
8	15	29	20
9	38	30	29
10	29	31	47
11	35	32	25
12	39	33	26
13	53	34	31
14	63	35	17
15	100	36	30
16	37	37	13
17	39	38	20
18	44	39	36
19	20	40	26
20	63	41	45
21	11	42	40

Interpreting Your Results

The more change you have, the more likely you are to get sick. Of those people with a score of over 300 for the past year, almost 80 percent get sick in the near future; of those with a score of 200 to 299, about 50 percent get sick in the near future; and of those with a score of 150 to 199, only about 30 percent get sick in the near future. A score of less than 150 indicates that you have a low chance of getting sick. So the higher your score, the harder you should work to stay well. Stress can be cumulative. Events from two years ago many still be affecting you now. If you think this applies to you, repeat this test for the events of the preceding year and compare your scores.

Negative Effects of Stress

So what are the negative effects of stress? What can happen when stress overloads your coping resources, when your skills are inadequate to deal with the demands placed on you by circumstances? Stress negatively affects your physical, psychological, and occupational functioning in a variety of ways.

Physical Consequences

The relationship between stress and your health is neither simple nor straightforward. Stress will not automatically cause you to become physically ill. The impact of stress on your health is mediated by a variety of personality variables (which we will address in later chapters), as well as your genetic makeup and environment. But physically, it is clear that when you are under prolonged stress your immune system can be weakened, creating vulnerability to illness and bodily system breakdown. Recent research has revealed that chronic high levels of stress hormones, known as glucocorticoids, cause white blood cells to migrate to the bone marrow and hide out, making them less available for combating disease. This appears to be one specific mechanism by which chronic stress weakens immune functioning, leading to an increased susceptibility to diseases, including cancer. Furthermore, stress can create a wide assortment of psychosomatic problems in which the weakest link in your system of organs, muscles, and glands is affected. For some individuals the heart is affected, for others the stomach or the pancreas; thus, some develop heart disease, others ulcers or diabetes. The following list illustrates some of these problems:

- Eighty percent of all visits to doctors' offices are for stress-related disorders.
- At least 50 percent of all deaths in the United States are caused by cardiovascular diseases such as heart disease and stroke, in which stress plays a significant contributing role.
- Most heart attacks occur around 9:00 A.M. on Monday mornings.

- Severe stress is one of the most potent risk factors for stroke—even more so than hypertension—even fifty years after the initial trauma. A study of over five hundred World War II veterans found that the rate of stroke was eight times higher for those who were POWs.

- Hypertension (high blood pressure), a stress-related disorder, afflicts at least 30 million people in the United States, with some estimates going as high as 80 million.

- Cholesterol levels in the bloodstream rise during periods of stress.

- One of the top gastrointestinal specialists in the United States reports that 90 percent of all people with chronic diarrhea (irritable bowel syndrome or colitis) have no organic basis for their condition.

- Ulcers, spastic colon, and similar gastrointestinal disorders are the direct result of elevated acidity brought on by the stress hormone cortisol.

- There are fifty to one hundred million headache sufferers in the United States. Headache is the number one complaint seen by physicians in this country, and 80 percent of all headaches are tension headaches. Migraines compose 18 percent of headaches, but even these (despite the genetic predisposition) are often triggered by stress and tension.

- Fifty million Americans suffer from chronic pain, and lower back pain accounts for 50 percent of this total. Negative emotions and stress can aggravate pain and cause acute pain to develop into chronic pain. The stress hormone ACTH can impede endorphin production (endorphins are the body's natural painkillers), leading to increased pain and discomfort.

- Recent research indicates that stress plays a significant role in the development of osteoporosis in women due to increased levels of stress hormones.

- Dentists report that a high percentage of patients show signs of nocturnal bruxism (tooth grinding at night).

- Stress is implicated in rheumatoid arthritis. The hormone prolactin, released by the pituitary gland in response to stress, triggers joint swelling.

- Studies reveal that during college exam week, students possess lower levels of salivary immunoglobulin, a defense against respiratory infections. Studies also report that students' acne worsens when they are under stress.

Psychological Consequences

It is not surprising that stress is a key factor in the development of emotional difficulties and behavioral problems. Can you remember a time when you felt there were too many demands placed on you? What was that like for you? Did it affect your ability to relax and enjoy life? Stress clearly influences our psychological well-being in a host of different ways:

- Stress is a major factor in the development of anxiety, phobias, panic attacks, depression, PTSD (posttraumatic stress disorder), obsessions, compulsions, and all major psychiatric disorders. In 1996 it was estimated that 1.5 billion individuals worldwide were suffering from some form of psychiatric disorder, including 115 million dependent on alcohol and/or illegal drugs and 400 million suffering from anxiety disorders.

- According to the World Health Organization, depression, clearly a stress-related condition, is the number one cause of disability worldwide.

- It has been demonstrated that stress alters serotonin pathways. Imbalances in serotonin levels have been linked to depression and, in some cases, aggression.

- More than thirty million Americans suffer from insomnia. Sales of sedatives are second only to aspirin.

- An estimated twenty-four million Americans use drugs to cope with stress. The three best-selling drugs in the United States are Tagamet (for ulcers), Inderal (for hypertension), and the tranquilizer Xanax (for anxiety).

- Alcoholism is the third major cause of death in the United States. An estimated ten million Americans are alcoholic. Relief of stress and anxiety is one of the primary motives for the use and abuse of alcohol. Repeated use for that purpose is viewed as an important factor in the development of habituation and addiction.

- Fifty-five percent of marriages in the United States end in divorce. Experts report that stress is a major contributing factor to relationship conflicts and the rising incidence of divorce. Frustration tolerance decreases, and thus individuals are more likely to misattribute the source of their stress and blame their spouse.

Occupational Consequences

At times of stress, how well can you concentrate on the task at hand? Do you find thoughts, preoccupations, and fears interfering with your ability to function? The ability to concentrate is significantly affected by stress. It is no wonder that an inability to cope with life stressors leads to lowered productivity and an increased frequency of mistakes on the job. In addition, you are more likely to miss work due to both emotional and physical illness. As the following list demonstrates, this leads to major financial losses for business, industry, and employees:

- People are more accident-prone during periods of stress. U.S. businesses claim that most industrial accidents are stress-related, accounting for two million disabling injuries, more than fifteen thousand deaths, and three billion dollars annually in lost productivity.

- At least ten billion dollars a year is lost in industry to absenteeism due to physical or psychological problems. It is estimated that individuals suffering from chronic pain miss over 700 million work days per year, with a cost of sixty billion dollars per year. A 1995 estimate by the American Heart Association indicated that cardiovascular diseases alone cost the economy $20.2 billion in lost production for that year (Miller, 1988).

- Data suggest that 80 to 90 percent of all business dismissals are somehow linked to tension and subsequent mental and physical problems.

- Stress is eroding the bottom line for business. The combination of decreased productivity, absenteeism, and spiraling medical costs may be costing the economy as much as $150 billion annually, according to some surveys.

- At least 25 percent of the people in the United States suffer from stress overload at work. According to a 1995 Gallup poll, 37 percent of American workers reported daily job stress, while 75 percent reported significant stress at least once weekly. A study by the National Center for Health Statistics revealed that more than half of forty thousand workers surveyed reported experiencing moderate to severe job stress in the previous two weeks. A 1998 Gallup poll strongly suggested that stress continues to mount for American workers, as fully 80 percent reported being significantly stressed at work. This poll also revealed that women feel more "stressed out" than men and, interestingly, that stress increases as income levels rise (Underwood, 1999).

- Insurance companies have recently been plagued by a nationwide epidemic of sick, disabled, and wealthy professionals—especially doctors, but also accountants, architects, insurance agents, and lawyers—filing claims for disability due to stress-related disorders (Freedberg, 1996).

The Physiology of Stress: The Fight-or-Flight Response

There is more than sufficient data demonstrating that stress can lead to physical, emotional, and behavioral maladjustments. But how do changes in our lives lead to ill health? The answer lies in a physiological mechanism known as the *fight-or-flight response.* The fight-or-flight response is a survival mechanism present in humans and most animals that prepares us to deal with physical danger. Imagine our prehistoric ancestors, cavemen and cavewomen, exploring their terrain, perhaps even enjoying the wonders of their environment, when suddenly out of the corner of their eyes they spot a sabertoothed tiger, licking its lips in anticipation of a tasty human morsel. The fight-or-flight reaction would kick in, preparing their bodies to either fight or flee from the tiger, through a series of instantaneous physiological and psychological changes that prepare the individual to take immediate physical action in the face of danger. These changes and their resulting physical signs are outlined in Table 2.1, Table 2.2, and Figure 2.1.

In short, the fight-or-flight response shows a picture of autonomic hyperactivity. Returning to the example with the cave dwellers, the person's body and mind would be put on "red alert" in order to deal with the impending danger. This activation would not go on for long, however. If the tiger had its way and the cave dweller ended up serving as a meal, he or she would definitely be relaxed, as the deceased tend to show no autonomic activity. If, on the other hand, our friend was lucky enough to escape and tell the story to those back in the cave, his or her physiology would return to a state of

Table 2.1   Signs of the Fight-or-Flight Response

• Racing thoughts	• Narrowed attention span
• Rapid pulse	• Pounding heart
• Gritting of teeth	• Muscular tension
• Restlessness	• Clenched jaw
• Tremors	• Tightened stomach
• Rapid, shallow breathing	• Increased perspiration
• Serious, concerned expression	• Narrowed field of vision
• Numbness	• Cold, clammy hands
• Impulsive behavior	• Gripping emotions
• Inability to concentrate	• Dry mouth

Table 2.2   Anatomy of the Fight-or-Flight Response

- The breathing rate becomes more intense and rapid, increasing the oxygen supply in the blood.
- Breathing becomes more shallow, switching from diaphragmatic to thoracic respiration, again shifting the oxygen/carbon dioxide balance.
- Muscles tense in preparation for strenuous action.
- Heart rate speeds up, ensuring sufficient blood supply to needed areas, especially to the brain for optimized control over conscious functions, as well as to major muscles to prepare the individual for action.
- Peripheral blood vessels constrict to send the bulk of the blood supply and the oxygen it carries to needed areas. Blood-clotting mechanisms are also activated to prevent excess bleeding should the individual be injured.
- The increased heart rate and constriction of peripheral blood vessels cause blood pressure to soar.
- Digestion ceases, so blood may be diverted to muscles and the brain.
- Stored sugar and fats pour into the bloodstream to provide fuel for quick energy.
- The adrenal glands release the hormones epinephrine (adrenaline) and norepinephrine into the system.
- Triggered by the pituitary gland, the endocrine system steps up hormone production.
- All senses are heightened. Pupils dilate, making vision more sensitive. Hearing becomes more acute.
- Electrical resistivity (perspiration/galvanic action) and skin temperature change.
- Perspiration increases and saliva decreases.
- The urethra and anal sphincter muscles (controlling bowel and bladder function) initially loosen, in order to evacuate waste if necessary, but then constrict to prevent waste elimination when running or fighting. So when people say, "I was so scared that I peed in my pants," there is a physiological mechanism underlying this humiliating phenomenon.

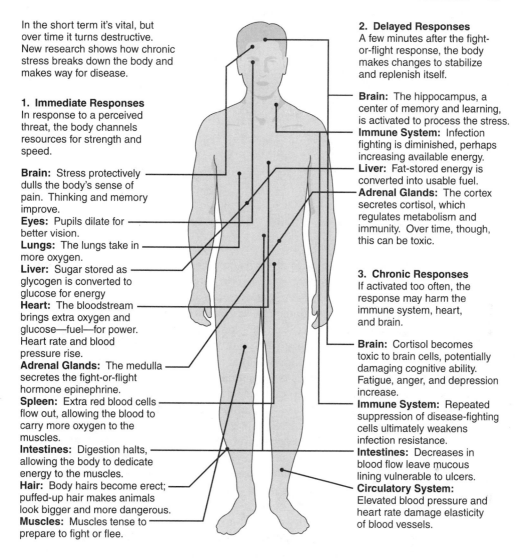

In the short term it's vital, but over time it turns destructive. New research shows how chronic stress breaks down the body and makes way for disease.

1. Immediate Responses
In response to a perceived threat, the body channels resources for strength and speed.

Brain: Stress protectively dulls the body's sense of pain. Thinking and memory improve.
Eyes: Pupils dilate for better vision.
Lungs: The lungs take in more oxygen.
Liver: Sugar stored as glycogen is converted to glucose for energy
Heart: The bloodstream brings extra oxygen and glucose—fuel—for power. Heart rate and blood pressure rise.
Adrenal Glands: The medulla secretes the fight-or-flight hormone epinephrine.
Spleen: Extra red blood cells flow out, allowing the blood to carry more oxygen to the muscles.
Intestines: Digestion halts, allowing the body to dedicate energy to the muscles.
Hair: Body hairs become erect; puffed-up hair makes animals look bigger and more dangerous.
Muscles: Muscles tense to prepare to fight or flee.

2. Delayed Responses
A few minutes after the fight-or-flight response, the body makes changes to stabilize and replenish itself.

Brain: The hippocampus, a center of memory and learning, is activated to process the stress.
Immune System: Infection fighting is diminished, perhaps increasing available energy.
Liver: Fat-stored energy is converted into usable fuel.
Adrenal Glands: The cortex secretes cortisol, which regulates metabolism and immunity. Over time, though, this can be toxic.

3. Chronic Responses
If activated too often, the response may harm the immune system, heart, and brain.

Brain: Cortisol becomes toxic to brain cells, potentially damaging cognitive ability. Fatigue, anger, and depression increase.
Immune System: Repeated suppression of disease-fighting cells ultimately weakens infection resistance.
Intestines: Decreases in blood flow leave mucous lining vulnerable to ulcers.
Circulatory System: Elevated blood pressure and heart rate damage elasticity of blood vessels.

Figure 2.1   Stress: The General Adaptation Syndrome

homeostasis or balance. After a slight period of recovery, our cave dweller would be no worse for the wear. Visually, this may be represented as shown in Figure 2.2.

Downside of the Fight-or-Flight Response

The fight-or-flight response is clearly an adaptive response to the presence of physical danger. The problem is that the response is triggered not only by actual physical danger, but by perceived danger. The tigers that chase modern humans are not made of flesh and blood; they are things like deadlines; unpaid bills; confrontations with others;

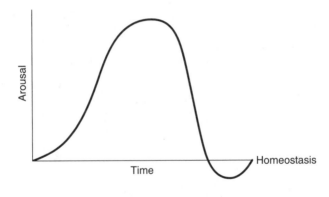

Figure 2.2

rush-hour traffic; and demands from children, spouses, and bosses. All these and many more trigger the fight-or-flight response in the person of today. But it gets worse, for not only are the tigers the actual events, but also those events remembered and anticipated by us. So not only does the act of asking the boss for a raise lead to increased autonomic activity, but also our anticipation of the meeting, along with the recollection of the event, particularly if we didn't obtain the desired results. The predicament lies in the fact that the fight-or-flight reaction prepares us to fight or run away, and neither of these responses is particularly useful nor adaptive for dealing with most of the stresses we face in our modern world. To further aggravate the situation, our cave dweller's stresses had a distinct beginning and a definite ending, whereas the tigers we face today seem to be much more ongoing. No sooner have we begun to recover from fight-or-flight activation when another event, real or imaginary, triggers the response again. Thus, we never really have the chance to fully recover and return to homeostatic balance before we are faced with the onslaught of new or old stressors recurring in our environment. This can be expressed visually as shown in Figure 2.3.

Day after day we are faced with a continuous barrage of stressors. We get some relief at night when we sleep, but even in our sleep we might dream about our stressors, again triggering the fight-or-flight response, and the next day we awaken with our physiology just a bit above homeostasis, to begin the whole cycle over again. After years of this pattern we forget what relaxation really feels like, as we habituate to a state of autonomic arousal. This state feels relaxed in comparison to full blown fight-or-flight activation, but in reality it is higher than true homeostasis, which we need to maintain health. This is illustrated in Figure 2.4.

Thus a person under chronic stress is like a car with its idle set too high. Imagine for a moment a car whose engine is idling just a little too fast. What would happen to it? For one thing, it would use more gas, just as we tend to spend more energy for diminishing returns when we are under stress. In addition, the engine would wear out prematurely, which similarly appears to happen to our bodies. Stress researcher Hans Selye, mentioned earlier, described this phenomenon as a three-stage process, which he named the *General Adaptation Syndrome (GAS)*, which is illus-

Figure 2.3

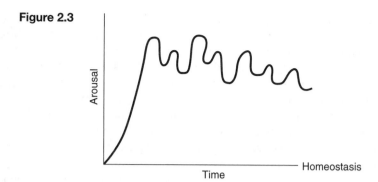

trated in Figure 2.1. The first stage of GAS, called the *alarm reaction,* is basically the fight-or-flight response. If the stressor continues, as is typical of modern-day tigers, we enter the *stage of resistance,* where our bodies habituate to the specific stressors. Overt signs of the fight-or-flight reaction disappear or go underground, but subtle signs persist (our neural and glandular systems remain hyperactive), leaving us overstimulated and vigilant. The last phase, the *stage of exhaustion,* occurs when stressors are prolonged despite our best attempts at coping. Just as we have to rest, so must our glandular system rest in order to regain balance. Without rest it wears down and eventually out, resistance deteriorates, and stress-related symptoms resurface. Clearly, if there is no relief, even death is possible (Selye, 1982).

Stress Sensitization

To make matters even worse, before the stage of exhaustion overtakes us, recent research indicates that we can become sensitized, or acutely sensitive, to stress. That is, we may respond to stress as we do to an allergy (Carpi, 1996). Once that happens, even the slightest stress can trigger a torrent of chemical reactions in both our brain and body that besiege us from within, making stress the psychological equivalent of ragweed. Even though at some level we realize that what we are facing is a normal,

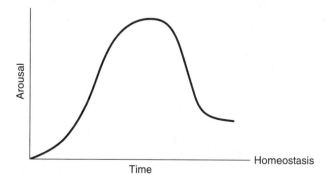

Figure 2.4

everyday stressor, our brain is signaling our body to overreact. We may not think we are getting worked up over running late for an appointment, but our brain is responding as though it were a life-or-death situation. Years of research have demonstrated that people become sensitized to stress, and this sensitization actually alters physical patterns in the brain. We may produce too many excitatory chemicals or too few calming ones; either way, we are responding inappropriately.

The fact that stress itself lowers our ability to cope with further stress leads to yet another distressing finding: Sensitization to stress may occur before we are old enough to prevent it ourselves. New studies suggest that animals ranging from rodents to monkeys to humans may experience still-undetermined developmental periods during which exposure to extreme stress is more damaging than in later years. For example, we have known that losing a parent when you are young is much harder to handle than if your parent dies when you are an adult. What we now believe is that a stress of that magnitude occurring in childhood may rewire your brain's circuitry, throwing the system off kilter, leaving you less able to handle normal, everyday stress. So clearly, stress does not just grab us for a time and then release us. It changes us by altering our bodies and our brains.

What Js Possible?

But enough of this doom and gloom scenario! Are we totally at the mercy of our past and current stressors? Is there nothing we can do? Research and an overwhelming amount of anecdotal evidence supports the idea that, just as we have the potential to slowly destroy ourselves, our mind-body system can also create miraculous beneficial results. What is possible can sometimes border on the unbelievable.

For example, you may have heard the story of Norman Cousins, who wrote about his remarkable recovery from a supposedly incurable and very painful connective-tissue disease that leads to spinal deterioration and paralysis in his best-selling book, *Anatomy of an Illness* (1981). Cousins refused to buy into the gloomy predictions of his physicians (who gave him a one-in-five-hundred chance of recovery), so he designed a regimen of self-healing based largely on using humor as a stress reducer. As part of his regimen he spent several hours daily watching movies of the Three Stooges and the Marx Brothers. Initially he reported that ten minutes of belly laughter had a powerful anesthetic effect, allowing him to sleep at least two hours without analgesic medication (painkillers). Laughter also reduced his inflammation, probably by stimulating the release of endorphins. Ultimately, much to the surprise of his physicians, he went into a complete remission.

The Power of Belief

Consider the amazing story reported by Ernest Rossi in his book *The Psychobiology of Mind-Body Healing*. Dr. Rossi recounted the story of Mr. Wright, as told by his personal physician, Dr. Phillip West, over thirty years ago. Mr. Wright suffered from an advanced malignancy of the lymph nodes known as lymphosarcoma. His condition was terminal and he had deteriorated to the point where his physician thought death was imminent. He had tumors the size of oranges in his neck, groin, chest, and abdomen. His spleen and liver were grossly enlarged. Copious amounts of fluid were drawn from his chest on a daily basis. He was bedridden and had severe difficulty breathing. All standard cancer treatments of that time, including radiation, had proved useless. Although his doctors had given up hope for his recovery, Mr. Wright maintained an optimistic attitude, for since the onset of his illness he had held fast to a belief that a miracle drug would come along to save the day.

This expectation was fulfilled when newspapers reported that a newly developed drug, Krebiozen, showed significant promise in the treatment of cancer. This hope was further heightened when he learned that the hospital where he was staying would be included in a research project studying the effectiveness of this new drug. Even though he did not fit the criteria for inclusion in the study (because of the advanced nature of his condition), he begged his doctors to include him in the treatment protocol. Against their better judgment his doctors included him in the study, fully expecting he would die within the week, thus freeing up a supply of Krebiozen for another patient.

His response to the drug was nothing short of miraculous! Within several days he went from death's door to walking around the ward, joking with nurses. His tumors were half their original size. After ten days of Krebiozen treatment, he was discharged from the hospital with his cancer in complete remission. In the meantime, early results of the study indicated that this miracle drug appeared to be ineffective in the treatment of cancer. Unfortunately, Mr. Wright became aware of these initial reports of the lack of effectiveness of the drug, and within a short period of time he completely relapsed.

Clearly, it wasn't the Krebiozen that was responsible for his improvement, but the power of his belief. In order to test this out, his doctors decided to see if they could recreate the previous results. They deliberately lied to him and told him not to believe the discouraging results he had read in the newspapers. They further informed him that Krebiozen was highly effective, and that his relapse occurred because his last doses had deteriorated on the shelf. They further added that he would be receiving double-strength dosages from a fresh shipment of the drug that would restore him to health. Then, with great fanfare, they proceeded to inject him with saline solution, nothing but a placebo. What do you think happened? Again he made a remarkable recovery, even quicker than the first time. He was discharged from the hospital and remained in complete remission for two months, until reports appeared in the press that Krebiozen had proved to be totally worthless in the treatment of cancer. Mr. Wright quickly relapsed and was readmitted to the hospital, dying two days later.

What can be learned from this? You could conclude that the lesson here is that Mr. Wright should have stopped reading the newspaper! But obviously what is evident, and rather amazing, is that it was purely the power of Mr. Wright's belief that affected his physiology. Doctors would dismiss this as a dramatic example of the *placebo effect*. We often hear our colleagues in the health profession refer to similar, if less dramatic, results with their own cases as "just a placebo." To us, the fact that *it's just a placebo* opens up a whole new range of possibilities. Rather than an area to be dismissed, we consider this a phenomenon to be explored fully. The consensus in the field is that 30 percent of the effectiveness of any treatment, including drugs, can be accounted for by placebo effects. One highly respected researcher in the area of stress reduction and the mind-body connection, Herbert Benson, (1976, 1985) believes the placebo effect is responsible for 80 percent of the success of all treatments.

The Mind-Body Connection

So clearly, just as we have the capacity to do ourselves tremendous harm through our reactions to stress, so too do we have the ability to create dramatic positive outcomes in our lives. The first step is acknowledging this possibility. Our mind and body are not as separate as was once thought. In fact, they are profoundly interconnected and interdependent. We now know enough of the necessary steps to harness this power. What remains is to learn and then practice these steps. If you follow the techniques and suggestions outlined in this book, we promise you will reap significant benefits. But let us caution you that knowing the steps is not enough; it is only in the doing that solutions are found.

Chapter Summary

You always need to consider that stress is an inescapable part of modern life. Stress is anything that requires an adaptive response, so all changes (even positive ones) are stressful. The more changes in your life, the more vulnerable you can become to illness, bodily system breakdown, or emotional difficulties. Stress negatively affects your physical, psychological, and occupational functioning in a variety of ways. This is due to a physiological mechanism known as the fight-or-flight response, an ancient survival mechanism that prepares you to deal with physical danger. Although this response is very useful if you are faced with physical danger, it is also triggered by perceived danger. Most of the stressors we face in our modern world are not physical; thus neither fighting nor fleeing is an adaptive response. Yet your body prepares you to do this anyway, and you are left in a state of heightened arousal or tension that, if chronic, begins to take a heavy toll. But just as you have the capacity to harm your body through your reactions to stress, you also have the ability to create dramatic positive outcomes in your life. Your mind and body are profoundly interconnected and interdependent. How you think and what you believe have a profound impact on the state of your health and your ability to cope with stress.

Chapter Questions

1. Define *stress*.
2. Distinguish between *eustress* and *distress*.
3. What level of arousal is associated with better performance?
4. Describe the physiological changes that occur during the fight-or-flight response.
5. Discuss the general adaptation syndrome (GAS).
6. What is stress sensitization?

Section 2

The Master Strategy: Stage 1

Breathing

What You Will Learn in this Chapter

- To discriminate between active and passive relaxation.

- To practice diaphragmatic breathing as a method for calming the fight-or-flight reaction and coping with stress.

- To practice other breathing techniques for lowering arousal.

- To explain the relationship between ultradian rhythms and relaxation.

As we mentioned before, the path toward stress mastery is lifelong. As the concepts and techniques become part of the daily fabric of your life, your capacity to thrive from stress continues to refine and become more elegant. Clearly, to deal with stress effectively, you must pay attention to both your body and your mind. A dramatic example of this is a study that showed that meditators tended to age more slowly than nonmeditators. During meditation one focuses on quieting both the body and the mind through the act of fixing on a single thought, image, or visualization.

Truth be told, the distinction between body and mind is really an artificial one. We now know that body and mind are really one, an intricately interrelated system where thoughts give rise to our physical reactions and, in turn, our physical reactions trigger our various thoughts. But for the purpose of learning how to begin traveling on the path toward stress mastery, it is useful to talk about addressing your body first. It is very difficult to change the way you think if your body is simultaneously sending messages of danger. Addressing the body is best accomplished by learning *active relaxation*.

Most people confuse inactivity with relaxation. You might say, "I do relax. I go home and sit down in front of the TV, watch my favorite programs, and let the stress of the day melt away." But the fact is that when subjects' level of stress, as indicated by physiological arousal, is measured while watching TV, a negligible, if any, decrease is evident. Passive relaxation such as this is not nearly as effective in reducing stress. What is needed is relaxation aimed at reducing the fight-or-flight response and thereby restoring balance or homeostasis. Active relaxation involves becoming aware of your body and your physiological reactions so that you may consciously reduce your level of arousal.

Diaphragmatic Breathing

Any journey that you undertake begins with a first step. The key to any practice of active relaxation is to relearn proper breathing patterns. Breathing slowly, deeply, and regularly is the easiest and most accessible relaxation technique (Loehr & Migdow, 1986). Most of the time you are no doubt oblivious to your breathing patterns. Let's first begin by discovering where you are now. Sit with your back supported, your feet flat on the floor, and your eyes closed. Put one hand on your chest and the other on your diaphragm, the muscle right above your stomach, as you focus on your breathing. Notice the pattern and rhythm of your breath as you breathe in and out. Then take a few deep breaths, noticing as you breathe in and out which hand moves more. Does the hand on your chest move up and down, with the shoulders rising and falling, as you breathe? Or does the hand on your abdomen do most of the movement? Take a few moments to do that now.

So what happened? Which hand moved more as you breathed deeply?

We notice in our classes and workshops that for the majority of students and participants, the hand on the chest evidences more movement. If you have ever seen a baby breathing while it is at rest or asleep, you may have noticed that the stomach moves up and down, while the baby's chest remains relatively still and quiet. This is called *diaphragmatic breathing,* and it is a natural antidote to stress. Diaphragmatic breathing involves deep, slow, rhythmic breaths.

Pay attention to what happens to your breathing the next time you feel stressed. You may notice that your breathing becomes quicker and more shallow and irregular. Some people even hold their breath or begin to hyperventilate under significant stress. For many adults, after years of frequently activating the fight-or-flight response, the fast, shallow breathing characteristic of this physiological reaction becomes a habit. This breathing is ineffectual, disrupting the proper balance of carbon dioxide and oxygen in your bloodstream and thereby creating a continual, if not full-blown, overactivation response. An optimal balance of oxygen and carbon dioxide needs to be maintained in your bloodstream for you to remain calm. Rapid, shallow breathing causes overoxygenation of the bloodstream. The side effects of too much oxygen include muscle tension, dizziness, and feelings of anxiety. That is why hyperventilation is so counterproductive. The more quickly you breathe, the worse you feel.

Practicing Diaphragmatic Breathing

Retraining yourself is, in most cases, a rather simple procedure that requires only about five minutes a day of conscious focusing on your breathing. You can do this by practicing the following technique, once a day, for three weeks. (Three weeks is generally required to bring tone to the diaphragm muscle.) We have discovered that a few minutes prior to going to sleep is a good time to practice for many people. Others prefer to take five minutes when they return home from work or school. It is important for you to discover which time is best for you.

Find a quiet place where you are unlikely to be disturbed and while reclining, put one hand on your diaphragm and one hand on your chest. Focus on allowing the hand on your diaphragm to rise as you breathe in, as if your stomach were a balloon filling with air. Then watch it go back down as you breathe out and the balloon deflates. Notice the rhythm of the rising and falling of your abdomen as you inhale and exhale. Focus on the particular feelings and sensations that you experience in your diaphragm as the breath comes all the way into your lungs and then completely empties from your lungs. Do this for about five minutes, gently focusing your attention on your breath.

If you find yourself having difficulty initially lifting your abdomen as you breathe, try imagining that you are putting on a tight pair of jeans, when they come out fresh from the dryer. You would let all the air out of your lungs first, as if you wanted to touch your spine with your bellybutton, then slowly inflate the balloon as you let the air come all the way into your lungs.

Yet another technique that has proven successful for many people is to use a heavy book placed on top of your stomach as you practice your breathing exercises. You could watch the rising and falling of the book as you breathe in and out. This method has the added advantage of providing a weight against which the diaphragm is rising and falling, thereby conditioning the muscle much more quickly. Most people find that with just a little attention and practice they can return to that slow, diaphragmatic breathing they knew as a child.

We cannot stress enough how important this first step is. Without shifting your breath to a calm, relaxed, diaphragmatic pattern, you will find it very difficult to start your journey on the path toward stress mastery. The type of breathing you employ is the key to unlocking the magic. We know it sounds simple, but it is nonetheless true.

Take as an example research done with people suffering from panic attacks, a disorder in which intense anxiety (often accompanied by hyperventilation) is experienced at various times, causing the individual to withdraw and increasingly restrict his or her activities in the hope of preventing the attacks. In the extreme, these individuals develop a condition known as agoraphobia, in which they become housebound as a way of coping with the fear of the attacks reoccurring. Developing appropriate diaphragmatic breathing patterns has been identified as essential in learning to overcome the panic.

Other research has shown that the speed of your breathing affects your perception of time. When you breathe faster, a typical by-product of shallow breathing, time seems to speed up. You are more likely to perceive a shortage of time, creating a sense of time pressure. This, in turn, increases your level of stress. As you slow down your breathing, time also seems to slow down, resulting in a much more calm and relaxed attitude.

Focusing on your breathing helps keep you in the present moment. Your worries, anxieties, and stress occur when you focus on either the past (that is, mistakes you have made or things you wish would have happened differently) or the future (that is, what is going to happen and how you will be able to survive). But the past has already happened; there is little you can do to alter that except change your attitude or perception about what happened. And the future is yet to come; you can only affect it by working in the present, the here and now. Breathing helps you exist in the now in a way that increases your effectiveness.

Most spiritual traditions recognize the importance of breath. It is often considered our direct link to God or a Higher Power. The word *inspiration* has a double meaning, being used both to describe breathing as well as being infused with spirit and motivation. Alterations in breathing can create dramatic effects on our consciousness. *Holotropic breathing*, an alteration in breathing in which controlled hyperventilation is employed, for example, has been shown to create dramatic shifts in consciousness in the practitioners, akin to, if somewhat less intense than, those experienced when using hallucinogens. So breathing is clearly a powerful tool that can create numerous changes in our body and in our experience of ourselves and our world.

Once you can breathe comfortably using your diaphragm as you think consciously about it, it becomes important to be able to generalize that response to your daily life. One easy way to do this is to set up a number of reminders in your everyday environment. For example, do you know those sticky colored dots that are often used in offices to color-code charts? You could take a few of these (three to five) and place them in different places around your home and work environment. We suggest that you resist the temptation to place these dots on the foreheads of people who are a source of stress to you. However, feel free to use your imagination. Each time you see a dot, stop for a second, take one or two breaths using your diaphragm, and then go on with your activity. This will allow you, with minimal effort, to remind yourself to breathe this way at different times during the day. In just a short time you will be pleasantly surprised, as you focus on your breathing, to discover that you are automatically breathing deep, diaphragmatic breaths.

Another way to ensure that you generalize the correct breathing response to a variety of situations is by using a higher-order classical conditioning principle. This principle states that when a new behavior is paired, and thus eventually associated, with a behavior that is frequently emitted, the new behavior becomes conditioned. Now to translate from psychologeeze, this means that you will learn how to breathe correctly faster and better if you do it at the same time that you are doing things that you do frequently, such as answering the phone, going to the bathroom, or stopping at red lights.

Another obvious way, and indeed the first building block, is to remember to breathe from your abdomen whenever you feel yourself becoming stressed. This will help interrupt the automatic cognitive and behavioral strategies you may be using now, which merely lead to an escalation of the stress response. Remembering to breathe correctly in these situations allows you a pause that opens up the possibility of thinking or behaving differently, thereby using the stress rather than being used by it.

We should caution you, however, that it is not wise to use only situations when you are feeling stressed as reminders to practice your breathing. You will clearly find it more difficult initially to successfully focus on appropriate breathing at these times. Until you have learned and feel comfortable with abdominal breathing, you need to practice in situations that are less demanding and in which the fight-or-flight response is not fully activated.

Breathing Variations

You need only do the most basic breathing awareness exercises to achieve a much more relaxed state of body and mind. As long as your breathing is becoming slower, quieter, and deeper, you are moving in the right direction. Quite frankly, the hardest part is remembering to remember to be aware of your breathing and then to practice. But the fact remains that wherever you are you still have to breathe, so you might as well practice doing it properly in a manner that will help you stay calm, yet alert. However, for those of you who would like to experiment with breathing further, you can play with these variations to give you increasing control over your breathing.

Variation 1
In this variation you are simply going to add the dimension of holding your breath for several seconds in between the inhalation and exhalation. In other words, slowly inhale until your lungs are full. This will take approximately three to four seconds. Then hold your breath for the amount of time it would take you to exhale, another three to eight seconds. Finally, exhale slowly and completely by pulling your stomach in to really empty your lungs. From this point you are perfectly prepared to slowly inhale and begin the cycle again.

Various yoga teachers recommend that you inhale through your nose and exhale through your mouth. They further suggest that it is also beneficial to do the exercises with the tip of your tongue pressed against the roof of your mouth behind your upper teeth, so that you do not deplete your body of energy in the course of practicing your breathing. Since they have been practicing for several thousand years, this is probably a worthwhile consideration. We do know that it will create a back pressure during the exhalation process and prevent you from expelling too much carbon dioxide too quickly and thus prevent hyperventilation. The main thing is to proceed slowly with awareness. If you feel lightheaded, go slower or do fewer repetitions. We suggest you start with four or five cycles and build to ten or fifteen.

Variation 2

In this variation the idea is to fill your lungs quickly in three to four seconds. You then hold the breath for three seconds and then, as slowly and quietly as possible, exhale through your nose or through a small opening in your lips. Exhale completely as in variation 1 and begin again. Begin with several repetitions and build to ten or fifteen.

When we were first taught this exercise we were given wax earplugs so that we could pay exquisite attention to the sounds of the breath. The feedback of sound enables you to really understand what we mean by making your breathing quieter. Any earplugs will do, but we recommend staying away from lima beans and raisins as they are very difficult to remove!

Variation 3

This exercise is very similar to variation 2. However, when you reach the point of exhaling, instead of quietly hissing the breath out, keep your mouth closed and hum any note, until you can no longer sustain the note. Then inhale quickly, hold for several seconds, and hum again. Variations 1 and 2 are subtle enough that you can do them anywhere quite undetected. If you begin humming in a staff meeting, however, your colleagues may be a bit perplexed. That's why we believe this exercise might be better done privately. It can have a very calming effect, is a nice change of pace in your practice, and provides you with a kind of internal massage. Try it; you'll like it.

Variation 4

This final breathing exercise will relax you quickly and allow you to focus on whatever task is at hand. This is especially useful for helping you focus your powers of concentration. Place the tips of your index and middle fingers of either hand on the center of your forehead. In this position you can use your thumb to close and open one nostril of your nose, and your remaining two fingers to close and open the other nostril. The exercise proceeds as follows:

1. Close your left nostril and inhale slowly and deeply through your right nostril.
2. When you have inhaled completely, close your right nostril.
3. Then slowly and quietly exhale through your left nostril.
4. Keeping your right nostril closed, slowly inhale through your left nostril.
5. When you have inhaled completely, close your left nostril and slowly exhale through your right nostril. This constitutes one complete cycle.
6. Repeat this exercise five to ten times.

Breathing and Ultradian Rhythms

You may be wondering, what possible relevance could breathing in and out of different nostrils have in terms of affecting your ability to relax or concentrate? Well, believe it or not, there is a growing body of research verifying the existence of *ultradian rhythms*. Ultradian rhythms are shifts in various body processes that occur approximately every ninety minutes. For our purposes, we are interested in how brain functioning is affected. As it turns out, our brain shifts from being dominated by left-hemispheric activity to right-hemispheric activity every ninety minutes. That is, we shift from a very logical, deductive, sequential, focused, externally oriented (left brain) way of being in the world, to a more intuitive, creative, dreamy, internally focused (right brain) way of being in the world. You have probably noticed that there are times during the day when you have been reading or concentrating very well, and then suddenly you find your mind drifting. You keep reading the same paragraph over and over, but it remains incomprehensible. Or you simply feel like closing your eyes and daydreaming. This is the feeling of the ultradian shift into a brain state dominated by right-hemisphere activity. In this state, you are particularly predisposed to relax and rest deeply. Any relaxation exercise is more easily accomplished.

So, what about your nostrils? Take a moment and notice which nostril is more open. That is, which nostril is moving more air through it? You can do this by simply feeling the comparative air flow when you close one nostril or the other. Or you can listen to the sound of the air as you close off one nostril. The higher-pitched sound is the more closed nostril, and the lower-pitched sound is the more open one. Your left brain controls the right side of your body and your right nostril; your right brain controls your left side and nostril. If the right nostril is the open one, then your left brain is more dominant now. If the left nostril is more open, then your right hemisphere is dominant. If they are equally open, your brain activity is relatively balanced.

The practical application of this information is that it seems likely that one can deliberately shift hemispheric dominance, or simply take advantage of the prevailing hemispheric dominance by breathing through the appropriate nostril (that is, the left nostril to stimulate the right brain, or the right nostril to activate the left brain). If you are in a situation that requires more focused attention, alternate-nostril breathing or right-nostril breathing should help. Relaxation is most accessible to you when the left nostril is open. As always, experiment and see if this works for you. For a more comprehensive treatment of this phenomenon, read *The Psychobiology of Mind-Body Healing* by Ernest Rossi (1986).

Chapter Summary

In order to counteract the fight-or-flight response and cope effectively with stress, you must learn how to relax your body. How you breathe is vitally important in this process. Proper breathing is the cornerstone of your successful stress mastery program. It is important to remember to practice diaphragmatic breathing, which involves breathing deeply, slowly, and rhythmically from your diaphragm. Quick, upper-chest breathing will only exacerbate your tension level. Remember to remember to practice proper breathing in nonstressful situations as well as when you are under stress.

Chapter Questions

1. What is the difference between passive relaxation and active relaxation methods?
2. How does diaphragmatic breathing differ from everyday breathing, anxious breathing, and hyperventilation?
3. What type of breathing is associated with panic attacks?
4. What are ultradian rhythms and how can practicing breathing techniques help you take advantage of your own biorhythms?

Cultivating Awareness

What You Will Learn in this Chapter

- To enumerate the value of self-awareness.

- To learn how adopting the *witnessing stance* facilitates the process of self-awareness.

- To explain how the three *stress hardiness attitudes* of *control, commitment* and *challenge* contribute to stress resilience.

- To assess your own level of stress hardiness using the stress hardiness inventory.

- To define an internal locus of control.

- To explain the relationship of an internal locus of control to proactivity.

By now you have become more aware of your breathing and you can notice just how you are breathing. Are you using your diaphragm or your thorax? Are you breathing deeply and slowly, with a comfortable rhythm? Or is your breath fast and chaotic? In any situation, if you notice that you are engaged in unhealthy, stress-producing breathing, this awareness allows you the opportunity to shift the pattern to a more appropriate one.

Can you do this? If you can't, we strongly urge you to continue your practice. Without the ability to breathe appropriately, it will be difficult for you to master stress. If you can, we congratulate you! You have taken the first and most essential step toward stress mastery. It is important that you now remember to do this throughout your day, in a variety of settings—that you think about it at work and at home, and that you notice your breathing as you are going to sleep and shortly after you wake up. It is important that you remember to remember to notice your breathing. The more you do this, the more you are cultivating awareness. You are replacing your automatic behavior with conscious behavior.

The Value of Self-Awareness

All human beings have the ability to be aware, not just of our breathing, but of a multitude of things that make up who we are. Let us demonstrate what we mean. Imagine, in your mind's eye, that a part of you can float out of your body, floating up to a particular corner of the room, so that you can see yourself, from that perspective, sitting there reading this book. What would it be like to do this? What would it feel like? How would you describe the particular sensations that the you who is sitting there is experiencing right now? Focus on a particular part of your body and become aware of your experience there. Perhaps you can be aware of pressure, or temperature, or some other sensation. It's not important what the specific sensation is, just your ability to notice it. How about your overall mood? How would you characterize that? What can you say about your thoughts? Are you thinking about what you are reading right now, and yet perhaps at the same time wondering what's the point of all this? As you answer these questions, make sure you get back into your body. We certainly wouldn't want you to remain floating around the room somewhere while you continued reading the book.

The Witnessing Stance

By doing what you just did, and answering the questions we just asked, you have demonstrated your ability for *self-awareness.* All human beings share the ability to be aware of ourselves. The fact that we can stand apart from our feelings and our thoughts suggests that we can have some control over them. Ram Dass, formerly known as Richard Alpert, a Harvard psychologist who studied extensively in India and is renowned for integrating both Eastern and Western techniques, describes our ability to stand apart from ourselves, to view ourselves from the outside, as assuming the *witnessing stance.* Whenever you are involved in the many experiences that make up your life, you have the choice to be a *witness* to your own life. This shift in perspective provides you with the possibility that you can change the particular situation. The fact is that you cannot always change situations (that is, external stressors or events) you are faced with, but you can always change your reaction toward the stressor. Assuming the witnessing stance allows you to make this shift.

Remember that, as we mentioned earlier, what inappropriately triggers your fight-or-flight response, and therefore your stress, is not actual physical danger. Not many of you have guns pointed at your head, at least not on a daily basis. What triggers your stress response is your perception of danger. And whether you perceive something as dangerous depends on the meaning you give the particular situation. Human beings give meaning to everything, and what we say, especially to ourselves, about a situation or event determines our attitude toward it. Assuming an observer perspective allows you to get a glimpse of the meaning you are ascribing and therefore provides you an opportunity to change your attitude.

Attitude Is Everything!

Research has revealed that the attitude you have at the beginning of a task determines the outcome of that task more than any other single factor. For example, if you believe you will be able to succeed at a particular undertaking and you approach the endeavor with a sense of excitement and joyful expectation, your chances of achieving success are much higher than if you face the task with dread and apprehension. Self-fulfilling prophecies can be positive or negative, depending on your expectations. So your attitude is more important than any other possible factor, both external and internal. In his book *The Seven Habits of Highly Effective People* (1991), Stephen Covey comments on the fact that everything is created twice—first in your head, then in physical reality. We believe that it is perhaps more accurate to say that everything is created three times. First, you create your reality by your thoughts, including what you think about the events that happen to you. Then you further give substance to these thoughts by your words—for example, when you describe the events in your life to others. Finally, your actions complete the process of creation. This is clearly true when it comes to stress and whether we thrive from it or are buried by it.

Remember Thomas Holmes and his research showing that there was a relationship between the number, severity, and pervasiveness of life changes and our physical and emotional health? We mentioned that the major flaw of this series of studies was a failure to take into account individual differences in abilities to cope with the changes and demands. This research focused only on the effects of external events or stressors.

Psychologist Suzanne Kobasa decided to focus her research interests on individual differences in coping skills. What makes some people capable of handling enormous amounts of change and demands without suffering the devastating physical and emotional consequences predicted by the Holmes research? Kobasa studied individuals whose lives seemed so filled with stressors that, according to Holmes, they should have been growing massive tumors on the sides of their heads. Yet these folks were successful in their endeavors and seemed to be suffering no apparent negative consequences from their demanding lifestyle (Kobasa, 1984).

Stress Hardiness Attitudes

Kobasa discovered three attitudes that these people all shared and that appeared to make them resistant to the negative effects of stress. She called these three attitudes *stress hardiness attitudes* because individuals who possess them appear to be "stress-hardy," that is, capable of dealing effectively with stressors. These three attitudes are *control, commitment,* and *challenge.* They are also referred to as the *three C's of stress hardiness* (Kobasa, 1979).

Control

Let's take a look at the first attitude, *control*. Stress-hardy individuals believe that they are in control of their lives, rather than that stressors have control over them. They recognize that they have resources and options that allow them to influence events in their lives. Although stress-hardy individuals recognize that they may not always have direct control over the actual onset or occurrence of an event, they certainly have control over their own response to the stressor. And this is not only true of humans, but also true of such higher life forms as rats. For example, let's hypothetically place two rats in cages capable of delivering an electroshock to their unsuspecting paws. (Psychologists do, indeed, do this and other perhaps less kindly things to these animals. That is why our standing as a profession is rather low in the rat community!) Using what is known in experimental psychology as a *yoked research design,* both rats are then shocked simultaneously at various intervals. One rat has a lever available in its cage that if pressed will discontinue the shock. The second rat has no such escape opportunity. When the first rat presses the lever, it stops the shock for both rats. This assures that both rats are exposed to the same level and intensity of the shock, but only the first rat has control over discontinuing the stressful event. Can you guess what happens? The first rat, the one with control, is minimally, if at all affected by the series of shocks. The second, "helpless" rat, on the other hand, suffers negatively, developing multiple psychosomatic symptoms such as ulcers.

These differences in stress response are maintained even when the escape lever is removed and replaced merely by a light that precedes the shock. In this design, the first rat has no means of escape, but is warned that a shock is imminent. Although the rat can do no more than dance around the cage, the effects of the stressor are somehow reduced perhaps because the rat knows it is going to be dancing around and is therefore more prepared to do so. Thus, our sense of control is also affected by the extent to which we can anticipate and prepare for the onset of stressors and change. Involvement in exercise is a perfect example of this. We know that physical exercise is stressful. Yet it is stress over which we have control because we typically can choose when to begin and when to end our exercise routine. Stress researchers conclude that this sense of control is at least partially responsible for the beneficial effects of repeated exercise.

Locus of Control
Stress-hardy individuals refuse to see themselves as victims, buffeted and abused by external occurrences over which they have no control. People with this attitude see themselves as active players in their own lives. They possess what Julian Rotter

(1966) described as an *internal locus of control.* Individuals with an internal locus of control believe that they are responsible for the ultimate outcomes in their life. They do not wait for fate to lead them in directions; rather they endeavor to take active control over their own life. When students with an internal locus of control fail a test, they do not blame the teacher nor the test questions. They take responsibility for the failure and attempt to determine what action is needed to avoid this in the future. This is the same attitude described by Stephen Covey as *proactivity.* Proactivity, simply defined, refers to the fact that as human beings we are responsible for our actions. What comes up for you when you hear the word *responsibility?* Perhaps you imagine a heavy ball and chain shackled to your ankle, impeding your freedom. But Covey means that we have *response-ability,* the ability to choose how to respond to any life situation. What about you? Do you look toward solutions, things you can do? Or do you focus primarily on the problem and how awful it is, and how things like that shouldn't happen to you? Take some time now and truthfully answer these questions. What would be your typical response?

What did you find? You see, whether you believe you are in control is a critical factor in predicting the outcomes of the various events in your life. There is no question that life is filled with waves that each of us must navigate during our personal journeys. You might not have the choice about when these waves appear or their strength, but you can certainly choose how you ride them—whether you travel on top of the water or underneath it; whether you have sails or oars to help you direct your way, or are merely carried away by the currents; and whether you enjoy the ride, in awe of the variety and beauty of it all, or are gasping for air, drowning in the tide.

Commitment

The second attitude characteristic of stress-hardy individuals that Kobasa identified is *commitment.* It is not merely persistence in following through with a goal; it is an attitude that expresses a real joie de vivre, a zest for life. Commitment involves believing that what you do is of value and importance. Individuals exhibiting this attitude seem to possess an almost romantic relationship to their own life and the pursuits they choose. When they wake up in the morning, they don't start their day with, "Oh God, I wonder what could go wrong today? What horrible ambush can life have planned for me?" Instead they wake up expectant of the possible surprises and wonderful experiences that the day has in store for them. They have an optimistic outlook. Stressors are viewed as potentially interesting and meaningful. Commitment is the opposite of alienation and is characterized by involvement.

It is not surprising that research has linked how a person answers two simple questions with the likelihood of developing heart disease. The two questions are: Are you happy? Do you like your job? If you answer yes to both of these, your chances of developing heart disease are much lower. Clearly the reverse is true when the answer is no. We are not implying here that overall life/job satisfaction causes heart disease; obviously there are many other factors operating in the development of cardiovascular problems. But your attitude toward your life is one important contributing factor. What is your attitude when you first open your eyes in the morning? We suggest you begin with an *attitude of gratitude*—one that says,

"Thank you. I'm glad I'm alive. I wonder what adventures and experiences this day has for me." You see, happiness is not a condition, but a decision. You can choose to focus on all that can make you miserable. If you do, you will get results fitting this attitude. Or you can choose to count your blessings, to be thankful for all you have, and all you still have coming. To quote the great comedian Gilda Radner shortly before her untimely death, *"Happiness is not about getting what you want, but about appreciating what you have."*

Another view of this attitude of commitment is expressed by Don Juan as told to Carlos Castaneda and reported in his book *The Teachings of Don Juan:*

> Each path is only one of a million paths. Therefore, you must always keep in mind that a path is only a path. If you feel that you must not follow it, you must not follow it under any circumstances. Any path is only a path. There is no affront to yourself or others in dropping it if that is what your heart tells you to do. But your decision to keep on the path or to leave it must be free of fear or ambition. I warn you! Look at every path closely and deliberately. Try it as many times as you think necessary. Then ask yourself, and yourself alone, one question . . . It is this . . . does this path have a heart? All paths are the same. They lead nowhere. They are paths going through the brush or into the brush. Does this path have a heart is the only question. If it does, then the path is good. If it doesn't, it is of no use. Both paths lead nowhere, but one has a heart and the other doesn't. One makes for a joyful journey; as long as you follow it you will be one with it. The other will make you curse your life. One makes you strong, the other weakens you. (Castaneda, 1998, p. 82)

Challenge

The third and final attitude that Kobasa discovered to be typical of stress-hardy individuals is that of *challenge.* This attitude can perhaps be best explained by considering the concept of *crisis.* The Chinese write this word using two characters, as illustrated in Figure 4.1. The first character is the symbol for *dangerous;* the second is the symbol for *opportunity.* Think about that, what a wonderful way to describe

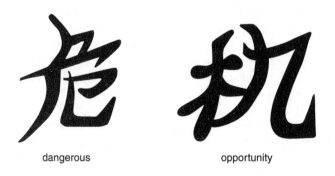

dangerous   opportunity

Figure 4.1

a crisis. Not a catastrophe, or a problem, but a *dangerous opportunity*. Individuals exhibiting the attitude of challenge focus not so much on the danger aspect of the crisis, but on the opportunities available as a result. Every crisis, no matter what, has inherent opportunities. Those who cope well look for these opportunities and capitalize on them. Those who cope poorly get paralyzed by the inherent danger. To again quote Don Juan,

> The basic difference between a warrior and an ordinary man is that a warrior sees everything as a challenge. While an ordinary man sees everything as either a blessing or a curse. (Castaneda, 1998, p. 82)

Or, to quote another colorful literary character, Zorba from *Zorba the Greek* by Nikos Kazantzakis, "Life is trouble, only death is not. To be alive is to put on your pants and go looking for trouble."

Stress Hardiness Inventory

Instructions: Use the following scale to indicate how much you agree or disagree with each statement:

0 = Strongly disagree	1 = Mildly disagree
2 = Mildly agree	3 = Strongly agree

_____ A. Trying my best at work and school makes a difference.

_____ B. Trusting to fate is sometimes all I can do in a relationship.

_____ C. I often wake up eager to start on the day's projects.

_____ D. Thinking of myself as a free person leads to great frustration and difficulty.

_____ E. I would be willing to sacrifice financial security in my work if something really challenging came along.

_____ F. It bothers me when I have to deviate from the routine or schedule I've set for myself.

_____ G. An average citizen can have an impact on politics.

_____ H. Without the right breaks, it is hard to be successful in my field.

_____ I. I know why I am doing what I'm doing at work or school.

_____ J. Getting close to people puts me at risk of being obligated to them.

_____ K. Encountering new situations is an important priority in my life.

_____ L. I really don't mind when I have nothing to do.

Scoring

To get your scores for control, commitment, and challenge, write the number of your answer, from 0 to 3, above the letter for each question. Then add and subtract as shown.

$$\frac{\_\_\_}{A} + \frac{\_\_\_}{G} = \_\_\_ \qquad \frac{\_\_\_}{C} + \frac{\_\_\_}{I} = \_\_\_ \qquad \frac{\_\_\_}{E} + \frac{\_\_\_}{K} = \_\_\_$$

$$- \qquad\qquad - \qquad\qquad -$$

$$\frac{\_\_\_}{B} + \frac{\_\_\_}{H} = \_\_\_ \qquad \frac{\_\_\_}{D} + \frac{\_\_\_}{J} = \_\_\_ \qquad \frac{\_\_\_}{F} + \frac{\_\_\_}{L} = \_\_\_$$

Control _____   Commitment _____   Challenge _____

Control + Commitment + Challenge = Total Hardiness Score _____

If your score is 10 to 18, you have a hardy personality.

If your score is 0 to 9, you are moderately hardy.

If your score is below 0, you are not very hardy.

Hardiness and Stress Resistance

Take a moment to fill out the Stress Hardiness Inventory. Research has documented an association between high hardiness scores and lower rates of physical illness among white-collar male executives and women in various occupations (Rhodewalt & Zone, 1989), blue-collar workers (Manning, Williams, & Wolfe, 1988), college students (Roth et al., 1989), and adolescents (Sheppard & Kashani, 1991). Hardiness is also associated with psychological health. Stress-hardy individuals report lower anxiety levels, less depression, greater job satisfaction, and lower levels of tension at work. In other studies, hardy subjects were shown to have stronger physical tolerance for stress. When exposed to a stressor they have a lower increase in diastolic blood pressure (Contrada, 1989) and a smaller increase in heart rate (Lawler & Schmied, 1987).

One interesting study (Allred & Smith, 1989) demonstrated that male college students who scored low on hardiness experienced high levels of tension before the onset of a stressor (that is, as they waited and anticipated), while those scoring high on hardiness displayed higher arousal only during exposure to the stressor. It appeared that the hardy subjects got aroused only when they needed an adrenaline surge to confront the stressor more effectively, while the others spent valuable energy worrying. Hardy individuals do get physiologically aroused, but at the right time and to the right level.

Strong resistance to stress is associated with optimism, and clearly the ability to think positively is a defining characteristic of the stress-hardy. Stress-resistant people are more likely to use problem-focused coping measures, positive thinking, and support-seeking strategies when faced with stress (Cohen & Edwards, 1989; Holt, Fine, & Tollefson, 1987; Nowack, 1989). Those scoring low on measures of hardiness tend to respond passively to stress, whether with avoidance or maladaptive behaviors. Hardy individuals are much more likely to take care of their health, which helps boost their stress resistance. A strong sense of personal control over one's life is associated with better health habits, such as exercise and good nutrition. Stress-hardy individuals are far less likely to utilize maladaptive coping strategies such as abusing alcohol, drugs or nicotine, or to act out aggressively when under stress.

The Three C's in Action

In August 1992, we had an opportunity to witness firsthand how stress hardiness attitudes affected the ability of literally thousands of people to cope with a monumental crisis. Being based in South Florida (specifically, the southern portion of Miami) we, along with thousands of other people, experienced Hurricane Andrew, one of the strongest storms ever to ravage the mainland United States. The scale of property destruction and disruption of normal life for months afterward was unprecedented. Just about everyone in the hurricane zone (ourselves included) suffered severe damage to their homes, businesses, cars, and personal property. Rebuilding took years, and normal routines were totally disrupted for at least six months for most people. As psychologists we paid close attention to how individuals coped with the aftermath and we found that three distinct styles emerged:

1. *The Whiners*—individuals who spent weeks and months bemoaning their plight and all the inconveniences, hassles, and property losses they suffered.
2. *The Stiff-Upper-Lip Crowd*—individuals who were very upset but focused on cleaning up and rebuilding and didn't spend an inordinate amount of time complaining. But internally they focused primarily on how awful it all was.
3. *The Adventurers*—individuals who did not deny the reality of the damage but who focused on how interesting, how exciting, what an adventure it all was. These people relished rebuilding their homes with insurance money. They delighted in the sense of camaraderie and community that developed between neighbors who found themselves in the same boat, and who previously had barely spoken to one another.

Needless to say, the latter group experienced far fewer emotional disturbances and physical illnesses than the other two groups. They believed that they could control their destiny, even in the face of incredible ruin. They were committed to making the rebuilding process as joyful as possible. And they viewed the crisis as a challenge and an opportunity to recreate their living situation and make new friends. For them the hurricane became an epic, fascinating story to share with friends, rather than merely a tragic event.

Clearly, you should be able to perceive the wisdom in Stephen Covey's oft-quoted phrase, *"The way you see the problem is the problem."* Ultimately, whether something is stressful depends on the way you look at the situation. Remember, it is not the world out there that makes you a victim, it is your perception of the circumstances and events that leads you either to be defeated by stress or to survive and thrive from the challenges and opportunities presented to you. You may not have control over all that happens to you, but you certainly always have control over the meaning you give to the events in your life. There is an old saying: *"When God closes a door, he opens a window."* Remember this as you face apparent hardships in your life. Always look for the windows; we guarantee that they will be there, no matter what the circumstances.

Chapter Summary

You cannot always control or change the stressors in your life, but you can always change your response toward these stressors. Adopt the witnessing stance (that is, becoming self-aware and viewing yourself and your situation from a distance) and notice how much easier it is to change your habitual responses. Developing the stress hardiness attitudes of control, commitment, and challenge will greatly improve your resistance to stress. Remember, it is important to believe that you have control, that you are responsible for the outcomes in your life, and that you have the resources to influence outcomes. It helps if you have a high level of commitment and involvement, a love of life, in which you believe that what you do is important and meaningful. As you face apparent hardships in your life, don't get stuck focusing on the potential danger. Instead view adversity as a challenge, focusing on the opportunities inherent in any difficult situation. A wealth of research indicates a clear relationship between stress hardiness attitudes and emotional and physical health.

Chapter Questions

1. What is the benefit of adopting the witnessing stance?
2. Define *self-fulfilling prophecy*.
3. Describe the three stress hardiness attitudes and how they contribute to stress resilience.
4. What is an internal locus of control?
5. What is proactivity?

Reviewing the Master Strategy: Stage 1

I. Breathing for Stress Mastery

    A. Differentiating ative relaxation and passive relaxation

        1. You must address your body. It's hard to tame stressful thoughts if your body is tense.

        2. Don't confuse inactivity with relaxation. Passive relaxation is not nearly as effective for reducing stress.

        3. You need active relaxation aimed at counteracting the fight-or-flight response and restoring homeostasis.

        4. Active relaxation involves becoming aware of your body and your physiological reactions to consciously decrease your arousal level.

    B. Diaphragmatic breathing

        1. Breathe from your diaphragm, not from your upper chest.

        2. Take deep, slow, rhythmic breaths; this counteracts the rapid, shallow, chest-breathing characteristic of fight-or-flight arrousal or anxiety. Shallow, quick breathing disrupts the oxygen/carbon dioxide balance in your bloodstream; deep, slow breathing restores the oxygen balance in your bloodstream.

        3. Remember the tips for facilitating diaphragmatic breathing.

            a. Imagine putting on a tight pair of blue jeans.

            b. Put a book on your abdomen and watch it rise and fall.

    C. Other benefits of proper breathing

        1. Helps overcome anxiety disorders such as phobias.

        2. Affects your perception of time; helps ease time pressure.

        3. Helps keep you in the here and now, and away from worrying about the future or lamenting your past.

        4. Can create powerful alterations in consciousness that facilitate spiritual exploration and growth.

    D. Generalizing proper breathing to your everyday life

        1. Set up reminders such as strategically placed dots.

        2. Practice it while doing things you do frequently.

        3. Remember to begin diaphragmatic breathing whenever you feel stressed, which will help interrupt your stress-inducing patterns.

        4. Begin practicing in nonstressful situations first, so you can master the technique and be able to use it readily when you are under stress.

    E. Breathing variations

      1. Add holding your breath.

      2. Slow it all down.

      3. Same as variation 2, but when exhaling, hum any note for as long as you can sustain it.

      4. Improve your focus and concentration by alternating breathing through each nostril.

II. Cultivating Awareness

    A. We all have the ability to become more aware of a multitude of things that make up who we are.

    B. Your ability to become self-aware, to stand apart from yourself and view yourself from the outside, is called the witnessing stance.

      1. You have the choice to be a witness to your own life.

      2. This shift in perspective provides the possibilty of change.

      3. You can't always change stressful situations, but you can always change your response toward the stressor. The witnessing stance allows you to do this.

    C. What triggers your stress response is not events themselves but your perception of events.

      1. By adopting the witnessing stance you can glimpse the meaning you give to a situation. You can then choose to change your perceptions.

      2. Use self-fulfilling prophecies to your advantage; your expectations significantly affect outcomes.

      3. Everything is created three times, including our responses to stress.

        a. First in your thoughts and expectations,

        b. Then by your words and descriptions,

        c. Finally by your actions.

    D. Stress hardiness attitudes are characteristic attitudes shared by individuals who appear very resistant to the negative effects of stress.

      1. Control

        a. Stress-hardy individuals believe they are in control of the stressors, rather than that the stressors have control over them.

        b. They know that if they can't control the stressor, they can control their response to it.

        c. Stress-hardy people refuse to see themselves as victims.

        d. Locus of control

          (1) Stress-hardy individuals have an internal locus of control—they believe they are responsible for the outcomes in their lives.

          (2) Stress-hardy people do not depend on fate; they endeavor to take active control over their lives.

      2. Commitment

        a. People who have this attitude possess a zest or enthusiasm for life along with persistence.

  b. Commitment is the opposite of alienation, characterized by involvement.
  c. Stress-hardy people begin with an attitude of gratitude.
3. Challenge
  a. In Chinese, *crisis = dangerous opportunity.*
  b. People with this attitude recognize that within every crisis there exists a multitude of opportunities.
  c. Those who cope well focus on opportunities rather than on danger or hardships.

E. Hardiness and stress resistance
  1. Research shows clear links between high scores on measures of hardiness and lower rates of physical illness.
  2. High hardiness scores are also associated with lower rates of psychological difficulties and stronger physical stress tolerance. Hardy subjects do get aroused, but at the right time to the right level.
  3. Optimism is an important component of stress hardiness.

Section 3

The Master Strategy: Stage 2

Acquiring Body Wisdom

What You Will Learn in this Chapter

- To explain the concept of *body wisdom*.

- To explain how adopting the *warrior's stance* facilitates the development of body wisdom.

- To practice progressive relaxation techniques to relax and release muscular tension.

- To practice intuitive stretching to release muscular tension.

- To list targeted stretches to prevent tension headaches.

If you have been applying what you have learned thus far, your breathing will be becoming slower, deeper, and quieter. Your awareness will be keener as you notice that you can observe and stand apart from your attitudes and emotions. It is from this very place that all systems of personal change and development begin. Now that you have gotten your feet wet, it is time to dive a little deeper and focus your new tools more intently on both body and mind.

Cultivating Body Wisdom

This chapter will focus on acquiring what we call *body wisdom*. Usually we think of wisdom as having an awful lot to do with the things we say and think. For many it is a measure of how many facts they know or how intelligent they are. Body wisdom, however, is not about how thoughts affect your body but about how your body affects your thoughts. We maintain that the body is intelligent, wise if you will, and that this wisdom can be tapped to improve your health, well-being, and performance.

Midway through graduate school one of the authors made a personal discovery that has guided his work as a therapist, trainer, and student ever since. The story illustrates the central premise of the chapter.

> It was the most difficult emotional period I had ever experienced in my life. I was a novice psychotherapist facing the pressures of a new job, a new relationship, physical illness, and the most difficult examinations of my academic life. My symptoms were classic: difficulty eating and sleeping, obsessive thoughts, a lack of energy, and feelings of hopelessness. Since I had never experienced anything like this before, I had no clear idea how to get better. The difficulties lingered for months, even after many of the problems had been resolved. It certainly didn't make sense to me that it just kept going on and on. It was as if my emotional life was going downhill and all I could do was watch. I was alternately frightened, sad, and bewildered by my inability to feel the way I used to feel—joyful and engaged in life.
>
> Finally, one afternoon as I sat alone in my office, particularly exasperated, I asked myself the key question, How did I act when I felt better? I was, as they say, sick and tired of being sick and tired. Thinking alone had not really changed anything for me. I knew I used to be different and I began to focus on *acting* that way again. Quite literally I decided to change my posture, the speed of my walk, the tilt of my head, the expression on my face. I walked out of my office *in character*, whistling a happier tune in my head, and asked the first person I saw how *she* was feeling. I played this part the remainder of the day and I noticed that I felt better.
>
> I decided to continue playing the role for a while longer and soon forgot that I was playing the role. I simply began to be the way I was, with one important difference: I now knew there was a way out of the darkness. I knew I would never be quite that lost again. This was the beginning of a series of physical and mental practices that have served me very well over the years. My body had led me out of the wilderness the way a horse carries an injured rider back to the stable.

The Warrior's Stance

Shakespeare once wrote, "If you lack the virtue, act the virtue." Today we say, "Fake it till you make it." What we are suggesting is that there is a stressed stance as well. If you act stressed, holding your body in the manner characteristic of the fight-or-flight response, you will feel stressed—even if there is no particular reason to be stressed. Luckily, there is an antidote for this: to discover what we call *the warrior's stance.*

At first blush, the notion of a warrior's stance leading to a more peaceful, less stressed existence may seem like an oxymoron. Why not a monk's stance or a gardener's stance? However, since life, business, and relationships are often presented in terms of struggles, battles, conflicts, and competitions, we might find it useful to examine this metaphor more carefully.

Contrary to popular belief, successful warriors are ultimately peaceful individuals whose primary battles are fought internally (Milman, 1991). They display a relaxed and balanced posture. This enables them to have exceptional reaction times and full freedom of movement. This capacity for relaxed balance also begets a fluidity of response that allows them to pull an opponent who pushes them or push one who pulls. It is a capacity to literally flow around obstacles. If you have gone whitewater rafting, you have been given the wise counsel to let the river carry you to a safe place when you have been thrown from the boat. To resist overpowering force is to risk being thrown into the rocks. A warrior knows that it is best to stay relaxed and alert and float feet first, in order to be aware of genuine routes of escape.

A warrior cultivates fearlessness. This does not mean recklessness. It simply speaks to the survival value of being able to notice the body's response to a threat and, by the force of the regular practice of a discipline, maintain the ability to choose a course of action. This grace under fire is often the difference between life and death in survival situations. Fear is a process that necessitates that we step out of the moment and contemplate the past or future. An intense focus in the here and now is the best way to keep fear at bay. The easiest way to maintain this focus is to cultivate the breathing and relaxed posture of the warrior. Warriors do not seek out or create conflict. Their preference is to walk away. But once engaged in battle, they are fully committed to their chosen course of action.

This is truly a critical piece of information for individuals who have attempted to change their lives by changing the content of their thoughts through endless affirmations. In our experience, "nice thoughts" have very little impact on someone's long-term well-being if his or her body is wracked with tension and stress-related hormones. You must actively change your physiology if you hope to contend successfully with stress. Consider a parallel from the study of communication. The best estimates that we have suggest that only 7 percent of the meaning of any communication is actually in the words themselves. The remaining 93 percent is communicated by our body language and the tone and tempo of our speech. In a similar vein, if we wish to communicate to ourselves the value of a more relaxed stance, we will need more than words. We need to speak to our bodies in a way that they will understand.

However, in the realm of relationships, the behavior that most of us need to cultivate is listening. This is no less true of our relationship with our body. The disorders that are brought on by chronic, excessive muscle tension begin as mere brief episodes of tension. We may grit our teeth in anger and still maintain some residual tension even after the cause of our anger is gone. Over time this can develop into bruxism, the grinding and gnashing of the teeth while sleeping. We may tighten our neck and shoulder muscles in response to fear or anxiety and again retain excess tension even after the threat has disappeared. This is how tension headaches begin. Why exactly does this occur?

You might say that in each of these cases, someone failed to listen to his or her body. Now the body's usual response is to continue communicating in its language of rising tension. Ultimately when we are stricken with a stress-related illness, the body is now screaming, "Why didn't you listen when I was whispering?" This is the primary aphorism of this chapter: *If you listen to your body when it whispers, you won't have to listen to it scream.*

Once again we return to the issue of awareness. To listen to the whispers of tension, we must be aware of what it means to be truly relaxed. Most people simply do not know what it means to be relaxed. We have seen many clients claim that they are relaxed, only to be shown otherwise when they are monitored by biofeedback equipment. As noted earlier, breathing is the starting point of your relaxation practice. But to go deeper into relaxation requires an additional practice, and we would like to introduce that to you next.

Progressive Muscle Relaxation

In his book *Progressive Relaxation*, Edmund Jacobson (1929), a Chicago physician, theorized that physical tension leads to mental tension, which further exacerbates physical tension. Therefore, learning to relax your body should promote mental relaxation and lowered stress levels. This technique has been used very effectively to treat a wide variety of stress-related disorders (Seaward, 1997). The theory of its use is simple: if you induce a feeling of deep relaxation in your body, you simply cannot be feeling stressed. As your body returns to homeostasis, your body's natural inclination toward healing and health is activated.

While we will present a formal protocol that you can follow to implement progressive relaxation, it is most important that you understand the principles and guidelines that will allow you to succeed as long as you commit to regular practice for several weeks. The reward for this short-term commitment is that you will be able to reduce the time needed to reach a relaxed state from twenty-five minutes down to five to seven minutes.

Practicing Progressive Relaxation

Before you begin, you may find the following guidelines helpful for your practice:

- Prepare a convenient time and place, and practice regularly. Remove distractions.
- Set up a regular practice schedule. Several times weekly is recommended until you have mastered the technique. You can then use it on an as-needed basis.
- Be comfortable. Wear loose-fitting clothing. Recline on your bed or sofa or in a cozy recliner chair. Some people place a rolled towel under their knees and lower back to maintain a comfortable spinal alignment.
- Avoid falling asleep, unless you are using this procedure to facilitate sleep.
- Don't try too hard. Paradoxically, if you try too hard to relax it will only increase your level of tension.

- Allow yourself to "let go." Sometimes people fear letting go, for it is equated with losing control. The only thing you have to lose here is unhealthy muscle tension. Learning to relax increases your control, but first you have to let go and allow this to happen.

- If you find your mind wandering, gently bring your focus back to your breathing and to this technique without scolding yourself or passing judgment.

- Finish your relaxation practice by coming back slowly. At the end of your practice session, slowly bring your attention back to the here and now, gently stretch your muscles, and open your closed eyes. If you are lying down, roll over slowly onto your side, pause, and then sit up. When your muscles are deeply relaxed, you do not want to contract them suddenly. Coming back slowly allows your relaxed state to linger for hours.

One goal of this procedure is to help you become aware of the difference between feelings of muscle contraction and muscle relaxation. Begin by taking a few moments to scan your body for tension and to focus your attention on any physical sensations. The basic method in progressive relaxation is to first carefully tense a particular muscle or group of muscles. This is to further develop your awareness of that part of your body, specifically when that part is tense. It is important that you contract the muscle only to a low level of tension. Be particularly careful not to overtense any muscle or muscle group where you are prone to experience muscle spasms. Contracting a muscle as hard as you can only leaves you more tense and does not cultivate relaxation. Tense each muscle group for five to seven seconds, and then release the muscle and focus your awareness on how the muscles feel as they relax for the next twenty to thirty seconds. Allow yourself to focus on any sensations of warmth and heaviness. As you continue from muscle to muscle, slowly but surely the sensation of warmth and heaviness will spread throughout your body. It can help to talk to yourself during this process with self-instructions such as the following:

> Clench your right hand into a fist. Tighten your fist and study the tension as you do so. Become aware of the tension and discomfort in your hand and forearm as you tense. Now let go of the tension and let your hand go limp. Pay careful attention to the feelings of relaxation spreading in your hand as the tension drains away. Notice the difference between the comfortable sensations of relaxation in your hand now, compared to the uncomfortable feelings of tension. Let go more and more, letting the muscles in your hand and forearm grow more and more deeply and fully relaxed.

The typical sequence of movements would be as shown in Table 5.1 on page 58. After you have become familiar with the sequence of movements in Table 5.1, you can try a number of techniques for coordinating your breathing, language, and imagination to creatively deepen and enrich your experience.

- Experiment with coordinating your breathing with the tensing and relaxing of each muscle group. Inhale and briefly hold your breath as you tense the muscle group. Exhale as you let go. Be aware of the sounds of the breath as you relax as well as the feelings of relaxation. Over time the hissing of the slow

Table 5.1   The Progressive Relaxation Sequence

Muscle Group	Activity
1. Hands and forearms	• Clench fists (left then right) • Bend hands backward at wrist (left then right)
2. Biceps	• Flex by bending elbows and bringing hands up to your shoulders
3. Triceps	• Straighten arms and push down against the chair or floor
4. Forehead	• Wrinkle forehead
5. Eyes	• Squeeze tightly shut
6. Jaw	• Press teeth together, then let jaw drop
7. Tongue	• Press into roof of mouth
8. Lips	• Press together
9. Head and neck	• Push head back • Bend head forward; touch chin to chest
10. Shoulders	• Shrug and try to touch ears
11. Chest	• Take three deep breaths; hold each several seconds
12. Back	• Arch
13. Abdomen	• Suck stomach in • Make stomach hard, as if it were going to be hit
14. Thighs	• Tense thigh muscles; stretch legs out
15. Ankles and calves	• Point toes toward face • Point toes downward

release of breath will become associated with relaxation and speed up the process of letting go.

• Some people prefer to visualize their breath as light that carries warmth and relaxation to their muscles. In this scenario, as you tense a muscle and inhale, you are pulling light to the muscle group. As you exhale, you expel darkness and tension from the muscles. Gradually you build an image of your body filled with light. If certain colors feel better to you, feel free to experiment. For instance, some people like to use the color blue to symbolize relaxation and red to indicate tension. Once you have reached a relaxed state you can really embrace your relaxation experience by imagining a scene that is pleasant to you (for example, lying on a beach or walking in the woods).

• There is also a time-honored method known as *autogenic training* in which you literally talk yourself into relaxation by repeating certain phrases over and over while focusing your attention on a particular muscle group. For instance, if after going through a progressive relaxation exercise, you still feel residual tension in a body part, then you would repeat to yourself, "My (arms, hands, thighs) feel warm and heavy." Or you could say to yourself, "My (arms) feel loose and relaxed." In fact, this method of systematically repeating relaxing phrases over and over again can be used on its own to induce relaxation. It can, however, be terminally boring, so be certain to tailor your program to your needs and interests. Create a routine that interests you, and you will increase the likelihood of following through and mastering this skill.

One main goal of progressive relaxation training is to help you achieve *differential relaxation* throughout your day. Accomplishing this means that you are able to contract only those muscles that are necessary to accomplish the task at hand, while keeping all other muscles relaxed (McGuigan, 1984). For example, there is no need to clench your jaw, stiffen your shoulders, or squeeze the steering wheel while driving. But your arm and leg muscles will certainly need to contract in order to operate a car.

The Importance of Stretching Your Muscles

As noted earlier, an intrinsic part of the fight-or-flight response is muscle tension. When muscles tighten, they also shorten. One way to reverse the fight-or-flight response is to lengthen your muscles. This is accomplished quite simply by stretching the muscles. Our goal here is not to provide a comprehensive manual on stretching exercises, but we would like to teach you several critical stretches that can help reduce or prevent tension headaches and mention some guidelines for stretching intuitively.

Intuitive Stretching

As you cultivate body awareness and relaxation, you will notice an urge to stretch your body in various ways. Many people notice that yawning is accompanied by an almost instinctual urge to lean back and extend one's arms. We are very aware of the need to stretch after sitting in a car or at a desk for a prolonged period of time. Anyone who has dogs or cats can watch them stretch when they awaken or when they anticipate they will go for a walk. While it is a good idea to read a manual on stretching or to take a yoga class to learn a specific routine, your body is actually a very good guide to this procedure if you pay attention to it. After all, someone figured this stuff out without referring to a textbook. Nor has anyone found the family dog curled up in front of the fireplace with an autographed copy of *The Autobiography of a Yogi*. This information is inside you. The following are guidelines for intuitive stretching:

- Set up a comfortable environment for your practice. This might include soft music.

- It is always easier to stretch muscles when they are warm. Thus, some light exercise such as walking until you begin to break a sweat is recommended. Another alternative would be to stretch after or while in a hot shower.

- Stretch on a firm padded surface, such as an exercise mat.

- Pay attention to what you are doing. It should not hurt when you stretch. Pain is a sure signal that you are doing something with too much intensity or in a direction that your body was not meant to accommodate. Progress in stretching will come rapidly, within weeks, but it is accomplished in small, incremental steps. Stretch and move your body until you feel a solid pull on the muscles and maintain that position as long as you feel comfortable. Return to your original position slowly.

- Move slowly, and do not bounce into any stretch.

- Do not hold your breath while stretching, but keep your breath flowing. Visualize or sense your breath carrying oxygen to the areas being stretched. See and sense them loosening.

- Rest for a short time after each stretch.

- At the end of your stretching period, take time to cool down and relax. An excellent time to do a breathing meditation or progressive relaxation is following stretching.

- While it is optimal to do a set stretch routine on a daily basis, do not limit your stretching to only one time or place. There are many moments throughout the day—at your desk, stopped in your car, and so on—when you can relieve the stress and tension in certain muscle groups with a quick stretch.

Stretches to Reduce or Prevent Tension Headaches

Muscles that are not strong and flexible tend to spasm and create pain. The muscles that support the head and neck are difficult to deliberately strengthen. These muscles are also intensely involved in the fight-or-flight response, as primates tend to pull their shoulders up to protect their necks and appear bigger when threatened. Over time, chronic tension shortens these muscles and leads to tension headaches. We have found several very simple exercises to be excellent for preventing tension headaches. These stretching exercises are most easily done in a standing position, but can also be done while sitting by moving up to the front edge of a chair or bed. Our favorite place to do this particular set of exercises is in a warm shower. Please follow the illustrations so that you stretch safely. Remember, no fast movements and no pain. Begin by placing both of your hands on your hips with your thumbs in front of your body and your remaining fingers on your lower back. Next, pull your shoulders back slightly. You are now in the correct position to begin.

Stretch 1

Fix your eyes on a point at eye level in front of you. While maintaining that visual anchor, move your head to the right as if you were attempting to touch your right ear to your right shoulder, as shown in Figure 5.1. You will feel the muscles stretching on the left side of your neck and shoulders. Hold this position *while breathing* for ten to twelve seconds, and then repeat this movement to the left (Figure 5.2). Repeat the complete sequence three times.

Figure 5.1

Figure 5.2

Stretch 2

From the start position, turn your head to the right as if you are looking over your shoulder and trying to see something behind you, as shown in Figure 5.3. Do not turn from the waist, but swivel your head from the neck up. Turn as far as you can without pain and hold this position for ten to twelve seconds *while continuing to breathe.* Then repeat the motion to the left (Figure 5.4). Repeat the entire sequence three times.

Caution: If your head should rotate completely around and face forward again, you should call a priest immediately. You may need an exorcist instead of stress reduction!

Figure 5.3

Figure 5.4

Stretch 3

The third stretch is clearly the geekiest of the stretches and definitely provokes laughter whenever we train people in its use. (This is also why we recommend doing these stretches in the shower.) Beginning from the starting position, push your face straight out as if you were trying to touch your nose to a point in space about three inches directly in front of your nose, as shown in Figure 5.5. You will feel the stretch at the back of your head, neck, and shoulders. You will also look like a chicken pecking for corn! Continue breathing, even if people are laughing at you. Hold this for ten to twelve seconds. Then reverse this movement, as if you were trying to pull your face and nose directly back from a really bad smell (Figure 5.6). You will tend to feel this stretch more in front of your neck and chest. Repeat this three times. You may now get out of the shower.

All kidding aside, if you are prone to muscle tension headaches, regular practice of these stretches will help elongate, strengthen, and loosen up the muscles in your head, neck, and shoulders. As a result, you can significantly decrease the frequency and severity of tension headaches and perhaps eliminate them altogether.

Figure 5.5

Figure 5.6

Chapter Summary

Remember that attitude change follows behavior change; therefore, act how you want to be until it comes naturally for you. Learn to adopt the stance of a peaceful warrior. Focus on the here and now, really listen to your body, and actively cultivate relaxation skills. Practice progressive muscle relaxation, in which you systematically tense and relax each muscle group from head to toe, to facilitate awareness of bodily tension and to release muscular tension. Remember to integrate proper breathing with your practice of releasing muscle tension. Get into a regular routine of stretching your muscles to release tension. It is much harder to feel stressed out when you are adept at relaxing your body.

Chapter Questions

1. How does body wisdom differ from the typical conception of wisdom?
2. How can acting as if you feel better before you actually do feel better promote positive changes?
3. Describe the warrior's stance.
4. According to researchers, what percentage of the meaning of our communication is actually transmitted by our body language and voice tone?
5. What is progressive muscle relaxation and how does it work?
6. What is the value in stretching your body, either by following a prescribed routine or by following your intuitions?

Looking at the World Differently

What You Will Learn in this Chapter

- To explain the concept that *the way you view the problem is the problem.*

- To practice using reframing strategies as a method for shifting your frame of reference.

- To explain how reframing lowers stress and facilitates problem solving.

- To enumerate the importance of being willing to give up being right.

- To explain the value of seeking win-win outcomes.

- To practice stepping into the shoes of another person.

- To practice optimistic thinking using the chapter guidelines.

- To explain how optimism relates to stress resistance.

- To practice cognitive restructuring techniques to challenge irrational thinking.

There is nothing either good or bad but thinking makes it so.

Shakespeare

If you have taken the challenge we set for you at the beginning of the text, you are amassing critical skills that will enable you to execute our Master Strategy for managing stress. Your breathing is becoming slower, deeper, and quieter. You have discovered the critical ability to observe your experience as you cultivate a change in your attitudes. Gaining a sense of control, commitment, and challenge moves you into the realm of the stress-hardy. In the preceding chapter you learned how to acquire body wisdom and the stance of a peaceful warrior; from this stance, the remaining options of the strategy are utilized. This chapter revolves around the simple question that completes the Master Strategy: Is there another way of looking at the world? The answer, of course, is always yes. Few of us would dispute that extremes of temperature, sound, or bodily injury are stressful. But the vast majority of that which is stressful to us is truly a matter of perception. If you perceive a situation to be threatening to you in some way, then you will react with the fight-or-flight response and experience stress. If you perceive it as nonthreatening, then you are not going to be stressed by it. This is what separates stress-hardy individuals from those who seem to be highly susceptible to stress. In fact, the way you think about things determines how you will experience your world. This is not a recent development in psychology, but a longstanding insight wherever people have acquired wisdom about the human condition. Thus what we are after here is helping you build your skills at changing the way you think. You absolutely do have a choice.

Reframing

There is an oft-repeated story of a Chinese farmer that goes something like this:

> A farmer and his only son were busily plowing their fields when their horse broke free from its harness and ran off into the nearby hills. When their fellow villagers heard of their plight they began to commiserate, "Oh, what terrible luck! How unfortunate! What will you do?" To which the farmer responded, "Good luck, bad luck—who knows?" Several days later the farmer's horse returned with two other horses in tow. His fellow villagers were astonished as they exclaimed, "What wonderful luck! You lose your only horse and end up with three!" To which the farmer responded, "Good luck, bad luck— who knows?" Several days later the farmer's son was attempting to break one of the horses so as to put it into service on his land. The son was thrown from the horse and broke his arm. All the villagers were united in their opinion that this was indeed bad luck. The farmer as usual responded, "Good luck, bad luck—who knows?" The very next week the imperial army marched through the village conscripting all the ablebodied young men into the service. The farmer's son was spared due to his broken arm. The villagers were once again impressed with this man's extraordinary good luck and told him so. And he replied, "Good luck, bad luck—who knows?"

This story illustrates a skill psychologists call *reframing*. Because the farmer was able to see things differently (that is, think about them differently than his fellow villagers), he was able to respond differently and experience an emotional calmness and equanimity that evaded those around him. As you get control of your breathing, relaxation skills, and awareness, you can notice what thoughts lead you to feel fear, anger, jealousy, confusion, and so on, and experiment with changing the way you look at things.

As with most things, this is easier said than done. However, be assured that it is definitely easier on you to learn to do it than not to do it. Reframing is like trying on different pairs of glasses and paying close attention to your responses. We've all heard of "looking at the world through rose-colored glasses" as a way to describe chronically optimistic people. And all of us have heard of people who act as if they have blinders on, because of their refusal to see things that are readily apparent to everyone else around them. We would like to offer you some different pairs of glasses to try on and experiment with their effects.

Entering the Funhouse

An older gentleman approached his doctor with a problem. "Every morning at 8:00 A.M. I have a regular bowel movement," he complained. His doctor was somewhat perplexed and responded, "That doesn't seem to be a problem to me. Most of my patients would be thrilled to have a regular bowel movement at 8 A.M." The patient replied, "The problem is that I don't wake up and get out of bed until 9 A.M.!"

Humor is the most familiar way in which reframing is used. We are led to believe a situation is one way and then suddenly we see it differently through an amusing lens. This contrast leads to the experience of laughter (a great stress reducer in itself). Whenever we can bring humor to our perceptions, our emotions shift and stress is reduced.

Consider the American amusement park phenomenon of the funhouse. We enter, frequently in the dark, and are beset by all manner of stimulation. The ground is unsteady, strange noises and blasts of air occur seemingly at random intervals, scary images jump in and out of our visual field, and bizarre mirrors distort our reflection. We are alternately scared, startled, and laughing, and emerge having had a pretty good time. Sounds a lot like life. Often our most interesting and funny tales are our descriptions of harrowing or embarrassing moments from our past, told from the safety of the present moment. As we step outside the experience and see ourselves in it, we see it differently and we can therefore feel differently. Remember what you are after here. In most stressful situations you will not be served well by the fight-or-flight response. In fact, trying to change your feelings by acting out this response will create problems. You need strategies for modifying your feelings and emotions so that you can choose an appropriate response. Here are some ideas to help you create your own personal funhouse.

Life as a Sitcom

The "life as a sitcom" approach is a simple strategy for changing your point of view. Imagine that your life is being videotaped and consider what this difficult moment might look like to your viewers. One of us discovered this strategy accidentally while moving a very heavy sofa with several friends.

The sofa was so awkward and heavy that everyone had to stop periodically to rest and readjust their grip. While we were doing this, I was intermittently warning all my friends to be careful not to set this large object on their feet. At that very moment I proceeded to lower the sofa onto my own foot! (And I realized that, indeed, it really was a very heavy sofa!) Just as my mouth was opening to ask for help, I mentally shifted to an outsider's view of my situation and started laughing hysterically. I had become Jerry Lewis or one of the Three Stooges, and I simply could not stop laughing long enough to speak. Luckily, my friends, also laughing now, realized I was pointing at my foot and removed the couch.

While we still recommend being careful with heavy objects, this incident demonstrates the power of shifting your point of view. The pain and upset would have been far more intense had the person not been caught up in the hilarity of the moment.

Life as a Novel

Frequently, when going through prolonged difficulty we tend to put ourselves down and create stress by seeing ourselves as failures, now and forever. It is as if we have forgotten that *things have not come to stay, but have come to pass.* Try considering your current difficulties as one chapter in a long autobiography. This gives you a different perspective and reminds you to *take a longer view of your life's possibilities.* Think about the life stories of great men and women. Almost invariably they are stories of failures that were converted into learning experiences, which then led to success. For example, were you aware that Abraham Lincoln lost eight elections, failed in business, went bankrupt, and suffered a nervous breakdown before he was elected president? There was a guy who didn't let failure get in the way of his success. His numerous failures built his character and made for a fascinating life story. Let your imagination roam into a successful future and look back at this time. What are you learning? In what way will it lead to your success?

Special Effects

The two reframing strategies discussed earlier are essentially about viewing your life literally from an outside or observer perspective. The next strategy includes playing with this perspective over time. This grouping of strategies is built upon a simple realization. Consider the fact that every special effect you have ever seen in the movies was first imagined by someone. This means that your imagination is capable of duplicating anything you have ever seen and fully capable of changing your experience in any given moment. For example, a very popular method of disrupting anxiety over public speaking is to imagine that your audience is nude. (A minority of people find this particular image really scary.) It is important to remember that we are in the funhouse to play and experiment. The next time you are bothered by a thought about the past or about the future, play with some of the following special effects:

- Change the voices in a memory to sound like Donald Duck and his nephews.
- Imagine that someone who is being particularly critical of you is suddenly seized with an attack of belching or flatulence.

- Add circus music to the soundtrack.
- Go beyond observing yourself. Watch yourself watching yourself.
- Imagine that an individual who always manages to intimidate or anger you is wearing a clown hat or mismatched clothes with dirty smudges, or is half-nude, and so on. The idea here is to create an image that is so ludicrous that it evokes your amusement rather than your anxiety or your anger.
- Pretend. Pretend. Pretend. Be childlike.

Case Study in Reframing: Using Special Effects

Julie was happily engaged to her boyfriend, and he had given her no concrete reasons to be jealous or to doubt his fidelity. Nonetheless, she found herself feeling quite jealous of an attractive, younger girl who lived in the same apartment building as her fiancé. Often she and her fiancé would run into this girl in the building or at the pool, and she would feel angry when her boyfriend chatted with her, although these conversations were not flirtatious and not of the sort that should have aroused her suspicions. When she confronted her fiancé with her feelings and asked him not to speak to this girl, he was annoyed and advised her to work on her feelings of jealousy. Since his actions were totally innocent and just friendly, he felt it was unfair to have to totally ignore this girl just to make Julie comfortable. When Julie considered the situation, by putting herself in her fiancé's shoes (a technique discussed in more detail in the next section), she decided there was merit to his point of view and suggestion that she work on her jealousy. To facilitate this end, she used reframing strategies to counteract the anxiety she felt when she saw the girl. Since the most common place she ran into this girl was in the elevator in her fiancé's building, she used that as the setting for her visualization. Julie imagined that she and her boyfriend ran into the girl on the elevator. Once the doors shut, the girl was immediately beset with an uncontrollable fit of gas, resulting in both audible flatulence and burping. Imagining this ridiculous scene made her double over with hilarity, and also resulted in Julie feeling sorry for the poor girl and her embarrassment. Julie was amazed that when she next saw the girl in question, all feelings of anxiety and jealousy were replaced by amusement and recollections of her silly, yet very useful, fantasy.

Giving Up Being Right

The number of different ways of looking at the world is limited only by your imagination. There is no substitute for your willingness to experiment with different pairs of glasses and notice what happens when you do. In other words, *there is no right way to see things*. In fact, we are going to recommend that you give up needing to be right. Of all the possible ways of looking at the world, the one most guaranteed to cause you stress and strife is the one that insists that your way of seeing things is the right way (Osterkamp & Press, 1988).

Giving up trying to always be right is a really hard thing to do. Why? We all love being right. Right? We've been taught since our youngest days to do the "right thing" according to the authority figures that surround us. We are rewarded for it. We feel good about ourselves for doing it. We try to figure out what the right thing is because we want to succeed, to win. Our culture worships winning. We remember the winners and display their names prominently in our stadiums, magazines, and commercials. Winners generally make a lot of money. Losers don't get the endorsements and the high praise. When you win, you typically feel good about yourself. Losing often hurts. And losing can be threatening to your self-esteem. Remember, any time you feel threatened you begin to engage the fight-or-flight response.

Looking for Win-Win Outcomes

If you are playing tennis or chess or any other competitive event, we recommend that you still put your focus on winning. However, we recommend extreme caution in trying to win in the arena of interpersonal relationships at home or at work. Operating out of a win/lose framework in relationships ultimately leads to all the players losing. Frequently, spouses with troubled marriages enter marital counseling with the hope that the therapist will choose sides and please explain to the other one how wrong he or she is. It is explained rather early on in the process of marital therapy that to ask who is winning in a marriage is an absolutely ridiculous question. A marriage built upon winning and losing is a marriage built upon conflict and threats. By definition it is then built upon stress. Our bodies respond to the ongoing battle of wills to be right as if it were a battle of the flesh, and once again the fight-or-flight response is engaged.

Good relationships embody the ability to compromise, to find ways that allow each party to get some of what he or she needs. Great relationships embody the ability to synergize. That is, they find ways for both parties to collaborate and create ways that allow the needs of each to be met. In other words, they find a way for everyone to win. As Stephen Covey has said in *The Seven Habits of Highly Effective People*, this requires courage and consideration. *Courage helps us stand up for what we need. Consideration allows us to honor the fact that others feel their needs as deeply as we feel ours.* Consider this story for a moment:

> Two young girls are fighting over a single remaining orange. Both simply insist that they need it. In a win/lose relationship, one of the children will end up with the orange, and one will end up with nothing but bad feelings and a desire to win the next time. In a good relationship they will cut the orange in half and share it. They will compromise and this is better than one of them losing. Neither, however, is completely satisfied. In a great relationship they speak to one another about why they want the orange. As it turns out, one of them needs the peel for a recipe and the other simply wants some orange juice. Both can have everything they want because they had the courage to speak up for themselves and the consideration to listen.

Stepping into the Other Person's Shoes

We maintain that looking for win/win outcomes in all relationships reduces stress. But practically speaking, how do you give up the need to be right, to win in your personal relationships? As with virtually everything else we have related to you, this too begins by breathing and becoming aware of the cause of your rising level of tension.

When we are trying to be right, by definition we see the other person's point of view or way of thinking as wrong. In order to go for a win/win solution to a problem, it helps to be able to *step into the other person's shoes and experience the world through his or her eyes*. This requires the funhouse skills we discussed earlier—that is, you need to pretend.

As you do your relaxing breathing, begin to allow a sense of the other person to form in your mind. See her in detail. Notice her expressions. Pay attention to the language she communicates through her body and her nonverbal communications. Hear not only the words she speaks, but the tone, tempo, and volume of her speech. Speculate about what she is feeling. As you do this, imagine that you can step into her body and look out of her eyes. Hear yourself saying the words and thinking the thoughts she might be thinking until you can feel what she is feeling. Do this until you can feel her sense of being right. Then step back into your own body and notice whether you feel any differences. Could she possibly feel as strongly as you do? Is it possible that her position has merit as well? Remember, the idea is not necessarily to give up your position and adopt hers (though that might happen). The idea is to move yourself to a place where you can work toward both of you meeting your needs, where both of you can win. Allowing yourself to feel, think, and experience the other person's viewpoint is a powerful way of facilitating the process of win/win.

Dealing with Irrational Beliefs

Another powerful way humans create stress for themselves is by doing what Albert Ellis (1975) called *catastrophizing*, which happens when you give yourself messages that a situation is too awful or overwhelming to bear, or that the worst is about to happen. These messages, also termed *self-talk* by Ellis or *automatic thoughts* by Aaron Beck (1970), refer to running commentary that goes on in your head during the course of the day. Most of it is mundane and benign, but problems arise when your perceptions are influenced by automatic thoughts that reflect irrational beliefs. Many studies have documented the link between irrational beliefs and anxiety (Bonner & Rich, 1991), but not all irrational beliefs cause stress. Those that do typically fall into two general categories: (1) beliefs that the world, someone, or something should be different; and (2) beliefs that your perceptions reflect reality rather than your subjective impressions of reality. Many times these irrational beliefs operate on a subconscious level, yet guide your emotional reactions nonetheless. Self-talk tends to be circular in nature, often creating a vicious cycle that can heighten your stress level (Bourne, 1990). Figure 6.1 illustrates this cycle. It begins with events in the environment that have no positive or negative value until you are there to interpret them or ascribe meaning to them. Next, we have your sensory impressions of the event (that is, your perceptions and sensory input). This is followed by your cognitions and interpretations of your perception of events (that is, your self-talk about the event), which may include irrational ideas or self-statements. The next step is the reaction of your emotional and physical system, not so much to the events themselves, but to your interpretations (self-talk) about the events. These physical and emotional reactions then feed back into your self-talk. For example, if you are feel-

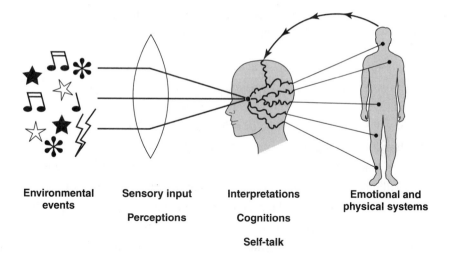

Environmental   **Sensory input**   **Interpretations**   **Emotional and**
   events   **physical systems**

               Perceptions   **Cognitions**

                               Self-talk

Figure 6.1   The Irrational Self-Talk Cycle

ing disappointed or depressed because of how you have interpreted an event, this sadness will then further influence your self-talk, predisposing you to further negative cognitions—and the cycle goes on. Negative thoughts create unhappiness, and depression stimulates further pessimistic thinking.

At the root of all irrational thinking is the assumption that things are done to you, rather than recognizing that events happen in the world (McKay et al., 1981). You experience those events (A), engage in self-talk about those events (B), and then experience an emotion (C) resulting from your self-talk. A does not cause C; rather it is B that causes C. If your self-talk is irrational and unrealistic, you create negative emotions.

The two common forms of irrational self-talk are statements that catastrophize or revolve around absolutes. Catastrophic thinking involves expecting the worst and/or giving nightmarish interpretations of your experience. Thus, a momentary chest pain becomes a heart attack; your boss's bad mood means you are going to get fired; your spouse is going out of town on a business trip and you assume you will be miserable if you are alone. The emotions that follow such expectations are very unpleasant, but you are responding to your own description of the world. Irrational self-statements involving absolutes typically include words such as *should, must, ought, always, and never.* Here you assume that if things are not a certain way, or if you do not conform to some standard, it is disastrous. Any deviation from that particular value or standard must be bad.

Cognitive Restructuring

A potent strategy for refuting irrational beliefs and changing your self-talk involves the use of *cognitive restructuring techniques* (Ellis & Harper, 1961). The first step in this process is to attempt to identify the irrational belief that is underlying your reaction. Once you have uncovered this belief, you may immediately notice the absurdity of it. Common irrational beliefs include the following:

1. Everyone needs to like you. It is awful if someone dislikes you.
2. You must be competent and perfect in all that you undertake.
3. Mistakes are sure proof that you are a failure.
4. You should never hurt anyone or refuse a request or favor.
5. It is horrible if things don't turn out the way you want.
6. You are helpless and have no control over your feelings or experiences.
7. You will be rejected if you don't go to great lengths to please others.
8. There is a perfect love and a perfect relationship.
9. You shouldn't have to feel pain. Life should always be fair.
10. Your worth as a human being depends on how much you achieve and produce.

The next step is to examine and challenge the irrational belief with your rational mind. Notice how so many of the irrational beliefs above revolve around a *should,* or a *must,* or the idea that it is catastrophic if something doesn't turn out in a particular way. Challenging irrationalities can be facilitated by asking yourself the following questions:

1. Is there any reason to think that this belief is true?
2. Is there evidence that this belief might not be true?
3. If I reject this belief, what is the worst that could happen to me?
4. If I reject this belief, what good things might happen as a result?

The third step is to substitute a new, rational belief in place of the old, irrational idea. Initially this may seem artificial, a bit phony. But replacing the negative thoughts that led to painful emotional responses with more positive and rational alternatives is a good start, even if you don't completely believe them at first. In time you will start to believe your rational thoughts, particularly after you experience improvements in your situation reflecting the change in you. Remember the lessons from Chapter 5 about "faking it till you make it." This principle applies to cognitions as well as overt behavior. The changes in your thinking patterns will become natural and comfortable after a while. With practice, it will get easier and easier to reframe reality and to view things from a more positive viewpoint. Cognitive restructuring does not imply that you should repress your thoughts. It is a process of acknowledging those thoughts and feelings that increase your stress level, then examining and challenging them, and finally replacing them with more rational thoughts when appropriate. For example, the following rational statements can be substituted for each of the preceding irrational thoughts. These are not the only options. We invite you to create your own rational alternatives if these choices do not fit for you. Notice that these rational statements use elements of reframing. Oftentimes, the process of thinking rationally involves the process of reframing, of learning to view a situation from a different, more rational perspective.

1. It is impossible to be well liked by everyone. No one achieves that. It certainly isn't the end of the world if _____ (insert the name of the person in question) doesn't like me. And, who knows, next month the situation could be totally different.

2. It is impossible to be good at everything. Besides, if I did succeed at being extremely competent in everything I did, many people would no doubt resent me.

3. Everyone makes mistakes. Mistakes can be learning experiences that lead to eventual success. *Failure* is just another word, not an enduring part of my character.

4. _____ will surely survive if I don't do things his or her way.

5. It is unfortunate if things don't turn out the way I would like, but it is hardly the end of the world and I can handle it. By this time next year I will no doubt be completely indifferent to this whole situation.

6. I *always* have a choice over how I respond to situations.

7. If I don't go out of my way to please someone there is a chance I might get rejected, but it certainly is not guaranteed. And if I need to go to great lengths to please someone in order for that person to like me, then that individual is not someone that I care to have as a friend. I want to be liked and appreciated for who I am, not for what I can do for someone.

8. There are no perfect relationships. I will focus on making this a healthy, honest, enjoyable relationship and learn to accept the inevitable disappointments and imperfections.

9. Life isn't always fair. Feeling pain is part of being human. If I never experienced sadness or despair, I would not know what it means to be happy and content.

10. My worth as a human being is much more dependent on my capacity to be fully alive and to feel everything it means to be human, the good with the bad. My worth depends more on how I am in relation to the people who are important to me.

David Goodman, in his book *Emotional Well-Being through Rational Behavior Training* (1974), offers six guidelines for rational thinking. You may find these rules to be quite useful for guiding you to think rationally and challenge your irrational beliefs.

1. *It does not do anything to me.* That is, the situation does not make you anxious or afraid. The things you say to yourself are what produce the negative emotions you may feel at any given moment. In the same vein, no one can make you feel anything. How you feel is always your choice. Other people may provide provocation, but ultimately you always choose how you feel in response.

2. *Everything is exactly the way it should be.* The conditions for things or people to be otherwise do not exist. To say that things should be different is tantamount to believing in magic. Things are the way they are because of a long series of causal events. To say that things should be different is to throw out causality.

3. *All humans are fallible creatures.* This is an inescapable truth. If you have not set reasonable quotas of failure for yourself and others, you increase the prospects for your disappointment and unhappiness.

4. *It takes two to have a conflict.* Before pointing your finger in blame, consider the 30 percent rule: Any party to a conflict is contributing at least 30 percent of the fuel to keep an argument going.

5. *The original cause is lost in antiquity.* It is a waste of your time to try to discover who did what first. It is often impossible to find the original cause of chronic painful emotions, as such dilemmas are usually extremely complicated and often the product of multiple interactions. The best strategy is to decide to change your behavior now.

6. *We feel the way we think.* To again quote Covey, "The way you see the problem is the problem." What you say to yourself determines your feelings.

The Map Is Not the Territory

We offer a final word on perception. Remember, your perceptions of reality are just that: your perceptions. Your perceptions are colored by your beliefs, expectations, biases, and so on, and that is true for all of us. That is why eyewitness accounts of crimes or car accidents are often so different from one another. Your perceptions are like maps you use to get around in your world. Remember that a map is not the territory. It is just one representation of a territory. And some maps are more useful than others, depending on the circumstances. If you want to drive from Atlanta to Washington, D.C., you will need a good road map. A topographical map of the southeastern United States will be useless. On the other hand, if you want to trek across the Appalachian Trail, a good road map will not help you, but a topographical map will come in very handy. The same is true of your perceptions. Given that we each have a unique set of blinders that influence our perceptions, it is useful to don that set of blinders that will be most useful in a given situation. *We recommend that you consciously choose to adopt optimistic perceptions. Why? Because that particular map of the world will be the most useful for helping you resist stress and achieve your goals.*

Optimism

Stress-resistant individuals develop the habit of perceiving and interpreting potential stressors in ways that give their life meaning and a sense of control. That is, they look for reasons to be happy and satisfied with life, imperfect as it is. They have become adept at turning lemons into lemonade and finding the proverbial silver lining in every cloud. There is a parallel between stress resistance and the quest for happiness. What makes people happy? Obviously, there is no easy answer to that question. Does money guarantee happiness? We all know of millionaires who are miserably unhappy. Does fame or success ensure satisfaction? What about all the movie stars who loathe their celebrity and yearn for obscurity? Does beauty make us happy? What about all the beautiful people who worry that they are appreciated only for their looks? Does getting a great job mean you will be content? What about all those stressed-out "success stories"? Clearly, your objective life circumstances do not define or ensure happiness or lack of stress. This is determined by your perceptions.

Happy people are optimists. Optimists tend to have lower stress levels and better coping skills because of how they perceive the world and their positive outlook. Optimists are not necessarily unrealistic or unwilling to accept or face negative circumstances; rather, they choose to focus on what is right rather than bemoaning all that is wrong. It is a matter of focus. They look for evidence that life is good and that they are doing all right. When misfortune strikes, as it does in everyone's life at some point, optimists recover more quickly because they find lessons in adversity that continue to give their life meaning. An optimistic world view naturally incorporates the stress hardiness attitudes of control, commitment, and challenge. In fact, *one could define optimism as habitual reliance on the three C's, combined with positive expectations.* Just as irrational or negative self-statements can create depression, anxiety, or other negative emotions, positive or optimistic self-statements can create and reinforce happiness and relaxation.

We encourage you to test your own level of optimism by completing the Optimism Questionnaire on page 76. There are no right or wrong answers to the questions. It is important to take the test prior to reading the interpretation of scores, in order to assure that your answers will not be biased.

There is a whole school of metaphysical thought that presumes that you create your own reality with your thoughts. If this is indeed true, then by adopting an optimistic world view you are maximizing your chances for success, happiness, and getting what you want. What have you got to lose by trying? Some of you may answer, "If I expect a positive outcome and it does not happen, then I will be disappointed." You would be a subscriber to the "Don't expect anything and you will never be disappointed" philosophy of life. But if you are really honest with yourself, you will admit that even if you truly expect nothing, if what you hope for fails to materialize, you are still disappointed. The problem with expecting nothing is that you might not do what is necessary to get what you want in life. There is an old saying: "If you want your ship to come in, you must go to the dock." The problem with being a pessimist is that you might not bother to go to the dock. Optimists go to the dock and find ways to enjoy their time there whether their ship comes in or not.

When to Be Optimistic

In what situations is it most effective and useful to be optimistic? Martin Seligman, Ph.D., in his book *Learned Optimism* (1991), advises that first you need to ask yourself what you want to accomplish. If you are in an achievement situation (a sports competition, a promotion at work, and so on), you may increase your chances for success if you are optimistic. If you are concerned about your feelings

Optimism Questionnaire

Instructions: Read the description of each situation and vividly imagine it happening to you. It is likely that you have not experienced some or even most of these situations, but that does not matter. If neither response seems to fit for you, go ahead anyhow and answer either A or B, choosing the one that seems more likely. You may not like some of the responses offered, but don't choose what you think you should say or what would sound right to other people; choose the response that would be most likely for you.

1. You get a flower from a secret admirer.
   A. I am a popular person.   1
   B. I am attractive to someone.   0

2. You run for a community office position and you win.
   A. I devote a lot of time and energy to campaigning.   0
   B. I work very hard at everything I do.   1

3. You miss an important engagement.
   A. Sometimes my memory fails me.   0
   B. I sometimes forget to check my appointment book.   1

4. You fail an important examination.
   A. I wasn't as smart as the other people taking the exam.   0
   B. I didn't prepare for it well.   1

5. You prepared a special meal for a friend and he or she barely touched the food.
   A. I made the meal in a rush.   1
   B. I wasn't a good cook.   0

6. You lose a sporting event for which you have been training for a long time.
   A. I'm not good at that sport.   1
   B. I am not very athletic.   0

7. You ask someone out on a date and he or she says no.
   A. I was a wreck that day.   0
   B. I got tongue-tied when I asked him or her on the date.   1

8. Your boss gives you too little time in which to finish a project, but you get it done anyway.
   A. I am an efficient person.   1
   B. I am good at my job.   0

9. You save a person from choking to death.
   A. I know a technique to stop someone from choking.   0
   B. I know what to do in crisis situations.   1

10. Your employer comes to you for advice.
    A. I am an expert in the area about which I was asked.   0
    B. I am good at giving useful advice.   1

11. A friend thanks you for helping him or her get through a bad time.
    A. I care about people.   1
    B. I enjoy helping him or her through tough times.   0

12. Your doctor tells you that you are in good physical shape.
    A. I make sure I exercise frequently.   0
    B. I am very health conscious.   1

13. You win a prestigious award.
    A. I was the best employee.   1
    B. I solved an important problem.   0

14. A store won't honor your credit card.
    A. I sometimes overestimate how much money I have.   0
    B. I sometimes forget to pay my credit card bill.   1

15. Your stocks are at an all-time low.
    A. I didn't know much about the business climate at the time.   0
    B. I made a poor choice of stocks.   1

16. Your romantic partner wants to cool things off for a while.
    A. I don't spend enough time with him or her.   0
    B. I'm too self-centered.   1

Scoring

If your score is 14 to 16, you are very optimistic.

If your score is 12 to 13, you are moderately optimistic.

If your score is 8 to 11, you vacillate between optimism and pessimism.

If you score is 6 to 7, you are moderately pessimistic.

If your score is below 6, you are very pessimistic.

(for example, trying to avoid depression or anxiety), adopting an optimistic frame-work will help considerably. If you are concerned about your physical health, by all means use optimism. By the way, optimism is one of the major emotional factors af-fecting how long cancer patients live and whether they survive. If you want to be in a leadership role, or to influence or inspire others, you will be far more likely to suc-ceed with an optimistic approach. On the other hand, in some situations you would be well advised to avoid optimism. If your goal is to plan for a risky or uncertain fu-ture, it is not wise to rely solely on optimism. This is not to say you should mire your-self in pessimism, but rather that you need to make a realistic assessment of the risk of negative contingencies and plan accordingly. If your goal is to give support or ad-vice to others with a grim future, do not use optimism initially. It is wiser to begin by being empathic to the person's situation. However, once you have established rapport it may be helpful to introduce some optimistic reframes after some time. Dr. Seligman teaches that the fundamental guideline for when to choose to be an optimist involves assessing the cost of failure in a particular situation. If the cost of failure is high for you, then optimism is definitely the wrong strategy. But if the cost of failure is low (that is, if all you have to lose is some of your time, or the chance of suffering some mild embarrassment), then go ahead and be an optimist.

How to Become an Optimist

Dr. Seligman offers a variety of suggestions for channeling your thinking in an opti-mistic direction. Many of the cognitive techniques for doing this are similar or iden-tical to the cognitive restructuring methods for defusing irrational thinking. This is not surprising, because in many instances pessimism is just one form of irrational thinking. Optimism is not about being unjustifiably positive about the world, but rather about learning to challenge negative thinking. Learning to think optimisti-cally involves learning to dispute pessimistic thoughts. Dr. Seligman recommends the following four strategies for defusing negativity.

Look for Evidence
The most convincing way of combating a negative belief is to show that it does not fit the facts, that it is clearly incorrect. Since pessimism is usually either an over-reaction or dead wrong, the facts will typically be on the side of a more optimistic viewpoint. This does not mean that we are recommending that you blindly repeat positive affirmations to yourself in the hope that it will somehow change your life. Most educated people are too scientific-minded or skeptical to blindly believe a positive affirmation without some confirmation that it could be true. Just repeating positive thoughts to yourself is not a guarantee of success or happiness. Rather it is how you deal with your negative thoughts that determines whether optimism or pes-simism will rule. In general, negative beliefs that accompany or follow adversity are almost always untrue. For example, let's say you fail an important exam. Common negative thoughts include assuming you are stupid, or that you can't cut it in college, or that you are destined to flunk out so why try at all. This is another example of cat-astrophizing, of picking the worst possible alternative from all the possibilities. One of the most effective techniques is to look for evidence pointing to the distortions

in your catastrophic explanation of events or catastrophic expectations of what will occur. Evidence to the contrary might include the fact that you got a B on a test last week, or that failing one test does not necessarily mean that you will fail every test or flunk out in general. Our professors in graduate school continually reminded us to *never generalize from one piece of data*. You could also remind yourself that even smart people can have a bad day and do poorly at times.

Generate Other Alternatives

Most things that happen in life have multiple causes rather than just one cause; they are a product of interactions among many factors. It is useful to keep this truism in mind. Pessimists make a habit of latching onto one cause and one cause only, and typically it is the worst of all the possible causes. They usually pick the cause that it is the most *permanent, pervasive,* and *personal.* Challenging this habit typically has reality on its side. To effectively challenge your negative thoughts, look for all the possible alternatives. What else could have caused the situation? What else could happen as a result? Focus on what is *changeable*, what is *specific*, and what is *nonpersonal*. Returning to our failed-exam example, you could focus on the fact that you didn't study hard enough (a condition that is changeable), that the exam was unusually hard (a specific instance that may not repeat in the future), and that many other students also fared poorly on the exam (a nonpersonal explanation for your poor grade). You may have to work hard to generate alternatives, and you may not be thoroughly convinced they are accurate. But the process of searching for alternatives trains you to think differently, and often you will come up with an alternative that makes a lot more sense than your worst-case scenario. But you have to look for the alternatives to get to that place. Latching onto the worst possible alternative and stopping there is a sure-fire recipe for increasing your stress level. Learning to generate alternatives will help you reduce it.

Realistically Assess the Implications

What do you do if the facts are not on your side, if your negative belief turns out to be true? In that case you need to use a technique called *decatastrophizing.* Ask yourself what the implications are if your belief is true. Generate a variety of alternatives. Challenge the most negative alternatives by asking yourself just how likely those implications really are. For example, let's say that you haven't just failed an exam, but that you are actually in danger of flunking out of college altogether. What does this mean? Is it a catastrophe that guarantees that you will never get a good job, that you will be a failure in life? Of course not; having a college degree certainly helps, but with the right attitude and willingness to do what is necessary, anyone can succeed, even without a college degree. This is not to say that flunking out is a good thing, but it is also *not the end of the world.* Other people have gone on to success without making it through college. And you need to remind yourself that flunking out is not a foregone conclusion. You have some choice in the matter, depending on how seriously you take your studies from this point forward.

Evaluate the Usefulness of the Belief

Occasionally there are situations where the consequences of holding a belief are potentially more problematic than the belief itself, true or not. You need to evaluate whether the belief is potentially dangerous. For example, if you truly believe you are stupid, even if you are not a rocket scientist, the damage to your self-esteem could be heavy. There are other instances when the best strategy is to distract yourself from a belief, rather than taking time to challenge it. This is the case when negative thoughts interfere with your performance, when you are on the spot to perform now. Engaging in negative thinking or the evaluation of such is not useful in a situation where you need to perform now. Distracting yourself and focusing on the task at hand is the most useful response.

Reframing Exercises

1. Is there a situation where you are habitually stuck because you are totally unwilling to part with your point of view about it? We guarantee that if you think hard enough you will find that the answer to this question (for everyone) is typically yes. Can you think of a particular instance? Pick one of the reframing techniques and practice shifting your perspective on this issue. If you are at a loss for how to proceed, experiment with reframing a past mistake or failure as a valuable learning experience. Think about how your life might have improved or been enriched today, either directly or indirectly, as a result of this experience. You may have to dig deep to adopt this perspective, or to see connections between past mistakes and current successes, but if you persist you will be rewarded.

2. The next time you find yourself feeling anxious or depressed, look deeper into yourself, and determine whether any irrational thoughts are fueling your feelings. Look at the list of irrational thoughts and check whether any of your unconscious cognitions are a close match. If so, follow the three-step cognitive restructuring technique to counteract those irrational messages.

3. Identify the area of your life about which you are most pessimistic. Experiment with the four techniques presented earlier and notice how you are able to shift your perceptions or expectations in a more optimistic direction.

Chapter Summary

"The way you see the problem is the problem." That is, problems are not what happens to you, but rather what you tell yourself about what happens to you. Your perceptions and expectations in great part determine whether you will experience stress and to what degree. To reduce your stress level, you can alter your perspective by practicing the art of reframing, which involves using various strategies for shifting your point of view. Oftentimes a helpful shift involves giving up being right. Being able to step into the shoes of the other person, to really understand his or her perspective, helps you work toward win/win solutions. Stress is also caused by conscious and unconscious irrational beliefs, which often lead to catastrophizing about situations. Learn to refute irrational beliefs by first identifying them, then challenging them, and finally substituting more rational alternatives. Remember, the map is not the territory. Your perceptions are not reality, only your subjective interpretations of reality. Adopting an optimistic map will be most useful for mastering stress and achieving your life goals. Practicing optimism is more about challenging nega-tive beliefs or expectations than mindlessly repeating positive statements. Learn to dispute negativity.

Chapter Questions

1. How does your perception of events influence how stressful those events will be for you?

2. Describe the process of reframing and how it can prove useful for reducing your stress level.

3. Describe several strategies for creating reframes.

4. What is the value of looking for win/win solutions to interpersonal conflicts?

5. What strategy can be helpful for allowing you to think in ways that promote win/win solutions?

6. What types of irrational beliefs contribute to increasing your stress level?

7. Describe the three steps of cognitive restructuring.

8. How does optimism differ from repeating positive affirmations to yourself?

Pathways Through Anger

What You Will Learn in this Chapter

- To identify what contributes to anger on a physical and psychological level.

- To assess your own level of anger using the hostility scale.

- To explain the relationship between anger, Type A personality, and cardiac disease.

- To practice using reframing strategies to defuse anger.

- To describe the value of forgiveness for stress reduction.

Have you experienced times when you were quick to anger, either in the workplace or at home, as if your fuse had become significantly shorter? Unless you are a yogi master and have achieved perfect balance and enlightenment, of course you have. All of us have had periods when we were more irritable and less tolerant. Have you noticed that there is a direct relationship between these periods and the level of stress in your life? Undoubtedly, a very common response to stress is anger and irritability. But why? Remember, stress is our body and mind's response to perceived threat. If you consider that for our ancestors, threat frequently represented attack from animals or other tribes; then anger was an adaptive reaction that mobilized them to take defensive action. Therefore, anger had survival value because typically, for our forebears, the appropriate response was to physically fight for their lives. But in today's world, physical confrontations are no longer useful in most situations. Yet we are left with this holdover emotional baggage of anger. Verbal expression of this anger, particularly if unmodulated, is certainly not much more adaptive, either in your work environment or in your personal life.

Violent, unrestrained expression of anger, both rational and irrational, has been at the forefront of national headlines and at the core of many of the most serious problems faced by today's society. As population swells, often leading to overcrowding or congestion, and cultural shifts appear to occur at an ever-quickening pace, many individuals become overwhelmed and resort to violence. While terrorist attacks typically intend to make particular political statements, we all struggle to understand why adolescents have engaged in countless school slaughters over the last few years. Meanwhile, adults bring firearms to work and shoot co-workers and innocent bystanders. Is domestic abuse, of both children and spouses, on the rise? Or is domestic violence just more routinely reported and publicized? Either way, it is clear that violence is a serious problem with which we must all contend, to avoid becoming either a victim or a perpetrator. Learning to co-exist is of paramount importance, and preventing violence first involves learning to handle anger.

The Nature of Anger

Physiologically, anger is arousal. When you are angry, the fight-or-flight response has been activated. Something has stressed you, and your body has prepared you to either fight or flee. Clearly, anger helps you if you need to fight. The problem is that when we are stressed we tend to look around to see what is making us angry. That is, we tend to externalize the sources of our anger or stress. We assume that something out there is causing our arousal. This is true not just with humans, but with our animal cousins as well. For example, imagine a lab rat in a box whose floor is covered with an electric grid. If that rat is alone and we shock it, the rat will jump, look for an escape route, and manifest clear signs of arousal. If we put another lab rat in the box with our first rat, and then shock them both, the rats will attack each other. It's as if the rats are blaming each other for the shock.

Frequently when under stress we behave just like our friends the rats. We look around for who is to blame for our uncomfortable feelings and sensations without being consciously aware of what we are doing. Yet even more problematic, para-doxically, those with whom we feel most comfortable are the most likely targets of our direct aggression. The old saying, "You always hurt the ones you love," is really true. Don't get us wrong. You may also get angry with people with whom you are not close or comfortable, but you are more likely to express your anger toward them in-directly. This is particularly true if they are in a position of authority over you. So in-stead of telling your boss how angry he or she makes you, you might just complain to your cronies at the water fountain or over lunch. Then when you go home at the end of the day and your spouse or significant other does something even mildly an-noying, you are ready to literally bite his or her head off.

This tendency to attribute the source of our uncomfortable feelings to an external agent further aggravates the problem because "putting it out there" lowers our control. Remember that in the three C's or stress hardiness attitudes, the first C is *control*. If we perceive that we are not in control in a particular situation, we are more likely to fall prey to the devastating effects of stress. And as we men-tioned in Chapter 4, we feel we are in control when we believe we have a choice. Well, the fact is that whether or not you get angry or stay angry is really *always* your choice. Being able to recognize this gives you control. It is not the event out there that causes you to flare; it is your interpretation of the situation that ulti-mately leads you to be angry—or not angry. We know that this might initially be difficult to accept, but the fact is that human beings give meaning to everything. And that meaning leads you to blowing your top, so to speak. The difficulty in rec-ognizing this is that we are typically unconscious of the interpretation or meaning we give a particular situation, as it lies outside our awareness and occurs almost instantaneously.

The fact that we have choice as to whether we feel anger, or any feeling for that matter, is the reason why two people can be faced with the same situation yet respond in ways that are diametrically opposed. For instance, imagine that you are driving in your car and someone cuts you off, almost causing an accident. The common response is to react with immediate anger and to grumble or even scream at the inconsiderate son-of-a-gun who dared to intrude on your sacred vehicular space. You tell yourself, or him, what an idiot he is, perhaps questioning how he ever obtained a driver's license or commenting on his dubious parentage. The incident may even become an indictment of all the drivers in your city, none of whom are as skilled as you. Meanwhile you are stewing in your own juices and continuing to aggravate yourself. You are well on the way to experiencing road rage.

Can you see how the meaning you gave this situation led to your angry re-sponse? Is it possible that another meaning that also explains the other driver's be-havior could lead to a different response? What if, instead of assuming incompetence or inconsideration on the part of the other driver, you said to yourself, "Poor guy, he must have a lot on his mind. I wonder what is going wrong for him?" Undoubtedly, were you to ask yourself these questions, your response to the same event would be quite different. Once again we are reminded of Stephen Covey's motto: "The way you see the problem is the problem." Not surprisingly, the solution invariably lies in changing the way you view the situation.

Anger and the Type A Personality

But you might be sitting there saying, "Why should I change? I have a right to be angry!" You are correct. You do have a right to be angry—but are you happy with the results? Persistent or frequent anger has serious deleterious effects on your emotional and physical well-being, as well as on your ability to be effective. There is no doubt that anger and resentment damage your health. A convincing example of this comes from what we have learned about the Type A personality. In the 1970s, cardiologists Meyer Friedman and Ray Rosenman (1974) noticed that their patients tended to share certain personality characteristics. They called this cluster of behavioral traits the *Type A personality.* Type A individuals tend to be very hard-driving, achievement-oriented, compulsive, overly concerned with time pressure, and easy to anger, as compared to Type B individuals, who are laid back, easygoing, and less concerned with time. A strong relationship was discovered between the Type A orientation and cardiac problems. But later research revealed that the only aspect of Type A behavior that was really related to heart disease was the hostility component. That is, one could be hard-driving and compulsive without incurring a greater risk of heart disease if hostility was not present. Take out a moment to fill out the Hostility Scale to help determine whether anger and hostility are a problem for you.

Hostility Scale

Instructions: Answer each question true or false.

_____ I often get annoyed at checkout cashiers or the people in front of me when I'm waiting in line at the supermarket or other stores.

_____ I usually keep an eye on the people I work or live with to make sure they're doing what they should.

_____ I often wonder how extremely fat people can have so little respect for themselves.

_____ Most people will take advantage of you if you let them.

_____ The habits of friends or family members often annoy me.

_____ When I'm stuck in traffic, I often start breathing faster and my heart pounds.

_____ When I'm annoyed with people, I always let them know about it.

_____ If someone wrongs me, I'll get even.

_____ I usually try to have the last word in an argument.

_____ At least once a week, I feel like yelling or even hitting someone.

Scoring

If you answered true to five or more of these questions, you may qualify as excessively hostile.

The fact that anger is a risk factor for heart attacks is well documented. Anger sets off a physiological mechanism that makes your heart beat faster, your blood pressure rise, your coronary arteries constrict, and your blood get stickier. A recent study of more than one thousand patients at Mount Zion (Illinois) Medical Center who had survived heart attacks found that those who had counseling to reduce their anger, aggression, and hostility had half the rate of recurring heart attacks of those who received no such help dealing with anger.

Likewise, it is known that persistent anger is linked to ulcers and other psychosomatic conditions. Similarly, psychotherapists often find that anger is the flip side of depression. That is to say, often depression results from unresolved anger that is turned inward toward the self. Nor does anger fare much better in relationships. Ultimately, the art of nurturing relationships depends on your ability to establish trust. It is about building bridges between yourself and others. When angry, you draw sides, which keeps others on their side of the conflict. You enter into interactions with the goal of "getting your way." Even if you are successful in achieving your ends, if you "win," so to speak, the relationship often ends up losing. So if your long-term goal is a happy and satisfying relationship, anger typically won't get you what you want.

But is anger always bad for you? Actually, the answer is no. Anger is a normal human reaction. It becomes problematic when it is chronic, persistent, and unresolved. In fact, there are instances when anger can be useful. Anger can be helpful for mobilizing your energy so that you can take appropriate action. If you were never able to get angry, you might become so complacent that you would never seek to resolve issues in your life.

The task is not to always prevent anger, but to learn how to move through it efficiently and effectively. A former mentor of ours, Jacqueline Small, teaches that "*the only way out is through.*" You need to be aware of your anger and, rather than getting mired in it, recognize it as a signal that something is amiss and must be addressed. Then you can use the energy it creates to mobilize you to take appropriate action.

Coping with Anger

Reframing Revisited

We have found that the most effective way of beginning to use anger, rather than be used up by it, not surprisingly involves beginning with the Master Strategy. First, remember to breathe. Take a couple of deep diaphragmatic breaths and then shift your attention to your muscles, particularly the muscles in the shoulders, neck, and jaw. Take a moment to relax these. Then assume the witnessing stance. Look at the situation from the outside. Ask yourself, "How can I look at this differently?" We talked about reframes in Chapter 6. Reframing is a powerful method for dealing effectively with anger. We would like to offer you a couple of reframes we have found particularly useful for working through anger.

Look for Comedy
One approach involves viewing your life as a sitcom in progress. It asks that you think of yourself as a comedy writer of your own life. In almost all situations, an element of humor or absurdity can be found if you look at it from a different perspective, and

seeing the humor inherent in a situation effectively defuses much of the anger. Think for a moment; if you were an objective, uninvolved bystander witnessing your situation, could any aspect of your circumstance be seen as humorous? Who is your favorite stand-up comedian? If that person were observing what was happening to you, what pithy or funny remarks would he or she make about you or your dilemma? You can probably remember times when you witnessed an event where a friend, colleague, or relative became angry, while you had a hard time keeping a straight face because you could see the absurdity in the situation. You can do this with yourself as well. As a matter of fact, almost any situation will seem funny when you are looking back at it after the passage of time. Realize that you have the choice to imagine that time has already passed when you are involved in your particular dramas.

The Unfolding Drama Viewpoint
Yet another useful reframe involves looking at your situation from a frame of reference in which you view your life as an unfolding drama for the benefit and entertainment of a higher being. And why not? Your life is God's gift to you. How you live it is your gift to God.

Write a Chapter in Your Life
A related reframe is to consider that your life is a novel in progress, and what is happening to you at any moment can make for a fascinating chapter in the book that is your life. How can you write this chapter, taking into account what you will ultimately learn from the experience?

We find that any of these perspectives will help to get you unstuck from the anger of the moment. If none of these appeal to you, can you think of others that would serve you better? Take some time to reflect on this now.

Case Study 1 in Anger Control: Road Rage

Sally is a high-powered executive who works downtown in a major metropolitan area. She enjoys the excitement and cultural amenities of the big city, but she prefers to live in a more rural atmosphere. To accomplish this aim, she purchased a home on the outskirts of the suburbs in an area that still feels like the country. This also enables her to have a lot of land and a barn in which to keep her horse. The price of this is that she has a very long commute, in rush-hour traffic, to and from her job. On a good day it takes her forty-five minutes to get to the office, and most days it takes over an hour to reach work. She hates the drive, but she is very satisfied with her job, and has no desire to move closer to work and lose the country environment she cherishes.

Lately Sally has found herself frequently engulfed in road rage, getting furious at bad drivers or inconsiderate motorists who cut her off. She found herself often screaming in her car, leaning on the horn unnecessarily long, making obscene hand gestures to other motorists, and then feeling agitated throughout the drive and even after she reached her destination. She was very concerned about her feelings and her behavior. She feared that she might anger strangers with her offensive gestures, who might then attempt to retaliate in some fashion. Mostly she was upset about the holdover agitation she felt even after getting out of the car. Her blood pressure was up and she was getting frequent tension headaches during her drive home which lingered all night.

Assisting Sally to work through road rage to achieve road peace first involved helping her to recognize that she had a choice whether to respond with anger to difficult driving situations. Sally was encouraged to identify the underlying assumptions that were fueling her anger. She believed that she had no control in the situation; after all, she couldn't stop lousy drivers from making driving mistakes, going too slow, or cutting her off. But the thought that triggered the bulk of her anger was her assumption that "they got away with it." That is, the person driving like a madman got away scot-free while interfering with her and putting her in danger.

Sally was able to overcome her road rage by being willing to shift her thinking. She began to acknowledge that while she certainly had absolutely no control over the driving behavior or competency of other motorists, she always had control over how she chose to respond to any given driving situation. She then searched for a way to reframe the trigger assumption: that bad drivers get away with it. She recognized that if a given driver was really that unskilled, then it was just a matter of time before that person was either ticketed by police or hospitalized from a traffic accident. The next time she witnessed a bad driver (a speeder weaving dangerously in and out of lanes on the expressway), she fantasized that that driver got a speeding ticket later that day. She further realized that when drivers are not incompetent but just inconsiderate (for example, those who cut you off because they are in a hurry), this inconsideration will catch up with them in other areas of life, particularly in interpersonal relationships. People who always put their needs above those of others rarely can sustain lasting relationships. So the next day, when a dapper businessman in a new Mercedes almost ran her off the road to cut into her lane, Sally imagined that he returned home that night and discovered that his wife had left him for being such an insensitive cad.

Sally was amazed at how adopting these alternative perspectives and engaging in these reframed fantasies defused her anger. Remembering to breathe slowly from the diaphragm when the driving got tense helped her to keep her mind open to new perspectives, rather than engaging in knee-jerk reactions of rage. She also began using her time in the car more constructively. She began listening to books on tape, rather than complaining that she didn't have time to read. She also began carrying a tape recorder in the car and periodically dictating reports that she didn't get to finish at work. Using her time more productively lowered her stress level and reduced her feeling that she was wasting two hours a day in the car. The distraction value of these activities was such that she stopped spending time searching the landscape for bad drivers or driving errors, as she had before. Within two weeks of adopting this change in perspective, Sally was free of road rage.

Case Study 2 in Anger Control: Workplace Anger

Carlos had been working at his sales job for a mid-sized manufacturing company for two years and had enjoyed phenomenal success. He had quadrupled his earnings in that time, due to his high sales figures and the company's commission structure, and he was the top salesman in the company. His forte was in developing new accounts and generating increased orders from existing customers. Rather than enjoy his success, Carlos became even more driven and began having inappropriate temper outbursts at work when other workers did not meet his expectations. He became enraged when other workers made minor errors that delayed the processing of orders for his customers. He would often yell at these co-workers and insult them. What upset him the most was what he perceived as the meddling behavior of the sales manager, his immediate boss. When his boss would attempt to assist him on an account (to help with paperwork), Carlos took offense. He assumed that his boss was implying that he couldn't handle it by himself. Mostly he was worried about getting fired either because of his temper outbursts or because he was disliked. He feared that the bosses wanted to can him so they could hire someone else at a much lower salary level. He knew he had to deal with the situation when his boss took him aside and told him that he needed to work on his attitude. Carlos was having problems sleeping at night and relaxing on the weekends with his family because he was so caught up in anger and worry.

Carlos was encouraged to use diaphragmatic breathing and to wait ten minutes before responding to any mistakes made by co-workers or perceived slights by his superiors, so he would have time to cool down. Using cognitive restructuring, he confronted his irrational expectation that people should always be perfect and never make mistakes. He was also encouraged to identify the other assumptions that were underlying his anger.

The first assumption was that he was soon to be fired despite his success. To find a reframe to combat this, he was encouraged to think of everything his company had to lose by firing him. He quickly realized that the company stood to lose a lot of money and a lot of business if he was let go, even if they did hire a lower-paid replacement. He had to admit that it would be a very foolish move for his employers to fire him, even if they did find him to be a "pain in the butt."

The second assumption involved his belief that his boss's efforts to help him with paperwork implied that he was not competent. When reflecting upon alternate explanations for his boss's behavior, Carlos realized that when his boss helped with paperwork it freed him up to do what he did best (that is, develop new accounts and increase orders from existing accounts). Therefore, his boss's assistance could help both Carlos and the company increase earnings.

When Carlos returned to work, he practiced breathing techniques and taking a ten-minute breather to walk around the office if hassles arose. Using the guidelines in Chapter 13 for practicing assertive (as opposed to aggressive) behavior, he approached his co-workers diplomatically and calmly. When his boss came to assist with his paperwork, rather than resenting it and glaring at him as he had done previously, he thanked him. Within a week he and his boss were on much better terms. They had a heart-to-heart talk in which his boss confirmed that he wanted to pitch in so as to enable Carlos to focus solely on selling. Carlos suggested a brainstorming meeting between the sales and shipping departments to foster improved communication and problem solving to expedite timely shipment of orders. At the meeting Carlos practiced empathic listening and began to understand why his co-workers made many of the errors. This meeting was very productive, and as a result numerous suggestions were made to help fix the existing problems. Carlos acknowledged that mistakes would still occur, but he was hopeful that the frequency could be significantly reduced by implementing the ideas offered at the meeting.

Lastly, Carlos kept reminding himself that he was a very valuable employee who had control over whether he was fired by how he chose to behave in the workplace. Several weeks after his change in attitude, his bosses took him aside and praised his work and the improvement in his attitude. From the discussion it was abundantly clear to him that he was, indeed, a very valuable employee with a secure job. Within two weeks he began to enjoy going to work again. His sleep normalized and he began to relax and have fun on his weekends.

The two case studies presented here are actual cases presented by patients in our Stress Mastery practice. The names and some details have been changed to protect the confidentiality of the participants, but the methods and outcomes are stated as occurred.

Developing Your Own Plan to Defuse Anger

Take a moment and think about a situation or a person that often triggers your anger. (Notice that we did not say something or someone who *makes* you angry. No one can make you angry; whether you respond with anger is always your choice.) Now, take a few moments to practice diaphragmatic breathing, and consciously release the tension from your muscles to better prepare you to deal with the stress of these thoughts. If it is a situation that you are thinking about, what alternate perspective or reframe can you create to help you view things differently? Are you harboring any irrational ideas that contribute to your anger and could be challenged? Spend a few minutes pondering the situation from this new frame of reference. What happens to your anger? Do you find it diminishing or perhaps even fading entirely? If you have been thinking about a person who often triggers your anger, make your best attempt to put yourself in the shoes of that individual. What feelings or motivations might that person have that led him to behave in ways that anger you? This does not mean that you have to agree with that person or condone his behavior; the only requirement is that you spend some time viewing the world from his eyes. Do you notice that it is harder to generate anger when you understand where someone else is coming from, even if you don't agree with him? Does that person's point of view have any validity, given that person's experiences or beliefs? Now that you have likely attenuated your anger by thinking differently, could you adopt any other alternative behaviors that might help you cope? For example, would being more assertive help you to deal better with the person or situation? If your answer is yes, pay special attention to Chapter 13.

Viewing Criticism as Feedback

One of the stressful things that often triggers our anger, particularly in a job setting, is criticism. It goes without saying that no one really likes to be criticized, particularly about our work or our on-the-job behavior. But some individuals handle criticism better than others. Why is it that some people seem to take negative feedback in stride and even appear to benefit from it, while others are overwhelmed with anger and self-doubt? Again the answer lies in the meaning attributed to the criticisms. One of the main reasons is that often people tend to equate criticism with themselves rather than their actions. Therefore, they view negative feedback as a statement about their self-worth rather than an observation about their behavior. When viewed this way, criticism tends to remind us of our inadequacies.

However, if we realize that it is not us but our actions that are being critiqued, it becomes easier to consider the possibility that there is validity to the complaint. You no longer need to feel as though there is something wrong with you, or that you are a bad or worthless person; rather, you need to focus your attention on the appropriateness, effectiveness, or worthiness of a particular behavior.

You need to recognize that in any situation where you receive criticism, three possibilities exist: (1) Your behavior is definitely out of line and the other person's complaint is valid; (2) your behavior is questionable but the criticism is also a reflection of biases, difficulties, or neuroses on the part of the critic; or (3) your behavior is fine and it is the critic who has the problem. (Remember the old saying, "Criticism reflects the critic.") It is important to take a good look at your behavior, but how you respond will depend on which possibility you decide best fits the situation.

If you decide that your behavior has been inappropriate, you must be careful not to fall into the trap of taking this as evidence that you have done something wrong and should feel bad about it. This trap is avoided by remembering to look differently at mistakes. (Refer to the section in Chapter 6 on refuting irrational beliefs.) Mistakes are not necessarily always bad. They are not just evidence that we have done something wrong. You *can* decide to view mistakes as *feedback*—important feedback that helps train you how to do things properly. It is when we realize that our mistakes are invaluable teachers that we cease to continue to repeat them.

> I have not failed 10,000 times,
> I have successfully found 10,000
> ways that will not work.
>
> Thomas A. Edison

Forgiveness

If prolonged anger and resentment damages our health and contributes to our level of stress, then clearly the ability to forgive and let go of past hurts and disappointments is a desirable goal. Let's be clear about what forgiveness is and is not. Forgiveness is not forgetting what happened, thereby placing yourself again in a situation where you could be mistreated. It is certainly not about condoning behavior you find offensive or hurtful. It is the process of letting go of the energy invested in past hurts or disappointments so that you can free that energy for more productive, growth-oriented activities. The decision to forgive stems from the realization that anger and resentment have a damaging effect on you. There is an old Chinese saying: "When working for revenge, dig two graves." We wonder whether you or anyone you know has ever said, "I don't get mad, I get even!" As cool as that statement might sound, you must realize the eventual toll such an approach will take on you.

Although forgiveness begins with a decision to forgive, it is important to remember that forgiveness is a process. As such, it takes time and willingness to go through the particular emotions involved, be they hurt, anger, or even depression. The problem develops when you get stuck in this process because of righteous indignation. Do not get caught in the trap of believing that you can begin to forgive only when an apology is offered or amends made. When and how you forgive is totally up to you, whatever the circumstances. If you want to achieve stress mastery, a consistent attitude of forgiveness is extremely useful.

An important point needs to be made here. Not only do you need to forgive others; it is perhaps even more critical that you master the art of forgiving yourself. Too often we see people in our workshops and classes who claim to be great at forgiving others but who are harsh and unforgiving regarding their own past actions and perceived mistakes. Remember that the most important relationship in your life is the one you have with yourself. Be gentle with yourself. Remember that all the decisions you have made in the past have contributed to who you are today, and as such they all have their usefulness. A most important key to stress mastery is learning to forgive yourself, again and again and again.

To facilitate this process you could use a helpful visualization strategy discussed earlier, that of observer imagery. Imagine yourself sitting in front of yourself. Have your present self speak to your past self, the part of you that made those mistakes you have found so unforgivable. Visualize telling your past self that you are forgiven, that you are not pleased with the behavior and wish you had done it differently, but that you now recognize that we are all struggling human beings trying to do the best that we can. Furthermore, you consciously forgive your past self because you deserve it. Of course, this same process can be used not only with yourself, but with an image of anyone who has hurt or angered you.

Assertiveness

Some situations that anger you certainly call for some type of response beyond letting go of your anger. Many times you will need to respond to individuals who have angered you so as to rectify the situation or prevent future occurrences of whatever is provoking your hostility. This is best accomplished by dealing diplomatically and assertively with the other person, rather than passively avoiding conflict (and allowing your resentment to build and take a toll on you) or responding aggressively (where you risk alienating others, making the situation worse and later being ashamed of yourself). A comprehensive treatment of effective and responsible assertive behavior is the topic of Chapter 13.

Chapter Summary

Sustained and chronic anger negatively affects your health and your relationships. You always have a choice about whether to respond with anger, based on your interpretation of the situation. Anger is not always bad and not always preventable, but it is important for you to learn how to resolve it effectively. The only way out is to work through the anger. Reframing strategies can be very helpful for moving through anger. Learn to view criticism as feedback to minimize your knee-jerk anger response. Give yourself permission to be human and make mistakes, but learn from your errors. Learn to forgive, especially yourself as well as others. Forgiveness is more for you and your own health than for anyone else.

Chapter Questions

1. What happens to you physiologically when you get angry?
2. What is the relationship between your perception of a situation, the meanings you give to it, and anger?
3. Persistent anger and hostility have been linked to which physical problems? How does anger lead to ill health?
4. Describe the initial steps that are helpful for working through anger.
5. List some useful reframing strategies for defusing anger.
6. Why is it that mistakes are not always bad?
7. Who is the most important person you need to learn to forgive?

Reviewing the Master Strategy: Stage 2

I. Acquiring Body Wisdom

    A. Fake it till you make it. Act how you want to be until it comes naturally.

    B. Adopt the stance of the peaceful warrior.

        1. Focus on the here and now.

        2. Change your physiology.

        3. Learn to listen to your body. *If you listen to your body when it whispers, you won't have to listen to it scream.*

        4. Cultivate relaxation skills.

            a. Begin with breathing.

            b. Follow with progressive relaxation.

                (1) Use the systematic process of tensing and relaxing each muscle group slowly and individually, allowing you to develop awareness of bodily tension and then enabling you to release it.

                (2) Coordinate this with your breathing.

                (3) Combine with relaxing imagery.

            c. Use autogenic training—a process of repeating relaxing phrases to yourself regarding pinpointed muscle groups.

            d. Use stretching exercises to lengthen muscles and release tension.

                (1) Follow your intuition about which muscles to stretch.

                (2) Go slow—if you feel pain you are stretching too hard.

                (3) You can stretch anywhere, anytime if you feel muscular tension building up.

                (4) Use stretches 1–3 to help prevent tension headaches.

II. Changing Your Perspective

    A. Problems are not what happens to you but what you tell yourself about what happens. To a great extent, our perceptions determine whether we will experience stress, as well as the severity of the stress.

    B. The art of reframing is useful.

        1. Find a different perspective.

            a. The magical effect of humor

            b. Life as a sitcom

            c. Life as a novel

            d. Special effects

        2. Shift your point of view.

C. Give up being right.
  1. Operating in a win/lose perspective in interpersonal situations ultimately leads to everyone losing.
  2. Would you rather be right or happy?
  3. The question of who is winning in a marriage is ridiculous.
  4. Looking for win/win outcomes in relationships reduces stress.
  5. How do you give up being right?
   a. Begin with breathing.
   b. Learn to step into the shoes of the other person. Make an attempt to really listen to her concerns, to see out of her eyes, and to adopt her perspective. This does not mean you have to agree with her, but only that you really attempt to understand her point of view and feelings.
   c. Is there any merit or validity in the other person's point of view? The answer is almost always yes.

D. Deal with irrational beliefs
  1. Catastrophizing increases stress.
  2. Catastrophizing is triggered by self-talk or automatic thoughts.
  3. Irrational beliefs exacerbate stress.
  4. Use cognitive restructuring to refute irrational beliefs.
   a. Identify the irrational belief.
   b. Challenge the irrational belief with rational questions.
   c. Substitute new rational beliefs. In time this process will feel natural.

E. Remember that the map is not the territory.
  1. Your perceptions are not reality—only subjective interpretations.
  2. Some maps are more useful than others.

F. Optimism is the most useful map.
  1. Remember that optimism reduces stress.
  2. Assess the cost of failure to determine whether to be optimistic.
  3. Learn to become an optimist.
   a. Look for evidence contrary to negative thoughts.
   b. Generate other alternatives than negative ones.
   c. Realistically assess the implications of the situation.
   d. Evaluate the usefulness of a particular belief.

III. Pathways Through Anger

  A. The relationship between anger and stress
   1. Anger had far more survival value for our ancestors.
   2. Anger is physiological arousal leading to the fight-or-flight response.
   3. When under stress, we look around for who is to blame.

  B. The relationship between anger and control
   1. You always have a choice about whether to respond with anger.
   2. It is your interpretation of an event—not the event itself—which leads to anger. The way you see the problem is the problem.

C. You have a right to be angry, but are you happy with the results?

   1. Sustained and chronic anger negatively affects your health.

      a. The hostility component of the Type A personality is correlated with heart disease.

      b. Learning to control anger decreases the rate of recurrent heart attacks.

      c. Anger is linked to many other psychosomatic disorders.

   2. Anger leads to win/lose scenarios, which damages relationships.

   3. Anger is not always bad. It is harmful only when it is chronic and unresolved. Anger can help mobilize your energy to take constructive action.

D. It is not always possible to prevent anger, but it is important to learn how to move through it effectively.

   1. The only way out is through.

   2. Anger is a signal that you must address an issue.

   3. Use reframing strategies to help move through your anger.

      a. Be a comedy writer on your own life. Look for the humor or absurdity in the situation to help defuse your anger.

      b. View the situation as a chapter in your life. What is there to be learned from this dilemma?

   4. View criticism as feedback.

      a. Recognize that it is your behavior that is being addressed, not your worth as a human being.

      b. Criticism reflects the critic. Examine the validity of feedback without defensiveness, but take it to heart only if there is truth to it.

      c. Mistakes are not necessarily always bad. You are human and entitled to err. Mistakes are our teachers.

   5. Forgive

      a. Forgiveness does not mean forgetting, but rather letting go of anger.

      b. Holding a grudge takes a toll on you. Forgiveness is more for yourself than for the other person.

      c. It is totally up to you whether to forgive, whatever the behavior of the other (whether he or she is apologetic or not).

      d. The most important person to forgive is yourself, over and over and over again.

Section 4

Further Applications
of the Master Strategy

Nutrition

What You Will Learn in this Chapter

- To list the seven steps to good nutrition.

- To determine which foods and vitamins facilitate stress resistance and which heighten your stress level.

- To explain the role of setpoint in regulating weight and defeating diets.

- To describe how to modify your setpoint to lead to weight loss.

- To explain how weight affects your stress level.

- To calculate whether you are overweight using the BMI (Body Mass Index).

- To explain the role of activity level and exercise in affecting weight and setpoint.

- To practice stimulus control methods (behavior modification strategies) for controlling weight.

The old adage "You are what you eat" is more true than you might imagine. Why is this? Because how well or how poorly you eat has a direct relationship to your ability to handle stress. Your body needs forty to sixty nutrients to stay healthy. When you are under stress your need for all nutrients increases, especially the B vitamins (which help you combat stress) and calcium. Calcium is especially important because it counteracts the lactic acid buildup created by muscular tension. If your diet is deficient in milk and leafy vegetables you could be calcium deficient; therefore, your ability to reduce high levels of lactic acid related to stress could be impaired. This would leave you feeling more fatigued, anxious, and irritable when under stress than if your diet were more balanced. You also need to realize that certain foods provide the biochemical building blocks for the neurotransmitters (brain chemicals) that affect mood and behavior, and consequently your ability to handle stress. For example, your body synthesizes the neurotransmitter serotonin from the amino acid tryptophan, which is found in certain high-carbohydrate foods such as bread, potatoes, and pasta. Healthy levels of serotonin help you stay relaxed, sleep well, and have less sensitivity to pain. That is why we tend to crave carbohydrate-rich foods when we are in a bad mood—in order to get a temporary lift. And it is also important to know that protein-rich foods tend to improve concentration and alertness.

This chapter is geared to help you recognize whether and how your eating habits contribute to high stress levels and potentially limit your on-the-job productivity. You can learn to make changes in your diet that will help you cope with stress and increase your productivity level.

The Seven Steps to Good Nutrition

1. Eat a Variety of Foods

The forty to sixty nutrients necessary for maintaining good physical and emotional health include vitamins; minerals; amino acids from proteins; essential fatty acids from vegetable oils and animal fats; and sources of energy from carbohydrates, proteins, and fats. Most foods contain multiple nutrients; however, no one food supplies all the essential nutrients in the needed amounts. Thus, the greater the variety in your diet, the less likely you are to develop either a deficiency or an excess of any single nutrient. It is recommended that you select your daily foods from each of the major food groups listed here to ensure that you are getting all the necessary vitamins and nutrients.

Vegetables	3–5 servings
Fruits	2–4 servings
Breads, grains, and cereals	6–11 servings
Dairy products	2–3 servings
Meat, poultry, fish, eggs, beans, peas	2–3 servings
Fats, oils, and sweets	Use sparingly

The average American diet is very unbalanced. Overall, we tend to eat a lot more protein than we need and not nearly enough starches. Starches are also rich in fiber, which aids our digestion and may protect us from some cancers, such as cancer of the colon. Even more problematic is the fact that most Americans, especially fast-food junkies, eat far more fat than they need. The average American consumes 40 percent of his or her daily caloric intake from fat. It is recommended that no more than 20 to 30 percent of our diet come from fat, and that we minimize our intake of saturated fats as much as possible. Saturated fats, which come from animal sources, greatly increase our cholesterol level. No more than 10 percent of daily caloric intake should be from saturated fats. Whenever possible, consume unsaturated as opposed to saturated fats. Olive oil, an unsaturated fat, is both delicious and nutritious and can be substituted for saturated fats such as vegetable oils, salad dressings, or butter.

The relationship between diet and the development of serious diseases has been well documented. It has been estimated that about 60 percent of cancer in men and 40 percent of cancer in women can be linked to diet. Food preservatives, high intake of saturated animal fat, and vitamin deficiencies are likely culprits. High levels of cholesterol increase the risk of heart disease. On the other hand, vitamins, calcium, fruits, vegetables, and nonfatty fish appear to reduce the risk of cancer.

2. Eat More Whole Foods

Whole foods for good nutrition include raw or lightly steamed vegetables, fruits, whole grains and cereals, brown rice, beans, dried peas, nuts, and certain seeds. These foods are complex carbohydrates that contain a complex mix of starch, fiber, sugar, vitamins, and minerals. We recommend that you avoid simple carbohydrate foods such as white flour, white rice, refined sugar, sugar-coated cereals, processed fruit products, and over-cooked vegetables. These foods are so refined, processed, or cooked that most of the vitamins and minerals have been leached out, leaving only a little starch and a lot of sugar. These foods are higher in calories and lower in nutrients than the whole foods from which they are made. Complex carbohydrates also contain much more dietary fiber, which aids digestion and reduces the risk of colon cancer.

3. Avoid Caffeine

Coffee, black tea, chocolate, and many soft drinks (especially colas) are very high in caffeine. Caffeine is a stimulant that chemically induces the fight-or-flight response in your body and depletes it of B vitamins. If you are already having trouble coping with stress or with sleeping, caffeine will just make matters worse. Limit or eliminate your intake of caffeinated beverages if you are under stress or if you have difficulty relaxing, sleeping, or coping with the pressures in your life. However, low to moderate caffeine consumption (for example, one to two cups of coffee daily) can certainly help boost alertness and concentration. This should not be problematic unless you are caffeine sensitive and feel jittery; in that case, avoid it altogether. Green tea, containing a more benign form of caffeine, is an excellent substitute and has been shown to be high in antioxidants which can help slow the ravages of age on our bodies.

4. Avoid Alcohol

People often increase alcohol consumption at times of stress as a means of maladaptive coping. But even moderate alcohol use can interfere with your ability to deal with stress. Alcoholic beverages are quite high in calories but low in other nutrients. Alcohol also depletes your system of the B vitamins, which are vitally important for helping you cope with stress. If you must imbibe, do it infrequently and in moderation, and try to limit yourself to wine, which may, if taken in moderation, help prevent cardiovascular disease.

5. Take Vitamin and Mineral Supplements

When you are under stress you require more of all vitamins and minerals, especially the B vitamins. Deficiencies in the B vitamins, vitamin C, calcium, and magnesium have been linked to stress-related symptoms such as insomnia, irritability, depression, and fatigue. No single nutrient is the most important; they all work together to help us minimize stress and cope with the pressures in our environment. Thus, taking megadoses of any one vitamin or mineral will not give you an optimal benefit if you are deficient in a variety of vitamins and minerals.

There is controversy among nutritionists about whether we need to boost our diet with vitamin supplements. Some say that a balanced diet supplies all our necessary vitamins and minerals. Others argue that today's supermarket foods are so nutritionally inadequate and overprocessed that you would have to eat three times as much food as your grandparents consumed in order get the same level of nutrients.

If you decide to supplement your diet with vitamins, the question arises, "How much of which vitamins should I take?" Some researchers, such as Linus Pauling, recommend megadoses of certain vitamins (such as vitamin C) because there is a big difference between the minimum amount of a nutrient required to prevent the symptoms of disease, and the optimum amount of that nutrient necessary to maintain vibrant good health and resistance to disease. A reasonable place to start might be with a multiple vitamin containing a balanced stress formula of vitamins A, E, D, and C and especially the B complex. Supplement this with additional C, A, calcium, and magnesium. A daily vitamin formula especially designed to combat stress was proposed by Adele Davis in *Let's Get Well* (1965). She recommends that you consume the following:

- 500 milligrams vitamin C
- 100 milligrams pantothenic acid
- 2 milligrams each of vitamins B2 and B6

During periods of high stress or illness, she instructs that you take half these amounts six times daily, in conjunction with a daily multivitamin tablet containing vitamins A, D, and E and a diet high in milk, liver, fresh vegetables, and wheat germ. If you are averse to taking vitamin supplements, you can increase your intake of natural vitamins and minerals by adding the following to your diet:

- Cod liver oil—vitamins A, F, and D
- Raw wheat germ—vitamins E and B complex, proteins, minerals, and enzymes
- Rose hips—vitamin C and bioflavinoids
- Wheat germ oil—vitamin E and unsaturated fatty acids
- Bone meal—calcium and trace minerals
- Kelp—iodine and trace minerals and elements
- Lecithin—choline and lecithin
- Whey powder—iron, B vitamins, minerals, and lactose

Dr. Andrew Weil, an allopathic physician and expert on medicinal usages of plants and alternative healing methods, makes many dietary recommendations in his landmark book *Spontaneous Healing* (1995) regarding supplements to promote health and freedom from stress. Although a detailed account of his advice is beyond the scope of this book, we have included a brief summary of suggested dietary aids (which Dr. Weil refers to as "tonics") relevant to boosting your body's ability to deal with physical and emotional stress. If you are intrigued with these nontraditional remedies, we recommend you peruse Dr. Weil's books for more information on dosage, history of use, and so on.

- Weak or compromised immune functioning is a common by-product of chronic stress or a single episode of extreme stress. The following herbal and/or fungal supplements have been shown to have dramatic effects on immune functioning: *garlic, ginger, astralagus, echinacea, and the maitake mushroom.*
- For restoration of energy, eliminating fatigue, and combating stress utilize *ginseng* and *astralagus.*
- Strong antibacterial and antibiotic effects have been demonstrated with *garlic* and *echinacea.*
- Protection against heart disease can be afforded by *garlic*, which has been shown to lower blood pressure and reduce clotting. The following tonics have been linked to lowering cholesterol levels: *garlic, green tea, and Ho Shou Wu.*
- Use *milk thistle* to help normalize liver functions following exposure to environmental toxins or long-term alcohol abuse.

Other foods that fight stress, as recommended in the May 1999 edition of *Reader's Digest,* include the following:

- *Whole-grain breads* speed the amino acid tryptophan to the brain, which helps to increase levels of serotonin, which is thought to have sedating properties.
- *Oranges* are full of potassium, an electrolyte that conducts nerve impulses and helps keep your brain's neurotransmitters functioning properly. Other excellent sources of potassium include *milk, cheese, apricots, bananas, whole grains, nuts, legumes,* and *poultry.*

- *Fish* is a rich source of B vitamins, along with avocados, potatoes, and beef. Insufficient quantities of B vitamins have been linked to anxiety, irritability, and mood swings.

- *Rice* is rich in vitamin B1 (thiamine). Some research has suggested that thiamine deficiency may be linked to mental illness, particularly depression. *Pork, fish, beans, enriched breads, cereals,* and *sunflower seeds* are also good sources of thiamine.

- *Artichokes* and *spinach* are full of magnesium, which is crucial to your body's ability to combat stress. Other excellent sources of magnesium include *wheat germ, soybeans, bananas,* and *peanuts.*

In addition, we would like to mention another herbal remedy, *St. John's Wort,* which appears to be as effective as antidepressants, such as Prozac, for mild to moderate depression. St. John's Wort appears to elevate mood and increase energy. Oftentimes the reaction to prolonged stress is chronic low-level depression and fatigue. St. John's Wort can help jump-start your system if efforts to pull yourself out of your doldrums have been failing. A word of caution, however: If your depression is severe or has lasted for years, we advise that you consult a reputable health care professional to determine whether St. John's Wort is appropriate for your situation.

6. Eat Frequent, Peaceful Meals

It is preferable to eat frequent small meals four or five times daily rather than two or three large meals, particularly if you are under stress. Frequent eating minimizes hunger; keeps your blood sugar at an even keel, preventing hypoglycemic symptoms; and helps promote weight loss. Give yourself time to eat your meals slowly and calmly. Even if your workday is overwhelming and you are tempted to eat while working to save time, do yourself a favor. Move away from your desk. Go outside if the weather is nice. Go to a different room if possible and take a minimum of fifteen minutes (preferably thirty minutes to an hour) not just to eat but to relax, stretch, and recharge your batteries. Your productivity may actually rise as a result of taking this break and you will end up accomplishing as much as if you had eaten on the run, with far less wear and tear on your body.

7. Maintain a Healthy Weight

Consider the following facts:

- Forty percent of Americans consider themselves overweight, and 35 percent want to lose at least fifteen pounds.

- Of individuals age 25 and older, the most recent statistics indicate that 63 percent of men and 55 percent of women are overweight.

- Eighteen percent of American adults are obese, being more than 20 percent overweight, up from 12 percent in 1992.

- Eleven million American adults are severely obese, being more than 40 percent overweight.

- Twenty-one percent of Americans are on diets; the vast majority of these are women.
- Within a few years at least two-thirds of "successful" dieters regain every pound they have lost, and then some (Schultz, 1999).

The percentage of Americans who are overweight has been steadily climbing. Ironically, the growing pudginess of Americans coincides with the increasing idealization of thinness as a cultural standard. The pressure to conform to societal ideals about weight and body shape can be very stressful, especially for women. Thus the fact of being overweight simultaneously contributes to your stress level, and then inhibits your ability to cope with environmental stresses. For most people, weight is considered a critical variable in any assessment of the physical self. Being obese can profoundly affect your perception of your self-worth, and provides largely negative attributions from those around you.

Genuine obesity increases your risk of diabetes, high blood pressure, heart disease, stroke, gallstones, arthritis, and certain types of cancer. The risk is even higher for individuals who are apple-shaped and carry their weight in their stomach, compared to pear-shaped people, who carry weight in the hips and thighs. A fatty paunch increases risk because the fat surrounds the internal organs, releasing fatty acids that make their way to the liver and diminish its ability to process insulin, eventually causing diabetes. Likewise, fatty acids enter the bloodstream and can contribute to clogged arteries. Fat around the middle also affects how your kidneys process insulin, which appears to be a factor in the development of high blood pressure. For every 10 percent increase over normal weight, men and women have about a 20 percent jump in the risk for heart disease.

Not only does being overweight put stress on your body, but in our weight-conscious society it can threaten your self-esteem. It is estimated that food has replaced sex as the central source of guilt for many individuals. Obesity can also affect how you are perceived on the job, no matter how unfair that may be. One study (Gortmaker et al., 1993) of obesity and earning power for women revealed that in two comparison groups of obese and slim workers (matched for job level, aptitude, race, socioeconomic level, and so on), the overweight women were earning an average of $7,000 a year less than their normal-weight counterparts after seven years on the job.

It is recommended that your percentage of body fat not exceed 15 percent for men and 22 percent for women. Another way to determine whether you are overweight as opposed to obese is to calculate your *body mass index (BMI)*. To figure your BMI, take your weight in kilograms (1 kilogram = 2.21 pounds) and divide that figure by the square of your height in meters (1 meter = 39.37 inches). Ideally, your BMI should fall between 23 and 25. If your BMI is over 30 you are obese; if it is between 25 and 30 you may be overweight, particularly if your percentage of body fat is higher than recommended.

But for many people losing weight is a difficult, challenging endeavor fraught with short-term successes and long-term backsliding. Why is it so hard to lose weight? And why is it even harder to keep it off once we lose it? Everyone knows people who are constantly dieting and going up and down in weight like a yo-yo. Why do some people put on weight by just walking past the bakery section in the supermarket, while some eat twice what other people eat and never seem to gain a pound? Under-standing the answers to these questions is essential if you need to slim down and want to discover which methods will actually work, both in the short term, and more im-portant, in the long term.

Weight Control and Your Setpoint

The first thing you need to understand is that your body has a weight control system controlled by your hypothalamus. Your body weight is determined by a regulating mechanism known as a *setpoint* (Leveille, 1985). Your setpoint is analogous to the thermostat in your home. After setting the house thermostat at a certain tempera-ture, say 72°, your furnace then shuts off when the house is warm and turns on when the house cools off. The whole system is geared toward maintaining 72°. Your body works the same way in terms of body weight and metabolic rate. Each of us has our own biologically determined setpoint for weight and our body works to keep us at our particular setpoint, a process known as *homeostasis*. When you go below your setpoint (such as after a diet), your metabolic rate naturally slows down, calories are burned more slowly to conserve fuel, and you tend to gain weight until you return to your setpoint. This is why diets so often fail, especially when it comes to maintain-ing weight loss. Most diets, even the most outlandish and faddish, will work in the short run given reasonable motivation on the part of the dieter. But once you go be-low your setpoint, homeostasis sets in, thereby lowering your metabolism and re-turning you to your setpoint. This often occurs even if you are eating in moderation.

There is no magic way to lose weight. Quick-weight-loss diets are not recom-mended, because in the long run they simply do not work. Chronic dieting can also be hazardous to your health. Men who perpetually diet were found to have dramati-cally higher rates of heart disease and diabetes than men who never or rarely diet. And individuals who have widely fluctuating weights over long periods of time were found to have higher health risks than those whose weight was steady, providing yet another reason not to diet (Shapiro, 1997).

Thus the process of dieting can be very discouraging and self-defeating. Diets only lower your body weight; they usually do not lower your setpoint. In fact, diets can sometimes actually raise your setpoint. Very-low-calorie diets throw your sys-tem into a "starvation mode" and your body responds by continually lowering your metabolic rate to compensate for the reduced caloric intake. This is a primitive sur-vival mechanism, a holdover from ancient times when our ancestors routinely dealt with famine and drought. To combat this, the human body developed a fail-safe mechanism. When food was unavailable or in short supply for our forebears, their bodies responded by lowering metabolism, thereby conserving body weight and making the most of what food was available. This mechanism remains with us. Our bodies respond to a diet as if it were a famine. And if you continually diet or fre-quently start and stop diets, your body will then reset your setpoint at even higher levels to guard against future diets (which it interprets as starvation). Thus, contin-ued dieting may make you gain even more weight in the long run, which accounts for the yo-yo effect.

Although dieters are told that they will lose a pound for every 3,500-calorie reduction in their diet, this turns out not to be true once their metabolic rate slows down. As many a dieter can testify, the drop in resting metabolic rate can be particularly frustrating. After the rapid weight losses that occur during the initial three weeks or so of a rigorous diet, further weight loss comes slowly. In one study (Bray, 1969), obese patients whose food intake was reduced from 3,500 calories daily down to a near-starvation 450 calories daily lost only 6 percent of their weight, partly because their metabolic rates dropped about 15 percent. That is why reducing your food intake by 3,500 calories may not reduce your weight by one pound. And when your diet ends, your body is still conserving energy. The amount of food that maintained your weight before the diet may now increase it. Some researchers believe that the more your weight fluctuates from yo-yo dieting, the more quickly your body switches on its energy-saving metabolic slowdown with each new diet. This process was demonstrated in an experiment with rats (Brownell et al., 1986) who were fattened up considerably and then put on and off a diet, creating a cycle of weight gain and loss. On the first diet, rats lost their excess weight in 21 days and took 46 days to regain it. The second time, eating precisely the same amount of food, they took 46 days to lose the weight and only 24 days to regain it. It's as if our body learns from previous diets how to defend itself more vigorously from what it interprets as starvation.

Does this pattern of losing and regaining pounds, with your base weight gradually creeping upward apply to you or anyone you know? If the answer to this question is yes, then the value of learning how to adjust your setpoint downward should be obvious. To a large extent, but not totally, your setpoint is determined by biological genetic factors. Some people, those who are just naturally thin whatever they seem to eat, are blessed with relatively low setpoints (and high resting metabolic rates) due to hereditary factors. Others are biologically predisposed to be heavier due to genetically programmed higher setpoints (and lower resting metabolic rates). That is why it is possible for two people of the same height, age, body build, activity level, and food intake to maintain different weights.

Certain other biological factors also affect setpoint. Your bone mass and frame structure will certainly affect your weight. Age is a crucial factor. Setpoints start to creep upward for women after age 30 and for men after age 35. But the fact that your setpoint is partially biologically determined does not mean that you should throw up your hands in despair and give up if you are struggling with your weight. Other factors affecting your setpoint are under your control. For the fact is that *you can lower your setpoint!* And once you lower your setpoint, the task of weight reduction is much easier to attain and maintain.

Lowering Your Setpoint

By now you are probably wondering, "What can I do to lower my setpoint?" Actually, you can do quite a few things that also have the added benefit of helping you cope with stress as well. Drastic and dangerous fad diets are not the way to go. Successful weight control involves changes in your lifestyle that allow you to reduce and then maintain a healthy weight.

Increase Your Activity Level

A very important determinant of your setpoint is your activity level. Regular exercise, particularly aerobic exercise, can significantly lower your setpoint and thus help you lose weight and keep it off. In general, lean individuals have much higher activity levels than those who are overweight. If you are not currently involved in a regular aerobic exercise program, we strongly recommend you consider starting one. It will facilitate your ability to lose weight even more than reducing your caloric intake. In fact, sustained exercise can be a weapon against the body's normal metabolic slowdown when reducing caloric intake. The next chapter deals in much greater depth with the benefits of exercise for stress management. In this section we will focus on the role of exercise in weight loss.

Exercise promotes weight loss because it builds muscle tissue, which has a higher metabolic rate (that is, it burns calories faster) than fat tissue. Exercise of all types, but particularly strength training, builds muscle and improves the muscle-to-fat ratio in your body, thereby helping to increase your metabolic rate. Thus, moderate amounts of weight lifting should be included in any plan to lose weight because it builds muscle mass, maintains muscle tone, and prevents muscle mass from being replaced with fat as we age.

The amount of body fat you possess depends on the size and number of your fat cells. An average adult has approximately 30 billion fat cells. Fat cells can be relatively empty, or full like an inflated balloon. In overweight people, fat cells swell to two or three times their normal size and may divide, producing additional fat cells. If your total number of fat cells increases, due to overeating or genetic factors, it never decreases. Thus we cannot reduce the number of fat cells we carry (short of procedures such as liposuction); we can only affect the fullness of each fat cell. Since fat tissue has a lower metabolic rate, it needs less food to maintain itself than other types of tissue. Thus, once we become fat, we require less food to maintain our weight than we did to attain it.

Consider the perils of inactivity. Lack of exercise can lead to weight gain. When people feel fat, they are less likely to be physically active, setting up a vicious cycle of inactivity. Oftentimes it is easier to just sit and watch TV. But physical activity helps release the muscular tension produced by stress. A correlational study of TV watching and obesity among 12- to 17-year-olds found that obesity was more common among those who watched the most television. This association remained even when many other factors were controlled, suggesting that the tendency to be a couch potato in front of the boob tube actually contributes to obesity. It is likely that the rise in obesity in American society is as much a function of inactivity as reliance on junk food. As a culture we are addicted to the automobile. Rarely do adults do any significant walking, and the same is true of children who typically expect to be transported wherever they need to go. This lack of physical exercise also contributes to the fact that lifespans in America are among the shortest in the industrialized countries.

One of the few predictors of successful long-term weight loss is exercise during and after changing eating habits. Check out Table 8.1 to see how much energy is expended by various activities.

Table 8.1   Calories Expended in One Hour, According to Activity and Body Weight

Activity	Body Weight in Pounds				
	100	125	150	175	200
Sleeping	40	50	60	70	80
Sitting quietly	60	75	90	105	120
Standing quietly	70	88	105	123	140
Eating	80	100	120	140	160
Driving, housework	95	119	143	166	190
Desk work	100	125	150	175	200
Walking slowly	133	167	200	233	267
Walking rapidly	200	250	300	350	400
Swimming	320	400	480	560	640
Running	400	500	600	700	800

Decrease Your Intake of Refined Sugar

Another important determinant of your setpoint is your consumption of refined sugars. Too much sugar raises your setpoint. Lowering your intake of refined sugar or eliminating it altogether will help to decrease your setpoint. The average American adult gets 25 percent of his or her calories from sugar in various forms, consuming an average of 160 pounds of sugar per year! Sugar is a highly refined simple carbohydrate that provides absolutely nothing nutritionally but calories.

The stress hormone cortisol stimulates the hypothalamus, causing us to crave sugar for a temporary mood lift. But the downside is that this process also facilitates weight gain. Avoiding sugar is especially important if you are under stress and are one of the three out of five people who are pre-diabetic or pre-hypoglycemic. Some people have difficulty regulating their blood sugar level and are thus prone to hypoglycemia. When you eat foods high in refined sugar, your blood sugar level shoots up, giving you a little boost of energy along with a restless feeling. This sudden sugar increase stimulates insulin production, which counteracts the sugar in your blood. If too much insulin is produced, it leads to low blood sugar. This results in hypoglycemic symptoms such as anxiety, dizziness, irritability, depression, tremor, nausea, and hunger pangs. These symptoms are partly due to the effect of the hormone epinephrine, which is released when blood sugar levels fall dramatically. Epinephrine is also one of the hormones involved in the fight-or-flight reaction; its function here is to help raise blood sugar levels to give you the energy to fight or flee. This is why the side effects of hypoglycemia feel just like anxiety or panic. Low blood sugar also tends to prompt you to have another treat. If you add environmental or emotional stress to this vicious cycle, you can create an emotional roller-coaster that is hard to get off, and sugar is one of the fuels that keeps it running.

Did you know that soft drinks contain up to sixteen teaspoons of sugar per eight-ounce serving? Also, if you take the time to read labels you will discover that sugar is also a hidden ingredient in many food products, appearing under different names such as *dextrose, maltose,* or *corn syrup.* In general, any ingredient ending with the suffix *-ose* or *syrup* is a sugar by-product. Try sweetening your foods or beverages with *fructose,* derived from fruit sugar, instead of refined sugar. Fructose is metabolized more slowly by your body, so it will provide sweetening without triggering an increase in insulin production.

Decrease Your Consumption of Fats

Not all calories are created equal. Calories consumed from fats are more likely to end up on your belly or thighs than calories consumed from carbohydrates or proteins. A gram of fat contains twice the number of calories provided by a gram of protein or carbohydrate. If you can reduce your fat intake to 20 percent of total calories consumed daily, your setpoint will begin to lower on its own. Lowering your fat intake helps lower your setpoint, thereby promoting weight loss more effectively than just lowering your caloric intake. That is, a 1,200-calorie-a-day diet with 40 percent of calories derived from fat will lead to much slower weight loss than a 1,200-calorie-a-day diet with a 20 percent fat ratio.

When shopping for food, read the label on the can or package. Almost all canned or packaged foods now have a chart on the back listing total calories per serving and the grams of protein, carbohydrate, and fat per serving. To figure out the fat content of a particular food or ingredient, just multiply the number of fat grams by 9 to determine the number of fat calories per serving. Then divide the total calories per serving by the fat calories to get the ratio of fat to total calories.

For example, suppose your favorite cereal has 100 calories per serving and contains just one gram of fat. Multiply 1 gram times 9 and you get 9 fat calories per serving. When you divide the 100 total calories by the 9 fat calories you see that this food is only 9 percent fat and would definitely qualify as a low-fat food. In contrast, a typical cookie contains approximately 100 calories but usually has about 6 grams (or 54 fat calories) of fat. Therefore, the cookie has over 50 percent fat content and is therefore a high-fat food. Although each food has the same number of calories, one promotes weight loss while the other does not.

There is now a proliferation of low- and no-fat foods on the market from which to choose. Make sure they do not compensate for being low-fat by having a high sugar or sodium content (where you trade one dietary mistake for another).

Watch Your Salt Intake

Your intake of salt affects your weight as well as your ability to deal with stress. There appears to be an interaction between salt and stress, since the hormones that contribute to the fight-or-flight response also help regulate the salt and water balance in your body. A diet high in salt can lead to a tendency to retain water, which is particularly problematic for women who experience PMS symptoms. Water retention can lead to symptoms such as irritability and nervousness. In addition, a high-salt diet can damage your arteries even when your blood pressure is within normal range.

Drink Plenty of Water

Dehydration can lead to irritability and fatigue. You may not necessarily feel thirsty even if you are becoming dehydrated, so it is prudent to keep drinking fluids, particularly if you are exercising or exposed to hot weather. Water helps aid digestion and flushes toxins out of your system more quickly, including toxins built up by stress. All weight-loss programs recommend drinking four to eight 8-ounce glasses of water daily.

Use Behavior Modification Strategies to Change Your Eating Habits

There are many useful tips for helping you to get control of your eating. Some of the following recommendations will no doubt be quite useful; others may not apply to you. Review these suggestions carefully and try out the ones that are relevant for you. The first category of suggestions involves tips for reducing your triggers for eating. This is about breaking the associations between eating and certain places or activities.

- Eat in the kitchen or dining area only.
- Do not eat while watching TV, reading, or studying. If you tend to get hungry while watching TV in a specific room, such as the family room, switch to watching in the bedroom if possible. Avoid watching TV commercials about food or snacks. Play with your remote control.
- Avoid restaurants or snack shops where you are prone to indulge.
- When at a restaurant, do not read the menu. Order from a plan you have prearranged.
- Go to the grocery store after you have eaten, when you are no longer hungry.

Take steps to prevent yourself from caving in to the impulse to eat. *Response prevention* involves minimizing exposure to tempting food cues. Hunger can be triggered by external stimuli such as the sight of food. Overweight individuals seem more responsive than people of normal weight to external cues, such as the aroma or sight of food or the approach of the dinner hour. Normal-weight individuals are relatively more influenced by internal sensations, such as hunger pangs. The following response prevention tips may help:

- Keep fattening foods out of your house. If you must have snack foods around, purchase those that have to be prepared as opposed to just popped into your mouth.
- Prepare only as much food as you need.
- Use a smaller plate. It will make your portion seem larger.
- Do not starve yourself or skip meals. Avoid fasting all day and eating a big meal at night. This is a common eating pattern among people struggling with their weight. Skipping meals throws you into a deprivation state, which can trigger an impulse to overeat or binge.
- Eat only when you are hungry. Attend to your appetite rather than the time of day or whether others around you are eating. Lean individuals sometimes eat a lot, but only when they are genuinely hungry. Heavy individuals tend to eat for the sake of eating, whether they are truly hungry or not.

- Mentally rehearse your next visit to friends or relatives who usually try to stuff you. Visualize yourself politely but firmly refusing seconds or that fattening dessert.

Engage in competing responses. Do the following things instead of eating. Remember, you always have a choice in the matter.

- When hungry, snack on celery, carrots, grapes, and other high-water-content foods rather than on sweets or chips.
- Substitute fat-free snacks, such as fat-free potato chips. Take out a small helping and put it on a plate. Put the bag away before you begin eating.
- Ride your bicycle or jog for half an hour instead of eating. It may just kill your appetite; if not, the exercise will help burn up the calories you may later consume.
- Pick up the phone and call a friend. Go visit your neighbor. Play solitaire. Turn on your computer. Pick up a good book. It's amazing how hunger, especially hunger that is tied to boredom, vanishes once we are engaged in something interesting.

Learn how to feel satisfied with smaller amounts of food:

- Eat slowly. We can't emphasize this enough. It takes about twenty minutes after the beginning of food intake for your blood sugar level to rise to the point where your hunger diminishes. This is a function of time, not how much you have consumed. Therefore, if you eat slowly and lightly, you will feel satisfied in about twenty minutes. Individuals who are overweight tend to eat very quickly.
- Take small bites and chew your food thoroughly.
- Put your utensils down between bites.
- Take a five-minute break during your meal or talk a lot to your tablemates.
- Start each meal with a filling low-calorie appetizer such as clear broth, celery sticks, or salad with olive oil and vinegar or lowfat dressing.

Build your desired habits through a process of successive approximations:

- Set reasonable goals for yourself in terms of how much weight you want to lose and how quickly. Targeting an ambitiously low weight usually dooms dieters to eventual defeat. Do not try to lose more than one to two pounds weekly. It is much easier to maintain weight loss achieved slowly. When selecting a reasonable weight goal, you can use the standard height/weight charts, but your ideal weight also depends on how much muscle mass you have, because muscle weighs more than fat. *Did you know that a pound of muscle takes up half the space of a pound of fat?*
- Decrease your daily caloric intake gradually—for example, by 100 calories each week, so that you will not feel deprived by a drastic change.

- Allow yourself to have frequent low-calorie, healthy snacks (for example, fruits and other low-fat foods) as your dieting gets under way. Then gradually space them out and eliminate one or two. Research shows that we metabolize our food more efficiently when we eat several small meals as opposed to one or two big meals.

- Eliminate high-fat foods from your diet one by one. Learn to substitute (for example, ground turkey in place of ground beef, or olive oil in place of salad dressing or butter).

- Increase your exercise routine by a few minutes each week.

- No matter what diet plan you choose to follow, give yourself one day off per week where you can eat more, but still stay within the guidelines for good eating. The reason for this is twofold. First, we are much more likely to binge or give up good eating if we are in a "deprivation state." Scheduling a day off prevents our frustration levels from building to the binge point. Secondly, many dieters, once they have given in to temptation and break the diet (even slightly), feel that they have failed and often give up completely. If a day off is part of the plan, it will prevent you from giving up because you feel you have broken your diet.

- Track your progress in ways that will not discourage you. Do not weigh yourself daily. Weigh in on a weekly or preferably monthly schedule. An alternative is to track your body circumference measurements every three to four weeks. Many times you will be losing inches (particularly if you are exercising and converting fat to muscle) but the scale won't change drastically. The bottom line is this: If you are fit and look good, it doesn't matter what the scale says.

If you are a woman, you no doubt feel the strong cultural pressure to be slim. Our society glamorizes unrealistic levels of thinness. For example, fashion modeling actually requires women to maintain weights at anorexic levels. No wonder eating disorders such as anorexia and bulimia, virtually unheard of fifty years ago when societal standards were more realistic, are so prevalent today. It is far healthier to accept oneself as slightly plump than to diet and binge, bear the health risks of fluctuating weight, and feel continually out of control and guilty.

Lastly, avoid rigidity in your diet plan. The worst diet, no matter how superficially healthy, is the one that you are continually worrying about. Chronic ruminating about what you do and do not eat creates so much stress that it can counteract the benefits of eating healthy. Don't make dealing with food a threatening ordeal. The key is moderation. Remember the three C's. Take on healthy eating as a *challenge; commit* yourself to change (but not to perfection); and you will experience increases in your sense of *control* over your weight, your health, and the stresses in your life. Maintaining good nutrition and staying physically active (see the next chapter for more detail on this) will provide the essential vitamins, nutrients, and energy necessary to manage stress effectively. It will also boost your immune functioning, which will greatly reduce your chances of developing debilitating illness or physical problems. This will help spare you from the stress of dealing with poor health.

Chapter Summary

How well or how poorly you eat has a direct relationship to your ability to handle stress. The relationship between poor diet and ill health is well documented. Following the seven steps to good nutrition will help improve your stress resistance: (1) eat a variety of foods; (2) eat more whole foods; (3) avoid caffeine; (4) avoid alcohol; (5) take vitamin and mineral supplements (particularly the stress-fighting B vitamins); (6) eat frequent, peaceful meals; and (7) maintain a healthy weight. Losing weight can be a frustrating process because your weight is partially genetically determined by a setpoint that sets your metabolic rate. The changes necessary to lower your particular setpoint (and help you lose weight) have the side benefit of boosting your resistance to stress as well. These include getting plenty of exercise, decreasing your consumption of refined sugar, lowering your fat intake to 20 percent daily, minimizing your salt intake, and drinking plenty of water. Additionally, you can use stimulus control methods such as response prevention, competing responses, and successive approximations to help you gain better control over your eating habits.

Chapter Questions

1. What vitamin and mineral deficiencies contribute to difficulties with handling stress?
2. What are the seven steps to good nutrition?
3. How does alcohol consumption damage your ability to cope with stress?
4. Which vitamins are the most important for combating stress?
5. Which herb has antidepressant properties?
6. How does obesity interfere with your ability to handle stress?
7. Explain setpoint theory. What steps can be taken to lower your setpoint?
8. Why do symptoms of low blood sugar feel identical to anxiety or panic?
9. Name four behavior modification strategies that you would follow if you needed to lose weight.

Exercise

What You Will Learn in this Chapter

- To explain the role of regular exercise for increasing stress resistance.

- To list the benefits of exercise in general.

- To discriminate between the various types of exercise with respect to how each type affects stress resistance and setpoint.

- To identify how much exercise you need.

- To explain how to begin a regular exercise program.

- To compute a healthy level of exercise based on your heart rate.

- To maintain motivation to exercise.

- To practice stimulus control methods for improving sleep and combating insomnia.

By far, one of the simplest and most effective methods of stress management is to engage in regular exercise. Your body immediately reacts to stress by gearing up to respond physically to a stressor. Given that the original evolutionary purpose for the fight-or-flight response was to enable humans to fight or to flee physical danger, it follows that the natural outlet for built-up physiological arousal is some type of vigorous physical activity or exertion. Exercise releases pent-up muscular tension and allows your body to return to equilibrium.

Throughout most of human history, our ancestors got plenty of exercise while taking care of basic living tasks such as searching or hunting for food, walking from one place to another, chopping wood for fires, and so on. In current times the advent of modern conveniences such as the automobile, elevator, supermarket, and washing machine, have greatly reduced the need for physical activity in order to accomplish basic tasks. It has gotten to the point where we don't even have to move to change the channel on the TV, thanks to the ever-present remote control! Consequently, if you don't make a point of exercising you are probably leading a sedentary lifestyle, unless you are involved in a job or profession involving physical labor or physically exerting activities. But the vast majority of us have sedentary occupations, sitting behind a desk, barely flexing our arm muscles to push papers. The majority of college students train for and hold sedentary jobs after graduation. Leisure activities often involve sedentary pursuits as well.

A sedentary lifestyle, particularly under conditions of high stress and poor diet, is a major contributing factor to coronary heart disease, arthritis, obesity, depression, fatigue, and muscular tension. Thus, even though the tempo of modern life and the rate of change is accelerating (further adding to our stress), our activity levels are falling. And this comes at a time when our need for regular exercise to bolster coping resources is increasing.

The Benefits of Exercise

Is there proof that exercise helps to cope with stress? Research clearly indicates that exercise is an effective stress reducer. Indeed, many studies have found that one of the most reliable differences between individuals with high and low levels of stress resistance was exercise and activity level (for example, see Brown, 1991; Kobasa, Maddi, & Puccetti, 1982; and Roth & Holmes, 1987, just to name a few). In one study, McGilley and Holmes (1989), found that individuals who exercised regularly had lower cardiovascular and subjective responses to psychological stress than individuals who were not physically fit. Studies have also been done linking regular aerobic exercise to reductions in depression (McCann & Holmes, 1984), anxiety (Long, 1984), and improvements in self-esteem (Sonstroem, 1984). In addition, research has shown that exercise bolsters energy resources rather than consumes them. In a clever study carried on over a twelve-day period by Thayer (1987), subjects either ate a candy bar or took a ten-minute walk during the afternoon lull when people often feel tired. Those who ate the candy bars reported a short-lived boost of energy, but within an hour they were even more tired and tense. The walkers, on the other hand, felt increased energy and decreased tension for up to two hours after the walk. Furthermore, it is important to note that the amount and intensity of exercise necessary to produce stress-management effects need not be overly extensive.

Research suggests that regular exercise, even of only moderate intensity, provides a dress rehearsal for dealing with stress. Why is this the case? Because the way your body responds to exercise is very similar to the way your body reacts to stress. During exercise your heart rate increases, blood pressure rises, respiration quickens, stress hormones are released, and muscles tense to perform the activity. Does this sound familiar? Therefore, engaging in regular exercise gives your body practice in experiencing stress, allowing you to develop more strength and stamina to cope; therefore, your body can recover faster from stress. The theory of *cross-reactivity* postulates that regular exercise teaches your body how to recover more readily from emotional stress as well—that is, you become conditioned to handle stress more effectively due to repeated exposure to the stress of exercise.

It appears that the stress-reducing effects of exercise are both short and long term. Many people find a single exercise session to be an excellent way of releasing tension. Proponents of regular exercise who exercise at least three times weekly typically report lowered levels of tension overall, even on days when they are less active (Holmes & Roth, 1988).

There is ample proof of the benefits of physical activity and exercise for health and longevity. A landmark longitudinal study (Paffenbarger et al., 1986) of 17,000 Harvard University graduates revealed that graduates who walked nine miles or more per week had a 21 percent lower risk of death than those who walked less than three miles per week. Those who burned less than 2,000 calories per week in physical activity had a 38 percent higher risk of death than those who burned more than 2,000 (the exercise equivalent of jogging approximately 20 miles a week) calories per week. The active alumni lived two years longer, on average, than their more inactive counterparts, who also had the highest risk of heart attacks. An English study by Morris et al. (1953) found a strong relationship between cardiovascular disorders and physical activity among postal and transportation workers. Letter carriers, who walked daily, and bus conductors, who were continually in motion collecting tickets, had about half the rate of heart attacks of postal clerks and bus drivers, who spent most of their workday sitting.

Another experiment with monkeys (Kramsch et al., 1981) confirmed the cardiovascular benefits of vigorous, sustained exercise, even when diet was far from ideal. Three groups of monkeys were randomly assigned to the following conditions: (1) a sedentary group that received a low-fat diet; (2) another sedentary group fed a diet high in fat and cholesterol; and (3) an active group that exercised for an hour on a treadmill three times weekly and were also fed a diet high in fat and cholesterol. The animals were monitored over a three-and-a-half year period. The active monkeys, despite their unhealthy diet, had higher levels of "good" (high-density lipoprotein—HDL) cholesterol (which is linked to cardiovascular health) and lower levels of "bad" (low-density lipoprotein—LDL) cholesterol (which is linked to cardiovascular disorders) than their sedentary counterparts. In addition, arteriosclerosis and sudden death were significantly more frequent occurrences among the two groups who did not exercise.

Clearly, exercise has powerful positive effects on both our psychological and physical well-being. Table 9.1 lists some of the most notable cumulative benefits of regular exercise.

But is all exercise the same in terms of its effects on managing stress? Research has found that just about any kind of physical activity can help reduce stress. This is because exercise exerts its stress-management benefits in numerous ways. Exercise induces biochemical and physiological changes that help your muscles relax, help you recover faster from emotional stress, and provide health benefits that counterbalance the negative effects of stress. Because of the pain and strain inflicted on your body by exercise, chemicals known as *beta-endorphins* are released in your body. Endorphins, which are chemically quite similar to morphine, are your body's natural painkillers. These chemicals appear to help your body recover from prolonged exercise by raising your pain threshold, slowing your heart rate, and decreasing your blood pressure, while enhancing your parasympathetic response (which leads to the relaxation response) and simultaneously inhibiting sympathetic activity (the fight-or-flight reaction). Physical activity can also provide a welcome diversion from sources of stress, as well as relieving boredom and providing opportunities for social interaction. Exercise is often fun, and enjoyable activities help reduce your stress level. Exercise may help you feel better about yourself by improving your health, fitness, and appearance. And mastering a new skill or excelling in a sport can also improve your self-esteem.

Types of Exercise

Exercise represents one type of physical activity. In general, physical activity includes all kinds of movement—from cleaning your house, carrying bags of gro-

Table 9.1   The Cumulative Benefits of Regular Exercise

- Improved sense of well-being; decreased depression
- Lowered anxiety and muscular tension
- Greater ability to handle domestic and job-related stress
- Increased endorphin production (endorphins are the body's natural painkillers and mood elevators)
- Decreased production of stress hormones such as adrenalin and cortisol
- Improved concentration and productivity
- Increased metabolic rate, leading to decreases in setpoint and easier weight loss
- Quicker recovery from acute stress
- Less fatigue; more energy and stamina
- Higher levels of HDL relative to LDL cholesterol in the blood
- Stronger heart muscle that works more efficiently
- Reduced blood pressure and resting heart rate
- Improved cardiopulmonary functioning; lower risk of heart disease
- More restful sleep
- Fewer physical complaints in general; boosts in immune functioning
- Better self-image and more self-confidence
- A more attractive physique; improved muscle-to-fat ratio

ceries, mowing your lawn, and rocking a baby to the more structured workouts we associate with exercise or playing a sport. *Exercise* generally refers to physical activities performed intentionally to improve physical fitness or to control weight. *Physical activity* occurs because you need to get something done that requires movement and energy. But in reality all physical activity could be considered a form of exercise. Let's consider the different types of exercise. Physical activity can be divided into three broad categories: aerobic, anaerobic, and low-intensity exercise.

Aerobic Exercise

One type of exercise clearly linked to stress reduction is aerobic exercise. This involves the sustained, rhythmic activity of the large muscle groups, particularly the legs. In order to qualify as aerobic, an activity should significantly increase your metabolic rate for a prolonged period of time (fifteen minutes or longer) (Fixx, 1977). Popular aerobic exercises include running, jogging, brisk walking, in-line skating, swimming, cycling, cross-country skiing, and aerobic dance. Which aerobic activity you choose is not nearly as important as whether you do it regularly. Aerobic exercise uses up a large volume of oxygen. This increased demand for oxygen leads to increases in heart rate and respiratory rate, along with a relaxation and dilation of the small blood vessels (capillaries) to allow more oxygen-carrying red blood cells to travel to your muscles.

Aerobic exercise improves fitness and facilitates stress mastery because of a phenomenon known as the *training effect*, in which your cardiovascular system is strengthened along with your stamina. To produce the training effect, you need to engage in nonstop, aerobic activity for at least twenty minutes three to four times a week. You know that your aerobic fitness has improved when you can perform a given amount of work (such as climbing several flights of stairs) with less effort. Ideally, to produce the training effect, your heart rate should reach 70 percent of the maximum range appropriate for your age and remain at that rate for twenty straight minutes. Exercising below your aerobic heart rate will not create the training effect, and activity consistently above your recommended heart rate could put too much strain on your heart. Staying at the 70 percent level places moderate stress on your heart, which gradually will improve its efficiency.

To determine your recommended range based on your age, first you must determine your recommended *maximum heart rate*, the fastest that your heart should be beating. If you are free from cardiac problems you can determine this by subtracting your age from the number 220. In general, your maximum recommended heart rate decreases with age at the rate of one beat per year. Your recommended target heart rate for sustained exercise is 70 to 80 percent of your maximum heart rate. First, multiply your maximum heart rate by 0.70 to get the low end of your target range; then multiply it by 0.80 to determine the high end.

During cooldown from an aerobic workout your muscles can relax. One study found that aerobic activities such as walking, jogging, and bicycling reduced muscle tension by more than 50 percent for up to ninety minutes following the workout (deVries et al., 1981). Likewise, rhythmic aerobic activity such as rowing, swimming, walking, and running has been shown to increase alpha-wave activity in the brain

(Stamford, 1995). Alpha brainwaves are associated with mental and muscular relaxation. (A more comprehensive discussion of the relationship of brainwaves to relaxation and stress management is included in Chapter 10). The cardiovascular fitness that results from regular aerobic exercise reduces the risk for heart disease. Aerobic exercise increases HDL (high-density lipoprotein—the "good cholesterol") levels in your bloodstream. HDLs appear to transport cholesterol out of your arteries, helping to prevent artery disease. Aerobic activity also increases insulin sensitivity, thus stabilizing blood sugar levels and decreasing the risk of type 2 diabetes. Regular aerobic exercise helps prevent high blood pressure, and helps reduce hypertension in those already afflicted. Aerobic exercise also makes blood platelets (which are responsible for blood clotting) less likely to clump together, reducing the risk of obstructive blood clots (which could lead to heart attack or stroke).

Anaerobic Exercise

Anaerobic exercise, such as team sports, individual sports such as tennis and racquetball, or track-and-field activities, can be quite exerting, but basically consist of stop-and-go action. Bursts of speed and specific movements are followed by periods of virtually standing still waiting for the next play to begin. Although anaerobic exercise can burn many calories along with improving flexibility or specific skills, the training effect will not occur unless you engage in the activity for twenty minutes nonstop. Although activities such as bowling, archery, or golf, do not call for the level of vigorous physical action required in aerobic activity, they still have been associated with stress reduction. When you are actively engaged in tasks that demand your concentration and attention to motor skills, it is hard to keep your mind on your worries. Engaging in such activities is often a lot of fun and may provide opportunities for socializing. Any activity that is enjoyable and promotes social support is potentially stress-reducing.

Low-Intensity Exercise

Low-intensity exercises are geared to increase flexibility and strength. These activities are not vigorous enough or engaged in for a long enough period of time to promote the training effect; nevertheless, they can be potent stress reducers. There are three main varieties of low-intensity exercises:

1. *Calisthenics* consists of various exercises and stretches designed to improve muscle tone, flexibility, and range of motion of all your major muscle groups along with joint mobility. Focused stretching is an excellent way to release muscular tension. Refer back to Chapter 5 for recommendations on stretches to prevent tension headaches as well as guidelines for intuitive stretching. Stretching exercises are also recommended as a warmup and cooldown before and after aerobic activity in order to help prevent injury and muscle soreness.

    The ancient tradition of *yoga* (which combines stretching, meditation, and breath control) offers many stress-management benefits. *Hatha yoga* is a form of yoga that combines sophisticated stretches and postures with breath control. Stretches range from gentle and relaxing to very strenuous. Taking a yoga class is an excellent way to enhance your Stress Mastery skills.

2. *Isotonics* involves muscle contraction against a resistant object with movement. The most popular form of isotonic exercise is weight lifting. Weight lifting helps convert fat to muscle; thus, it can help increase your resting metabolism, because muscle tissue has a higher metabolic rate than fat tissue. Strength training is important to overall fitness and to maintaining a healthy muscle-to-fat ratio to prevent muscle deterioration and rises in setpoint due to aging.

3. *Isometrics* also requires muscle contraction against resistance, but without movement. Isometrics also increases strength but does so without enlarging your muscles. Isometric exercises can also be used for stress reduction. For example, progressive relaxation exercises (introduced in Chapter 5) are a form of isometrics.

All forms of exercise are potential stress reducers and each has specific applications. Clearly, aerobic exercise helps us manage stress because it increases our stamina and energy while releasing muscular tension. Anaerobic exercise does not necessarily improve stamina, but it too can help release muscular tension. Most of us engage in anaerobic pursuits because they are something we enjoy (for example, a rousing game of tennis or shooting hoops with friends), and engaging in any enjoyable, entertaining activity helps to counterbalance the stresses in your life. If you work hard, you may also need to play hard. Low-intensity exercises such as stretching are vital for stress reduction. Many ancient systems such as yoga or tai chi, which use sophisticated stretches and movements, are wonderful stress reducers, due to both their meditative aspects and muscular release. Progressive relaxation is basically a system of isometric exercises geared toward decreasing muscle tension. Even isotonic exercises such as weight lifting can be very useful for releasing pent-up muscular tension.

How Much Exercise Do You Need?

It is likely that you are getting more routine exercise than you realize, for activities such as cleaning your house, shopping, carrying bags of groceries, light gardening, and slow walking all qualify. But clearly this is not enough. To maximize your ability to cope with stress, you need to focus on becoming physically fit, which for most of us requires involvement in a regular exercise program. *The basic recommendation is that you engage in thirty minutes of physical activity each day.* These thirty minutes of exercise need not be performed at one time. You can increase your activity level by climbing the stairs instead of taking the elevator, walking a few blocks to the store instead of driving, taking the dog for a walk instead of letting him roam in the yard, doing yard work, and so on.

Ideally we recommend that you engage in the aerobic activity of your choice at least three times weekly. Begin and end your workout with stretching exercises for warmup and cooldown. On the days between aerobic workouts, engage in weight training. Practice stretching whenever your muscles feel tense, and in between as well. If you are really out of shape due to years of inactivity, obesity, poor diet, smoking, or advanced age, begin slowly with only low-intensity exercises or leisurely walking. If you have any heart problems that you are aware of, or if you are past 40 and have not exercised in years, consult your physician before embarking on any aerobic activity. If you have any concerns about your health, consult your physician before starting an exercise program, and always put medical advice ahead of suggestions in this book.

An ideal exercise program for a healthy young person that would provide the greatest amount of health and fitness benefits with the least investment in time would be as follows:

Aerobic activity	Three to five times weekly
	Twenty to sixty minutes per session
Resistance training	Twice weekly
	Eight to ten exercises, covering all major muscle groups
	Eight to twelve repetitions per exercise
Stretching	Three to five times weekly

Getting Yourself Motivated

You may already be involved in a regular exercise program. If so, we urge you to continue and make sure there is an aerobic component to your regimen. But if you are one of the many who sincerely want to start an exercise program, yet always find reasons to delay getting started, pay careful attention to this next section. Recognize that the reasons you give yourself for avoiding exercise are powerful and must be faced and challenged if you are to graduate from being a couch potato.

The most common excuse people cite for not exercising is lack of time. If this reason is familiar to you, take a moment to figure out how many hours weekly you spend sitting in front of the TV. The average American adult watches thirty hours of TV a week! Of those hours you spend in front of the boob tube, how many are truly essential to your well-being? Many times we fool ourselves and justify TV watching by assuming that we are "relaxing." But, as mentioned in Chapter 5, *do not confuse inactivity with relaxation.* It is quite possible to be sprawled in front of the TV and maintain high levels of tension. Exercise can release this tension. This is not to say that it is impossible to relax by watching TV, but television viewing is not a particularly effective stress reducer. There is a difference between active and passive relaxation. So if you are opting out of exercise in favor of the TV, it may be time to really look at your priorities. Without exercise, you will become increasingly tense and out of shape and your energy level will diminish. Can you really afford to continue on this path? Could you sacrifice a few of your TV hours to devote to exercise?

Once you begin an exercise program, you can take several steps to help maintain your practice:

1. Start out slowly and build up gradually to avoid injury or excessive soreness.
2. Set weekly goals (for example, walk briskly three times a week, increase by five minutes each week) and reward yourself for mastering your goals. Make your goals realistic.

3. Pay attention to the rewards of exercise (for example, increases in energy, stamina, clothes getting looser).

4. Publicize your goals to friends and family. Public announcement of goals makes it more likely that you will strive to meet your goals.

5. Visualize yourself succeeding. Imagine yourself meeting your exercise and fitness goals.

By all means, take the necessary precautions to avoid injury:

1. Do not overdo it. For aerobic exercises, start out gradually and build up to a minimum of twenty minutes of nonstop activity. For anaerobic exercises, build up slowly as well, depending on your skill level and stamina.

2. Use the proper equipment and clothing, especially shoes.

3. Stretch for five to ten minutes prior to beginning an aerobic workout in order to warm up your muscles. Walk or stretch for three to five minutes after an aerobic workout to cool down and avoid muscle cramps.

4. If you are ill, do not exercise. Take the day off.

5. If at any time during or after exercise you develop symptoms such as chest pain, dizziness, tachycardia (rapid heartbeat that does not slow down when you rest), or difficulty breathing, stop exercising immediately and consult your doctor.

6. Do not exercise after eating a big meal. Wait at least two hours.

7. Do not push yourself past your limit. Use common sense.

8. Do not smoke.

If you cannot spare thirty minutes daily to exercise, try fifteen or twenty minutes. Some exercise is much better than none. If you have been sedentary for a long time and are very out of shape, start out slowly, perhaps with just a fifteen-minute walk daily. Keep in mind that the worse your fitness level is, the sooner you will see and feel the results.

Achieving a Restful Night of Sleep

Have you ever wondered why we need to sleep? One outdated theory suggested that we sleep in order to rest our brain—but our brain cells are quite active even when we sleep. It appears that we sleep to rejuvenate our tired bodies and to recover from stress. During sleep, or any period of deep relaxation, our body's natural healing mechanisms are accessed and we are able to repair bodily damage and combat illness. That is why we generally need to sleep more when we are ill. Likewise, our need for sleep may increase during periods of change, stress, or depression as our body counteracts the wear and tear from our stressful day. Chronic lack of sleep or irregular sleep can have ill effects. Research suggests that people who sleep more than seven hours nightly live longer. Thus, long-term sleeplessness can subdue your immune system. But for the most part, most people can skip a night's sleep and still be functional the next day. Even people who remain sleepless for several consecutive days show few serious disturbances in functioning. Most often, the effects include temporary lapses in attention and concentration along with occasional confusion or misperception. These cognitive lapses may be episodes of borderline sleep. Oftentimes, the anticipation of the negative effects of a sleepless night is more damaging than the actual effects. That is, many people tend to catastrophize about how horrible it will be if they do not get a good night's sleep. If you expect the worst, that is often what you will get, via self-fulfilling prophecy. The truth is that most people can sustain a night without sleep very easily, with some afternoon fatigue being the main consequence.

One of the most common stress-related emotional problems is insomnia. It is quite common for most people to experience some form of insomnia during stressful periods. For some people, insomnia is a common occurrence and becomes a stressor as well as an effect of stress. There are three varieties of insomnia: (1) sleep-onset insomnia, which refers to difficulties with falling asleep; (2) frequent awakening with difficulty falling back to sleep; and (3) early-morning awakening. Sleep-onset problems are associated with anxiety and high levels of arousal, while early-morning awakening is more related to depression. Over thirty million Americans complain of insomnia; it appears to be a more frequent complaint for women. Poor sleepers are more ruminative, depressed, shy, and concerned with physical complaints are than good sleepers.

Insomniacs often exacerbate their problem by trying to force or will themselves to sleep. All that does is make matters worse, for efforts to will yourself to sleep only lead to further arousal and sleeplessness. Falling asleep is a process of letting go, of getting out of your own way and allowing sleep to happen rather than making it happen. Millions go to bed each night dreading the possibility that sleep will be elusive, and these very worries help create and perpetuate the problem. You cannot force yourself to sleep. What you can do is allow yourself to relax and let your mind wander elsewhere. If falling asleep or staying asleep is problematic for you, use the following suggestions to help ameliorate your difficulty. The key here is to follow the suggestions and let go of the need for any particular result. Trust your body to do the work for you if you make relaxation, rather than sleep, your primary goal.

How to Get to Sleep and Stay Asleep

1. *Challenge irrational beliefs.* Your concern over falling asleep only increases your autonomic arousal and muscle tension. Insomniacs often convince themselves that the following day will be ruined unless they get to sleep immediately. Do yourself a favor and remind yourself that a poor night's sleep is not a major catastrophe. You will function just fine the next day, albeit a bit tired at midafternoon, but overall you will survive and be okay. Also, remind yourself that your body will not let you die from lack of sleep. If you are totally exhausted, your body will find a way to get some sleep.

2. *Avoid sleeping pills.* Numerous problems are associated with reliance on sleeping medications, including (1) becoming dependent or addicted, (2) in-

creasing tolerance such that your dose has to be continually increased in order to get the same benefits, and (3) attributing your sleep to the medication rather than developing confidence in your own ability to relax and sleep.

3. *Limit caffeine and alcohol consumption.* Everyone is aware that drinking coffee or other caffeinated beverages shortly before bedtime can interfere with falling asleep. But what most people don't realize is that even if you are able to fall asleep readily following caffeine consumption, the quality of your sleep will be disturbed. Caffeine disrupts sleep architecture. That is, it interferes with your normal sleep cycles and rhythms, causing restlessness and less time spent in deep sleep. The result is that you feel less rested. Also, caffeine is metabolized very slowly by your body, so it exerts its effects hours after your caffeine buzz has worn off. Limit your intake of caffeinated beverages to two daily, and do not consume any after 6:00 P.M. if you are having any difficulties with sleep. Alcohol, on the other hand, may assist you in initially falling asleep (by knocking you out like any other sedative), but it also disrupts sleep architecture by causing light, restless sleep and promoting frequent awakening.

4. *Create an environment conducive to sleep.* It goes without saying that you need a quiet, comfortable place to sleep, but other factors are important as well. Most people sleep best in a fully darkened room. The presence of light causes biochemical changes that promote wakefulness and appears to disrupt your circadian rhythms. It is as if we are biologically programmed to be awake during the day. Incidentally, if you awaken at night to use the bathroom, don't turn on the light. You may find it harder to return to sleep following exposure to bright light. If your bedroom does not remain dark, or if your work schedule requires that you sleep during the day, invest in dark shades or curtains to block the light. You could even try draping towels over your window. Most people sleep better in a cool room (60° to 70° F). Another factor that helps you fall asleep quickly is the use of a constant sound, such as that generated by a white-noise machine. After only a short time, sleep becomes conditioned to the soft, soothing hum. A ceiling fan can serve the same purpose, and adds the calming breeze. In addition, most disturbing noises will be masked. If noise continues to be a problem, use earplugs.

5. *Time your eating and exercising appropriately.* Sometimes a small, carbohydrate-rich snack before bed can promote sleep (believe it or not, milk and cookies seems to be quite effective), but eating a large meal close to bedtime is a big mistake. Not only will it inhibit sleep, but you will be more likely to suffer gastrointestinal distress and gain weight. Engaging in a program of regular exercise will facilitate your ability to sleep, but exercising too close to bedtime will wind you up rather than down. Schedule your workouts at least three hours before you plan to retire for the night.

6. *Focus only on relaxation, not sleep.* When lying down to go to sleep make relaxation, rather than sleep, your goal. Practice your breathing exercises or progressive muscle relaxation. Remember, several hours of deep relaxation has virtually the same rejuvenating effect on your body as sleep. Progressive muscle relaxation exercises have been shown to reduce sleep-onset insomnia significantly in a number of studies (Lick & Heffler, 1977).

7. *Use participant imagery.* Another method for inducing relaxation is to let your mind wander to a pleasant scene or fantasy. Imagine yourself relaxing on a sun-drenched beach with waves lapping at the shore; visualize yourself walking in a lush forest or a fragrant garden; or create any relaxing scene that is meaningful for you. When doing this, it is important that you create a scene in which you are a participant. That is, imagine that you are directly experiencing the fantasy, enjoying the sights, sounds, smells, and good feelings associated with the imagery. It is the difference between imagining being on a quiet desert isle while being massaged and pampered, versus fantasizing about someone else in the situation.

8. *Use stimulus-control methods.* The key here is to convert your bed from a trigger for worry and restlessness to a place where you can relax and escape from worries. When you go to bed, focus on relaxation. If worries come up, focus on your breathing. If these thoughts return, imagine them as printed words on a movie screen that are passing you by. Watch the words disappear off the end of the screen and bring your focus back to your breathing. If worries persist or you are not asleep within fifteen minutes, get up and go somewhere else that you have designated as your "worry place." If worries still intrude, repeat the procedure. Allow your worry place to be associated with obsessive concerns and separate your bed from these intrusions. In the same vein, do not study or snack in bed; you run the risk of converting your bed into a trigger for hunger or concerns over everything you have to do tomorrow. For most people with sleep difficulties, this suggestion may be the most crucial one to follow.

9. *Establish a regular sleep pattern.* Create a regular routine, especially during the week. Avoid napping, which decreases sleepiness at bedtime. Try going to bed at approximately the same time and waking at approximately the same time, to get your body conditioned to a routine. Oversleeping in the morning to try to compensate for difficulty falling asleep the night before will make you less ready to sleep at your normal bedtime the following evening, and will thus perpetuate sleep-onset insomnia.

Above all, remember that it really does not matter if you do not get to sleep early this night. You will survive. Catastrophizing about a poor night of sleep creates more stress than losing a few hours of sleep.

Chapter Summary

One of the most effective ways you can master your stress is to engage in regular exercise. Physical activity releases muscle tension, and exercise provides a dress rehearsal for dealing with stress. You will notice varied benefits from exercise, including improved physical and emotional health and stress resistance. Any physical activity can help you to reduce stress. The types of exercise most closely linked with stress reduction include aerobics, resistance training such as weight lifting, and stretching. Buy any physical activity that is fun, provides a distraction from worries, and offers opportunities for social support is potentially stress-reducing for you. It is recommended that you exercise for thirty minutes daily to maintain fitness and maximize stress resistance.

Just as you need physical activity to remain healthy, you also need to sleep. Your body's natural healing mechanisms are activated when you sleep, but a similar thing happens when you relax deeply. An hour of deep muscular relaxation is almost as rejuvenating as an hour of sleep. Sleep is a process of letting go. You cannot will yourself to fall asleep. Focus not on falling asleep but on relaxation and breathing. Your body will allow you to fall asleep if you make relaxation your goal. Use stimulus-control methods to facilitate sleep. Above all, don't panic if you miss a night of sleep; catastrophizing creates far more stress than losing a few hours of slumber.

Chapter Questions

1. How does regular exercise help decrease your tension and stress levels?
2. What are some benefits of exercising regularly?
3. What are the three categories of exercise and how do they differ?
4. What is the training effect?
5. Progressive relaxation is a form of what type of exercise?
6. How much exercise do you really need?
7. Why is inactivity (for example, sitting and watching TV) not the same as relaxation?
8. How do caffeine and alcohol affect your sleep?
9. List three techniques for facilitating restful sleep that you would choose to use if you were having difficulty falling asleep or staying asleep.

Psychotechnologies

What You Will Learn in this Chapter

- To explain the role of high-tech devices and methods for facilitating relaxation and stress reduction.

- To describe the role of biofeedback technology for facilitating different forms of relaxation and ameliorating psychosomatic symptoms.

- To discriminate among the four types of biofeedback.

- To explain how hypnosis works.

- To explain how hypnotic tapes can foster relaxation and stress reduction.

- To enumerate the role of flotation tanks for creating relaxation and stress reduction.

- To explain how brainwave frequency ranges relate to states of consciousness.

- To summarize how light and sound (BWS) devices create a profound state of relaxation through the entrainment process.

- To explain the benefits of BWS usage.

- To list the rules for using BWS technology.

The obvious purpose of this book has been to help you understand stress, learn to limit stressors when possible, and learn how to counteract stressors that are inevitable. You have learned (and hopefully practiced) time-honored methods for relaxation, including breathing exercises, meditation, and various techniques for reducing muscular tension. A strong case has also been made for the value of physical exercise and eating a nutritious diet as part of your stress mastery program. You have been exposed to a wide variety of cognitive strategies for changing the myriad thinking patterns that help create, inflate, and perpetuate stress on the job and in your personal life. We hope that you have found these strategies useful for mastering the stress in your life.

This book would not be complete, however, without also introducing you to yet another avenue for stress management involving the use of recently developed high-tech tools. Basically, all methods of stress management are potentially highly effective (assuming, of course, that you engage in them with some regularity). Some will work better for you than others, and you may need to switch periodically depending on the type and amount of stress you are experiencing. All of the stress mastery techniques, methods, and tools presented here represent different roads to Rome. They will all get you to the same place (relaxation and peace of mind), but which road you should choose can vary depending on circumstances. New devices have been introduced that can offer shortcuts in the process of achieving deep levels of muscular relaxation, and it will be useful to familiarize yourself with some of these new alternatives.

High-tech relaxation tools, referred to as *psychotechnologies*, encompass a variety of devices and methodologies including biofeedback technology, flotation tanks, double-induction audio tapes, and (our personal favorite) light and sound machines, also known as *brainwave synchronizers*. One striking feature of each of these is that they offer the potential for finding nondrug shortcuts to achieving the relaxation response. In our high-pressure society, too many people resort to medications like common minor tranquilizers such as Xanax or Valium to achieve calmness or reduce stress. It is reassuring to know that powerful alternatives do exist, without the side effects or the possibility of addiction from drugs. The fact is that anti-anxiety medications come with lots of strings attached.

Biofeedback

It was traditionally assumed by physicians as well as psychologists that functions of the autonomic nervous system (ANS) could not be consciously controlled. After all, the ANS is also called the *involuntary nervous system;* it controls so-called involuntary bodily functions such as blood pressure and heart rate. Then, in the late 1960s, a series of creative experiments by psychologist Neal Miller, Ph.D., demonstrated that people can consciously affect and control autonomic functions after all. Miller was experimenting with what later became known as *biofeedback*, a system of recording, amplifying, and feeding back information about subtle physiological responses. The mechanisms whereby we control autonomic functions are still poorly understood, but it appears that it involves activation of the parasympathetic branch of the ANS (which mediates the relaxation response), along with deactivation of the sympathetic branch (which stimulates fight-or-flight activity).

Biofeedback instruments give you information (feedback) about what is happening in your body. You can then use this feedback to facilitate relaxation and to relax targeted muscles. Biofeedback technology involves attaching highly sensitive electronic sensors to your body to detect subtle changes in targeted body functions. These data are then fed into an electronic device that amplifies it and delivers it back to you, usually in the form of audio signals or visual displays. You would then exercise methods of altering your physiology, usually by practicing specific relaxation skills taught by the therapist or biofeedback technician, who also adjusts the instruments. By monitoring the audio or visual feedback, you can determine whether your efforts at relaxation are successful, and you can introduce modifications depending on the levels indicated by the feedback. In this way you can learn sophisticated relaxation skills, such as relaxing a specific muscle group or increasing blood flow to a particular region. Biofeedback offers users a powerful way to overcome certain stress-related disorders and to learn systems of relaxation with direct access to information about mastery (Miller, 1985). But while biofeedback can be highly effective, it does require a commitment of time and practice from the user in order to achieve results. These machines cannot make you relax; they only give you information about your progress.

Types of Biofeedback

There are four main categories of biofeedback equipment and training, each measuring different bodily functions and having different applications. The most common application of biofeedback involves the use of *EMG (electromyograph) training*. The EMG, which measures muscular tension, is especially useful for treatment of stress-related disorders such as tension headaches, bruxism (teeth gnashing), and TMJ (temporal mandibular joint) disorder, all of which are caused by excessive tension in particular muscle groups. Learning to relax targeted muscles can significantly improve any of these conditions. Physical pain can also be reduced by EMG biofeedback training. It is widely known that pain can be reduced by up to 40 percent just by relaxation alone, for tension increases our perception of pain. In fact, much of the effectiveness of major painkillers (such as opiates) is due to the fact that they induce relaxation. Relaxation also allows endorphins to be released more readily. EMG biofeedback can be used for general relaxation quite effectively, as well as for relaxing specific muscle groups that may be involved in pain.

Many stress-related disorders, from migraine headaches to menstrual cramps, are related to blood-volume changes. Vasomotor activity can be measured and modified with the help of *temperature biofeedback*, which employs the aid of a *thermistor* to measure subtle changes in the temperature of the skin, reflecting changes in blood flow. Skin temperature increases when *vasodilation*, the opening of peripheral blood vessels, occurs. The more relaxed you become, the greater your peripheral vasodilation. By learning specific relaxation skills (a process known as *autogenic training*, which was reviewed in Chapter 5) geared to increase blood flow to the hands or the feet, users can learn to decrease or eliminate migraine headaches, hypertension, and asthma.

EEG (electroencephalograph) biofeedback is useful in helping individuals modify brainwaves (which will be discussed in greater depth later in this chapter). Applications include treatment of insomnia (where muscle tension is not a problem), alcoholism, and ADD (attention deficit disorder). EEG biofeedback has been shown to improve attention and concentration. This application of biofeedback is relatively rare because few health care professionals have access to an EEG or the training to operate it properly.

EDR (electrodermal response) biofeedback has applications in the treatment of hypertension and hyperhydrosis (excessive sweating due to anxiety or arousal). Your electrodermal response reflects changes in the electrical conductivity of your skin due to the minute changes in sweat gland activity that occur in response to stress. Polygraph machines (lie detectors) also work on this principle. However, in general, this type of biofeedback is less reliable than the other forms, just as polygraph technology has been deemed somewhat unreliable and is therefore inadmissible as evidence in court.

Double Induction Hypnotic Tapes

Subliminal and hypnotic audiotapes for self-improvement have been on the market for many years. While some have been effective, the vast majority are of dubious quality for reasons that are beyond the scope of this book. However, within the last decade, hypnotic tapes have been developed that take advantage of powerful methods for promoting relaxation and planting suggestions. Basically, *hypnosis* is a method of pacing and leading you into a deeply relaxed state. There is nothing magical or mystical about the hypnotic state. It is just a state of profound relaxation whereby you become more suggestible or open to receiving suggestions. When you are hypnotized, your conscious mind is more easily neutralized and therefore cannot resist advice as easily. Your conscious mind is a pro at nullifying suggestions that are for your own good. That is why we cannot always rely on our conscious, rational mind to solve all our problems, or to provide motivation for beneficial change. Sometimes we have to access our unconscious, creative mind to help find solutions, increase motivation, or overcome fears or obstacles to our growth.

How Hypnosis Works

A useful analogy is to think of the human brain as a computer. Any computer, despite its hard drive, is only as good as its software and the data that we input. Garbage in, garbage out. Many times humans run into difficulties because of faulty programming earlier in life. We develop fears, insecurities, and thinking patterns that promote stress because of how we have been programmed. Hypnotic suggestions are a way of revamping or rehauling the old programming and installing new, healthier patterns. But the conscious mind is inherently conservative and reluctant to part with old, familiar programs to which it tenaciously clings. When we are relaxed, our conscious mind is more easily bypassed and we can access the unconscious processes that are more open to useful reprogramming.

Is Hypnosis Mind Control?

In case you are concerned, you cannot be made to do anything you do not agree with or do not want to do via hypnotic suggestion. Although being deeply relaxed or hypnotized may make you more open to suggestion, it does not render you helpless in the face of any suggestions that are antithetical to your beliefs, harmful to you or others, or offensive to you. We guarantee you would reject any suggestion that does not feel right for you, no matter how relaxed you might be. You will only adopt suggestions that you are ready and willing (but previously unable) to assimilate.

Within the last ten years, audiotapes have been developed that use a sophisticated hypnotic technique known as *double induction*. This method uses two separate voices weaving in and out rhythmically, often with each voice speaking to a different ear. The overall effect is often very confusing, for it is very difficult to follow two voices simultaneously, each carrying its own story line. It is meant to be confusing; this confusion helps neutralize your conscious mind, which eventually gives up the struggle of listening and enters a deeply relaxed state. Bypassing your conscious mind allows suggestions for beneficial change to be planted in the unconscious mind and take root.

These tapes also follow a form of hypnosis known as *Ericksonian hypnosis*, named after Milton Erickson, M.D., regarded by most people to be the greatest hypnotist who ever lived. The Ericksonian approach is far more effective than traditional forms of hypnosis. In Ericksonian hypnosis, suggestions are delivered in an indirect or metaphorical fashion, which is harder to resist than traditional hypnotic suggestions that typically take the form of commands. Most of us naturally resist commands. For example, let's suppose you have a tendency to procrastinate, which is starting to cause problems for you on your job. You listen to some hypnotic tapes in an attempt to motivate yourself to be more productive. To which suggestion do you think you would respond more favorably? On one tape you are admonished to "stop being lazy" and to "begin working now." On another tape you are gently encouraged to "plant some seeds, watch them grow, and take great pleasure in the task of watering and nurturing your plant." Obviously, the second suggestion is more alluring, but that does not mean you will take up gardening. Basically, your unconscious mind is being directed to begin a task, follow through, and gain pleasure from it.

Double-induction hypnotic tapes are available with a wide variety of applications: general relaxation and stress reduction, enhancing self-esteem and self-confidence, developing assertive skills, healing from illness and injury, pain control, facilitating restful sleep, overcoming specific fears, boosting creativity and problem solving, losing weight, conquering addictions, stopping smoking, mastering procrastination, boosting sexual responsivity, and many more.

Flotation Tanks

Another method for inducing profound relaxation involves the use of sensory deprivation. This is based on the discovery of the *Ganzfeld effect*, whereby individuals exposed to an unvarying visual field (such as in a white-out produced by a blizzard) enter an altered state of consciousness and begin to experience a wealth of internally stimulated visual imagery. The most effective application of the Ganzfeld effect involves the use of flotation tanks (Hutchinson, 1984).

The Float Experience

A *float tank* is an enclosed container roughly the size of a large bathtub with a lid. Inside is ten inches of warm water, heated to a constant temperature of 93.5°F (equal to the temperature on the surface of your skin) and inundated with Epsom salts to enable you to float effortlessly. When you shut the door you are enclosed in total darkness. All sounds are blocked out by earplugs. But this sensory deprivation chamber goes beyond a simple Ganzfeld situation by restricting other sensory input as well. Tactile sensations are eliminated by lying back and floating in a pool of water at body temperature, causing you to lose your sense of separation from the liquid. The boundaries of your body seem to disappear, thus eliminating sensations of touch, pressure, or friction. The effects of gravity are also nullified by the fact that your body is totally suspended in fluid. The result is that you are almost completely deprived of external sensory stimulation. Scientists estimate that at least 90 percent of our brain's activities are involved in processing the wealth of external stimuli that bombard us at any given moment. When we are freed of the need to monitor external stimuli, our mind opens up to internal, often unconscious mental processes that are ordinarily obscured. One of these processes is internal imagery.

Positive Effects of Floating

Numerous studies, as summarized by Michael Hutchinson (1991), in his books *MegaBrain*, and *MegaBrain Power* (1994) document that floating has dramatic stress-reduction effects. Most people find the float experience profoundly relaxing. Studies reveal that periodic float tank exposure leads to decreased heart rate, blood pressure, and oxygen consumption, along with reduced levels of stress hormones, such as cortisol and adrenaline, in the bloodstream. Furthermore, levels of stress chemicals remain lower for days, and in some cases weeks, after the float sessions. Float-induced relaxation also leads to vasodilation (enlargement of blood vessels, causing increased blood flow), which boosts the supply of oxygen and other nutrients to the brain. This, along with the effects of sensory deprivation, results in enhanced mental functioning.

Along with documented stress-reduction benefits, the flotation experience has been shown to produce many other beneficial effects. Studies have revealed that endorphin levels rise after float tank exposure, a common result of the deeply relaxed state. Floating also appears to increase access to right-brain functioning, thereby making it easier to get in touch with creative and problem-solving abilities, visualization skills, and memory functions. Many professional athletes who have combined visualization practice with floating have succeeded in improving their sports performance. Learning appears to be enhanced when floating. Many individuals combine floating with specific learning tasks, such as mastering a language or memorizing complex material. This involves taking advantage of what noted researcher

Thomas Budzynski, Ph.D., refers to as a "twilight learning state" where relaxation (in particular, the achievement of a theta brainwave state) leads to improved mental clarity, concentration, synthesis, and recall. In a study (Taylor, 1983) that compared the learning ability of a float group with that of a nonfloat group, the results revealed that people who floated learned at a significantly superior level. As the difficulty and complexity of the learning material increased, the superiority of the floaters over the nonfloaters increased sharply. Check out whether your community has a flotation center and treat yourself to this enjoyable and healthy relaxation experience.

Light and Sound Technology

Sound and light machines that alter brainwave activity via a combination of stroboscopic lights and synchronized rhythmic tones may seem new, but the knowledge that flickering lights and rhythmic tones can lead to profound relaxation, altered states of consciousness, and visual images is something humans have known since the discovery of fire. Can you remember staring into a campfire or fireplace and feeling a sense of calm and tranquility pervade your body? Meanwhile, you may have found yourself watching images dance in the glowing embers. When you first see a sound and light machine it may appear bizarre, like something out of a science fiction movie. But while the hardware is new, the techniques being used are ancient.

Human Brainwaves

To understand how light and sound machines work, you must first learn a bit about human brainwaves, which were first discovered in 1922 and can be measured by an EEG. Human brainwaves range from 0 to approximately 40 cycles per second (cps). They can be divided into four categories based on distinct changes in consciousness associated with different frequency levels. The following relationships can be observed between brainwave ranges and subjective states:

1. *Beta waves* (13–40 cps), the highest frequency range, are associated with normal, waking alertness. We operate within this frequency range during most of our waking hours. It is here that we carry on most of our daily living tasks. The high end of this range includes arousal frequencies, which can be associated with tension.

2. *Alpha waves* (8–13 cps) are generated while we are relaxed but alert and also when we are engaged in creative, absorbing endeavors. Meditators strive to achieve the alpha state. An excellent measure of whether you are relaxed involves determining whether you have reached an alpha state.

3. *Theta waves* (4–8 cps) are usually produced when we are just falling asleep or waking up (also known as the *hypnagogic state*), and rarely do adults manifest a theta state while fully awake. Waking theta states generally occur during bursts of highly creative activity or peak experiences.

4. *Delta waves* (0–4 cps) are produced when we are deeply asleep or in other similarly unconscious states.

Entrainment

Light and sound machines work by gently guiding your brainwaves into a slower frequency cycle, thus lulling you into a more deeply relaxed state. This is done with only gentle tones and flashing lights. The devices affect your brainwaves through a process known as *entrainment* (or the *frequency following response*), which is a very well researched and empirically validated phenomenon. Basically, your brain begins to match or mimic the flashing light stimulus that is presented to it. So if you are viewing a light flashing in the alpha range, after a while your brain begins to shift into an alpha frequency range to match the flashing light. That is entrainment. It is the same principle by which tuning forks work. Your brain essentially can resonate like a tuning fork, entraining to flashing lights, pulsating tones, or both. As your brain enters into an alpha or theta state, your muscles naturally relax.

Sound and light technology has a distinct advantage over relaxation exercises and biofeedback; where biofeedback merely measures levels of tension and relaxation and helps train you to relax by providing feedback, light and sound machines literally create a state of relaxation for you as a result of the entrainment process. Although practice on these devices is certainly recommended to maximize results and benefits, you do not have to go through a time-consuming learning process to learn to relax. Light and sound machines create the relaxed state for you, sometimes in as quickly as five minutes. Light and sound machines are also portable, unlike flotation tanks, and are available for home usage.

Do light and sound machines, also called *brainwave synchronizers (BWS)*, really work? Or are they simply a fancy placebo? Given that light and sound technology is quite new (having been developed in the 1980s), there is minimal controlled research. However, we conducted several unpublished controlled studies (Brucato & Abascal, 1990, 1991) documenting that light and sound machines do produce clinically significant levels of relaxation. In one study with college student volunteers, the effects of brainwave synchronizers were compared to the outcome of activities that are considered intrinsically relaxing, such as reclining in a comfortable chair or listening to soft music. The experimental group reclined in specially designed recliner chairs and received six light and sound sessions complete with melodious music. Subjects in control group 1 only reclined in the same chair as the experimental group and were instructed to relax. Subjects in control group 2 reclined in the same chair and listened to the same music as the experimental group. To minimize variations in subjects' expectations, all groups received a blurb about stress and the beneficial effects of relaxation, combined with an explanation that they would be receiving state-of-the-art relaxation treatments. The results indicated that the levels of relaxation (as measured by a variety of physiological and self-report indices) in the group receiving exposure to light and sound were significantly greater.

Researchers have gone beyond verifying the phenomenon of entrainment and have begun to document the effects of practicing relaxation with entrainment devices such as brainwave synchronizers. Michael Hutchinson (1991) summarized many of these findings:

1. Certain frequencies, particularly within the alpha and theta ranges, are associated with deep physical relaxation and mental clarity.

2. At these same frequency levels, anxiety levels are reduced.

3. Such reductions in anxiety or tension levels have been shown to linger for hours or up to several days following exposure to BWS stimulation.

4. In some cases the verbal ability and verbal performance of subjects was increased following stimulation.

5. Suggestibility and hypnotizability were markedly increased, especially by frequencies within the alpha and theta ranges.

6. The flickering lights could bring the two hemispheres of the brain into a state of greater coherence or synchronization. This state is associated with increased intellectual capacity or functioning.

7. Such exposure could help stimulate vivid, spontaneous mental imagery and imaginative, creative thinking.

Experiencing Light and Sound Machines

Sound and light devices have great potential as stress-management tools in that they produce relaxation in a more reliable and efficient manner than many other methods. This technology is also quite entertaining, as many people report seeing colors, shapes, or patterns during exposure. The visual experience has been likened to a kaleidoscopic array of vibrant colors and designs. Spontaneous dreamlike visual imagery is also possible, and for that reason BWS devices have been used to potentiate creativity and problem solving in addition to relaxation. Many individuals resist the regular practice of relaxation techniques or meditation because of the boredom factor. Light and sound machines, due to their entertainment value, are anything but boring, leading to higher compliance with routine relaxation practice. For these reasons, we highly recommend light and sound devices and feel that they represent the cutting edge in stress-management technology.

Using a light and sound device is as easy as pushing a button. The device consists of goggles and headphones that plug into a small, portable computer console. All you do is press a button to choose the program you desire. Preset computer programs exist within the machine, varying in length, modes of light presentation, and frequency ranges, allowing you to pick an alpha, theta, or delta program. Once you have chosen your program, you don the goggles and headphones, adjust the volume and light intensity to your comfort level, and close your eyes. It's that simple.

You can enhance your experience by playing melodic music (such as New Age or classical) through the machine to accompany your relaxation experience. Most light and sound devices are built to accommodate a patch cord that interfaces with a tape or CD player. An even more elegant approach is to combine light and sound technology with double-induction hypnotic tapes for self-improvement. Since brainwave synchronizers can create profound relaxation (analogous to a hypnotic state), it follows that listening to a hypnotic tape while already deeply relaxed will maximize the effectiveness of the suggestions on the tape. In our experience, using hypnotic tapes in conjunction with light and sound creates a synergistic effect where each is more powerful than when used alone.

Tips for BWS Usage

The following list offers several guidelines to enable you to get the most out of BWS technology, as well as to help you choose programs that will help you achieve your goals.

1. If you are not an experienced meditator, it is wise to begin with alpha programs of twenty to thirty minutes' duration as a good way to introduce yourself to this technology. Once you are comfortable with the process and aware that you have achieved a relaxed state, you can move on to other programs.

2. If you have a seizure disorder or a history of convulsions, these devices are contraindicated. Stroboscopic light stimuli can precipitate a seizure in individuals prone to them. These devices will *not* cause seizures unless you have a pre-existing seizure disorder.

3. Not everyone achieves the full depth of relaxation in the first experience with light and sound. Sometimes it takes a few tries to let go and trust in the process. If you try too hard, it is like trying to fall asleep. You cannot make yourself sleep, as it is a process of letting go; the same is true with relaxation. In our experience, light and sound technology is effective with 75 to 80 percent of the population. There is no right or wrong way to have a light and sound experience. You may also find that each experience you have with this equipment is different.

4. When using hypnotic or subliminal tapes in conjunction with light and sound, effectiveness is maximized by employing a theta program. You will be most receptive to suggestion while in a theta or hypnagogic state. A word of caution: in our experience subliminal tapes are not nearly as effective as advertised. Studies indicate that subliminal tapes can potentially carry some influence, but only if used properly—that is, listened to in their entirety daily for at least thirty days in succession.

5. When using BWS machines to potentiate creativity, imagination, or problem solving, it is also recommended that you choose a theta program (Budzynski, 1991). It is while in theta that we are most likely to get flashes of inspiration or develop creative solutions. Thomas Edison taught himself to fall asleep standing up against a wall while holding a hard rubber ball in one hand. As he began to doze off, his hand would open and release the ball, which would fall and strike a strategically placed metal plate at his feet. The resulting clatter would rouse him and he would immediately jot down any thoughts, ideas, or images that had occurred to him as he was nodding off. Many of his most famous inventions were first glimpsed in this fashion. Edison didn't know it at the time, but he was using the theta state to maximize his creative juices.

6. Delta programs are typically used for two major applications: to control pain and to facilitate sleep. Avoid delta programs otherwise, for they will make you too groggy.

7. Many light and sound devices also contain short wake-up programs within the beta range that can take the place of a coffee break. Especially during that late-afternoon lull, it can be useful to do a six- or ten-minute beta program to wake yourself up without the negative side effects of caffeine.

8. Depending on the nature of your job and the amount of privacy in your work-space, it may be possible to take a light and sound machine to work. If you feel fatigue catching up with you, it may be possible to do a short relaxation pro-gram (for example, fifteen minutes) to recharge your batteries and revitalize. Or you can wake yourself up with a very short beta program. Many profes-sionals use these devices regularly within their offices as a way of minimizing stress and anxiety and boosting energy.

9. The relaxed state produced by light and sound use often lingers for several hours up to a day or two after exposure. We recommend that you practice with the device two to three times weekly. This can reduce your baseline level of tension (your normal level of arousal) by linking together these periods of in-creased relaxation—the equivalent of giving your car a tune-up, increasing its efficiency and gas mileage and averting future breakdowns. If you are inter-ested in obtaining a brainwave synchronizer for your personal use, please re-fer to the appendix for more information.

Chapter Summary

New high-tech tools offer shortcuts for achieving the relaxation response. Biofeed-back technology involves learning to relax targeted muscle groups or change blood flow while your tension levels are monitored by electronic sensors. Information about your tension level is then fed back to you, assisting you in the process of mas-tering relaxation skills. Double-induction hypnotic tapes take advantage of sophis-ticated Ericksonian hypnotic techniques for relaxation, and reprogram your unconscious mind with effective strategies for self-improvement and stress reduc-tion. Flotation tanks help you achieve a deeply relaxed state through the effects of sensory deprivation. Our favorite high-tech tool is light and sound machines, also known as brainwave synchronizers (BWSs). These devices induce a profound state of relaxation for you through the use of light and sound stimulation; they work by altering brainwave frequencies via the entrainment response. BWS devices have been shown to help create alpha and theta brainwave states, which are associated with deep muscular relaxation, calmness, and a sense of well-being.

Chapter Questions

1. What is biofeedback? What are the four types of biofeedback devices and the applications of each?

2. Is hypnosis the same as mind control?

3. What is hypnotic double induction and how does it work?

4. What phenomenon is responsible for the relaxation produced by flotation tanks?

5. Which brainwave states are associated with relaxation?

6. What is the entrainment process and how do light and sound machines use it for creating relaxed states?

7. Light and sound machines can be used in conjunction with what other relaxation device?

Section 5

Workplace Stress

Stress Mastery on the Job

What You Will Learn in this Chapter

- To list the signs and symptoms of workplace stress.

- To assess your own level of workplace stress if you are employed using the inventory.

- To identify the factors contributing to the rising level of stress in the workplace.

- To list the faulty assumptions held by many workers that contribute to workplace stress.

- To substitute realistic expectations in place of faulty assumptions.

- To practice methods for pacing yourself on the job.

- To relieve muscular tension at work by using specific relaxation exercises designed for the workplace.

It will come as no great surprise to you that workplace stress has been rising and will continue to rise at an alarming rate. Each and every one of us is feeling the pressure. The National Center for Health Statistics, based on a 1985 study, reported that more than half of the workers surveyed admitted to experiencing severe to moderate stress in their jobs over the last two weeks. The National Institute for Occupational Safety and Health (NIOSH) reported that one-third of workers felt that their jobs were extremely stressful, and one-fourth of employees viewed their jobs as the *number one stressor* in their lives. NIOSH defines job stress as "the harmful emotional response that occurs when the requirements of a job do not match the capabilities, resources, or needs of the worker." Early warning signs of job stress include the following:

Headaches	Short temper
Sleep disturbances	Job dissatisfaction
Upset stomach	Low morale
Difficulty concentrating	

Job stress takes its toll. In addition to employee misery, billions of dollars are lost annually by business and industry due to lowered productivity and skyrocketing health care costs. Therefore, learning to master workplace stress makes all the sense in the world for you, personally and financially. To ascertain your personal level of workplace stress, complete the Workplace Stress Test.

Factors Leading to Increased Workplace Stress

Why is the level of workplace stress increasing with such velocity? To a great extent, it has to do with the acceleration of the rate of change (change = stress) in the world at large. There are three driving forces behind this ever-increasing speed of change:

1. *Population growth.* Although humans have inhabited the earth for millions of years, our total population didn't hit one billion until the 1860s. Within seventy-five years, the earth's population had doubled. By 1975 it had doubled again, this time only taking fifty years. And it continues to build. The more people living on our planet, the more competition we will face and more new ideas, changes, and developments will bombard us daily. Why? Because people are the major change agent.

2. *The information explosion.* More information was produced in the thirty years from 1965 to 1995 than had accumulated in the entire previous history of civilization, in the roughly five-thousand-year period spanning 3,000 B.C. through 1965! It now appears that the amount of available information is doubling every five years, further accelerated by our capacity for instantaneous communication via TV, the Internet, wire services, and so on. The more we learn and are exposed to, the more we must change or risk falling more and more behind.

Workplace Stress Test

Instructions: Rate your answer to each question according to the following scale:

1 = Never   2 = Rarely   3 = Some of the time   4 = All of the time

1. I feel tired at work, even with adequate sleep.	1	2	3	4
2. I feel frustrated in carrying out my responsibilities at work.	1	2	3	4
3. I am moody, irritable, or impatient over small problems.	1	2	3	4
4. I want to withdraw from the constant demands on my time and energy.	1	2	3	4
5. I feel negative, futile, or depressed about work.	1	2	3	4
6. My decision-making ability is less than usual because of my work.	1	2	3	4
7. I think that I am not as efficient at work as I should be.	1	2	3	4
8. I feel physically, emotionally, or spiritually depleted.	1	2	3	4
9. The quality of my work is less than it should be.	1	2	3	4
10. My resistance to illness is lowered because of my work.	1	2	3	4
11. My interest in doing fun activities is lowered because of my work.	1	2	3	4
12. I feel uncaring about the problems and needs of my co-workers, customers, clients, patients, and others at work.	1	2	3	4
13. Communication with my co-workers, friends, or family seems strained.	1	2	3	4
14. I am forgetful.	1	2	3	4
15. I have difficulty concentrating on my job.	1	2	3	4
16. I am easily bored with my job.	1	2	3	4
17. I feel a sense of dissatisfaction with my job—that there's something wrong or missing.	1	2	3	4
18. When I ask myself why I get up and go to work, the only answer that occurs to me is, "I have to."	1	2	3	4

Scoring

If your score is 0 to 34, you are not stressed.

If your score is 35 to 55, you are moderately stressed.

If your score is 55 or more, you are definitely stressed.

---

3. *Technological advances.* The rate of technological change is a direct outgrowth of population growth and information expansion. It is estimated that well over 80 percent of the world's technological advances have occurred in the last hundred years. Technology feeds on itself—one breakthrough leads to a host of other advances, which then spur on even more developments. This cycle is never-ending, and the pace will keep accelerating.

The Effects of Accelerating Change

One of the first places where accelerating change is often apparent is in the workplace. Businesses must constantly shift and adapt to stay competitive. We must continually upgrade our skills and knowledge, master new equipment, and make sense of new procedures if we are to keep pace and remain competent and secure in our positions. Sometimes the burden seems overwhelming.

One common result of job stress overload is burnout. But job stress alone does not inevitably result in burnout. Often a worker's perceived lack of control over the job situation leads to anxiety, frustration, decreased motivation, and burnout. It has often been said that jobs that combine maximum responsibility with minimal control are the most stressful. Middle managers (who shoulder lots of responsibility without the power of top management) often fall into this category. Health care workers involved with high-risk populations also fit here. But this can occur in any job—for example, if you cannot meet unrealistic expectations held by your boss, if your coworkers are undermining you, if you own your own business and can't pay the bills, or if your level of skills and training are not adequate for the demands of your position.

Minor factors can also add up to greatly increase your level of job stress. A long commute to and from work each day through rush-hour traffic can definitely contribute. Working in a job where you must continually deal with red tape and bureaucratic inefficiency can lead to frustration. Having to deal with frequent interruptions or multiple simultaneous demands on your time and attention can also take its toll. A very unpleasant work environment (for example, noisy, dirty, too hot or cold, or cramped) can also wear you down. The cumulative effect of annoyances such as these can raise your stress level significantly. Sometimes a job can be stressful because it is overly boring, failing to challenge your intelligence or to provide enough variety of tasks to keep things interesting. That is, being underloaded can be as hard to take as being overloaded.

Many times we add to our stress level by how we perceive a situation. Remember, stress is caused not by what happens to you but by what you tell yourself about what occurs. This self-induced job stress is fueled by a number of faulty assumptions, as highlighted by Price Pritchett and Ron Pound in their pamphlet, *A Survival Guide to the Stress of Organizational Change* (1996). Review the following misguided expectations and see which currently apply, have applied, or could apply to you in the future. Pay careful attention to the tips on how to neutralize these faulty assumptions and cope with stressful work situations more effectively.

Ten Faulty Assumptions and Effective Antidotes

1. Expecting Someone Else to Lower Your Stress Level

It is tempting to blame others for your stress—your boss or your supervisor, perhaps—and if they are to blame, then you might expect them to change or rescue you from your predicament. Keep in mind that changes or decisions created by top management are typically reactions to external events. It is likely that managers are trying to respond effectively to outside forces such as economic downturns, stiffer competition, marketplace shifts, or new technological advances. The changes they have wrought make sense from their point of view, and it is unlikely that they will backpedal just to make life easier for you. If they stagnate, it may ultimately be worse for you and your organization in the long run.

Blaming others for your situation further damages your sense of control, for you view yourself as a helpless victim without alternatives or choices. Blaming also triggers anger and the release of stress hormones that can damage your health and deplete your energy. It is unrealistic to expect someone other than yourself to rescue you from a stressful job situation or protect you on the job. Your bosses are too busy taking care of themselves and they, no doubt, feel as much or more stress than you. *You* need to take charge of managing the pressure, for ultimately you can only count on yourself to lighten your psychological load.

How do you go about doing this? First, assess whether you can take any reasonable steps to change the stressful conditions. If so, then take those steps. If not, then two choices remain: (1) adapt to the situation, or (2) find another job. Oftentimes adapting just requires a change in your perspective. Try to put yourself in your boss's shoes (using the techniques presented in Chapter 6) to understand why certain changes or new practices are necessary, even if you don't like them. And recognize that you are never really trapped. Your choices may be difficult, but choice always exists. You can weigh the pros and cons of staying with your job and learning to adjust if the pros weigh heavier, or you can begin searching for a new job if the cons win out.

2. Assuming That You Can Resist Change

It has often been said that *"the only constant is change."* You can attempt to resist change in the workplace, either consciously or unconsciously, directly or through passive-aggressive maneuvers. If you resist, you may decrease your anxiety or stress level in the short run, but in the long term you are setting yourself up for greater stress and eventual failure. The very act of resisting change is in itself stressful, and may prove more difficult for you than going with the flow. Many people waste far more energy clinging to old habits than it would take to accept and adapt to the changes. *Fighting change is almost always a losing battle.* Can you really expect to succeed in your job, in an ever-changing world, if you keep doing the same old things in the same old way?

The same thing applies if you decide to accept the need for change, but only at your own pace and according to your own schedule. Here the goal is to minimize stress by "pacing yourself." While this may be well-intentioned, it can often back-fire. Why? Because failure to keep up with your organization's rate of change is still resistance, however well-intentioned. You can slow things down for other people, cause backlogs for yourself and others, and risk the wrath of your superiors. If you are the boss, then you run the risk of falling behind your competitors.

You need to keep in step with the intended rate of change deemed necessary by your organization or your competitors. Some people, if allowed to go at their own pace, would take forever to change. If you lag behind you will eventually have to play catch-up, and there is no guarantee that you can successfully close the gap. Remember—you may not have control over the type or speed of changes thrust upon you, but you always have control over how you choose to react to the need for change.

However, the whole notion of "pacing yourself" on the job to lower stress is a good idea, but only if you pace yourself in the right way. Pacing yourself properly can enhance productivity and lower stress. Pacing yourself wisely is not a matter of slowing down, but rather using strategic planning for structuring your time. Here are some pacing tips that will enable you to recharge your batteries, revitalize your-self, and ultimately be more productive and creative.

1. Pay attention to your natural body rhythms to determine at what times you function at your best. Are you a morning person or a night person? When possible, schedule your most difficult tasks for your peak performance hours. Try to avoid tackling difficult or exhausting projects during the part of the day when your energy is at its lowest.

2. Shift between pleasant and unpleasant tasks. After finishing a difficult piece of work, switch to something mindless, easy, or pleasant.

3. Allow some time each day, even when you are swamped with work, for plea-surable work tasks, even if they are not highly productive.

4. Use your breaks and lunches to relax. Do not work over lunch unless it is ab-solutely essential.

5. Take mini-breaks for three to five minutes throughout the day to relax and bal-ance yourself. Talk to a co-worker, have a refreshing drink, and so on.

6. Choose leisure activities that balance the unique stresses in your line of work. For example, if you deal with people's complaints all day long, choose solitary, peaceful pursuits. Or if you are cooped up in a windowless office all day, choose outdoor activities. If you work alone, make sure your leisure time in-cludes social activities with friends.

7. Take vacations. Carefully consider the length and type of vacation you plan in order to balance work stresses. If your work is very sedentary, plan an active vacation. If your work is physically exhausting, plan a vacation where you allow a good amount of time for just kicking back and relaxing. If you work alone and feel lonely, visit friends or family or vacation with others.

8. If possible, take a break during your workday to exercise, do relaxation practices, or run an errand. Back in Chapter 5 we talked about the importance of stretching your muscles for decreasing stress and physical strain. The following six stretches are specifically designed for the workplace, to be done at your desk in your chair (Marshall, 1999). Take a few moments daily to do one or more of these stretches when you feel tense or fatigued, and notice the results.

Figure 11.1   Chair Twist

Chair Twist

Sit toward the front of your chair. Swivel your thighs toward the right side of the chair so you are sitting diagonally on the seat. Inhale and lift your right arm up to the ceiling. Exhale and move your arm to the back of the chair on the opposite side, taking hold of the chair back. Bring your left hand to your right knee. Inhale and lengthen your spine. Exhale and twist to the right, pressing your right hand against the back of the chair to deepen the twist. Breathe into your rib cage. Relax the muscles in your back and gently twist a little farther. Stay in the pose for four to six breaths. Return to your center with an inhalation and repeat on the opposite side. (See Figure 11.1.)

Shoulder Rolls

Sit upright and inhale while lifting your right shoulder to your ear. Exhale and slowly roll your right shoulder forward, around and back, dropping it away from your ear. Continue these shoulder rolls three more times, alternating right and left. Inhale as you lift both shoulders up to your ears. Exhale as you release them. Repeat the shoulder lift five times and then relax your shoulders. (See Figure 11.2.)

Figure 11.2   Shoulder Roll

Figure 11.3
Side Stretch

Side Stretches

Stand with your feet parallel. Inhale and stretch your arms out to your sides and overhead, with your palms facing away from your body. Exhale while holding your left wrist with your right hand and then inhale. Stretch the fingers of your left hand toward the ceiling. Exhale and stretch to the right. Pull your left arm with your right hand. Keep your left arm and head straight. Breathe softly as you stretch. Inhale as you come back to the center. Exhale and switch hands, holding your right wrist with your left hand. Inhale as you reach up through the fingers of your right hand. Exhale while stretching left and inhale and return to the center. Repeat this sequence on each side. (See Figure 11.3.)

Figure 11.4 Open Chest Stretch

Open Chest Stretch

Sit near the edge of your chair. Interlace your fingers behind you, palms facing your back. Lean slightly forward. Lift your arms and rest them on the back of the chair. Inhale and lift your chest. Exhale and relax your shoulders away from your ears. If your hands do not reach the top of the chair, clasp the sides of the chair back and press your chest forward, relaxing your shoulders and opening your upper chest. Hold this position for three to six breaths. With an exhalation, slowly release your hands and bring them down by your sides. (See Figure 11.4.)

Figure 11.5
Neck Stretches

Neck Stretches

Sit upright, with your head aligned with your spine. Inhale and on exhalation, drop your right ear toward your shoulder without lifting the shoulder or turning your head. You can use your left hand to gently assist your head and neck in stretching toward your right shoulder. Take several breaths in and out. Gently massage your neck and shoulders with your left hand. Slowly lift your head and switch sides to repeat the sequence. (See Figure 11.5.)

Figure 11.6 Back and Shoulder Release

Back and Shoulder Release

Part One: Sit on the edge of your chair, placing your feet about two-and-a-half feet apart, parallel to each other. Lean forward and place your forearms on your inner thighs. Press your inner thighs out with your forearms. Breathe deeply in and out.

Part Two: Make sure your knees are directly over your heels, and your feet are parallel to each other. Slowly stretch your arms down toward the floor. Rest your ribs on your thighs and your armpits on your knees. Cross your arms, placing your hands at the opposite elbows. Continue to breathe deeply. (See Figure 11.6.)

3. Believing That You Are a Victim

Viewing yourself as a helpless victim buffeted by the winds of change only maximizes your stress, allows you to feel awful, and guarantees failure. Victims maintain that life is unfair and there is nothing they can do about it. Victims revel in throwing a big pity party for themselves, focusing only on what they have lost and what sacrifices must be made. There is also the hope that others will feel sorry for them and perhaps come to the rescue. If you are a victim, you need to be saved.

Perceiving yourself as a victim totally disempowers you. Although you may do so to defend or soothe yourself, the reality is that you are only damaging yourself further. You are setting yourself up for even more victimization because victims do not make attractive employees. Acting like a victim will threaten your future.

This self-induced stress perpetuates itself and can end up in a vicious cycle that only you can break. Remember that the Chinese character for *crisis*, when translated, actually means "dangerous opportunity." Within every change or crisis there is opportunity. Look for these opportunities. Learn to view them as challenges. Remember the stress hardiness characteristics. Refuse to yield to the seductive pull of self-pity. Remaining productive and developing resilience will pave the way out of your doldrums. Accept the situation, pick up the pieces, and learn to make lemonade from lemons. You are a victim only if you decide to be one.

4. Thinking That If What You Are Doing Isn't Working, You Should Just Try Harder

If what you are currently doing in your job is not working, then what makes you think that trying harder will work any better? The key may not be to *try harder*, but rather to do *something different*. You cannot play a new game by the old rules. This "more of the same" strategy is destined to fail in a changing environment. On the other hand, if your current strategies are working, then by all means stick with them. If it isn't broken, don't fix it.

Struggling to do your job with methods that are not working can significantly increase your level of stress. Study your work situation to determine exactly what has changed and exactly what is not working, and then experiment with new ways of doing tasks. You must be willing to alter your old techniques and routines if you are to remain viable. Choose to view this as a creative challenge rather than a chore. If you are clueless as to what to do differently, ask a colleague or a co-worker who is highly competent about what he or she has tried that has proven fruitful.

5. Assuming That You Will Always Benefit from a Low-Stress Work Environment

Whether you search for a job with minimal pressure or work behind the scenes at your current job to lower stress (by slowing the rate of change, for example), you may only be hurting yourself in the long run. Beware of the trap of believing that there is such a thing as a low-stress organization that is on track to survive. All available evidence points to the conclusion that slow changing organizations are headed for trouble. If you opt to slow down change today, you can temporarily lower your stress, but you are sacrificing your future.

Clearly, working in an environment of rapid change is stressful. But you may be headed for greater problems and stress down the road if your outfit fails to change or responds too slowly to changes in the external environment. Remember that the stress of accelerating change is here to stay. The key to stress mastery is often less about avoiding environmental stressors and more about how you respond to the inevitable stresses you will face. You will actually serve your own best interests by getting involved with an organization with the courage to move ahead in a changing world. Concentrate on lowering workplace stress in ways that do not involve minimizing change. Refer to the tips in faulty assumption #2 for ways you can reduce workplace stress in a manner that is in your best interests.

Another way to lower your level of job stress is to lighten your workload by abandoning tasks that may be expendable. Many times workplace stress builds because employees are expected to produce a heavier volume of work, improve quality standards, and work faster, all at the same time. In this era of downsizing, more work keeps falling on fewer shoulders. Has this happened to you? If not, do not be surprised if it does in the future. Customers are expecting better services. Competition is rising in almost all sectors. Workloads naturally rise as a result. But we all have limits to the amount of work we can carry.

If you keep taking on new duties without giving some up, you will eventually become overloaded. If you overview your work and then reorder your priorities, you may discover that certain tasks or procedures are expendable, some can be streamlined, and still others can be delegated to other workers. But this is easier said than done. There is a tendency to hang on to old habits and familiar ways of doing things, even if they are inefficient. This is particularly true if it involves tasks you are good at and reluctant to part with, even if they have minimal importance for your job. Does any of this apply to you? If you eliminate that which is expendable, it will create valuable time for you to devote to projects and tasks that really count. Not only will it help relieve the pressure on you, and therefore lower your stress level, but it will also allow you to devote more time to the important work that higher management will use to evaluate your performance.

So creating a low-stress work environment often involves re-engineering your job by (1) getting rid of busywork, (2) ditching unnecessary steps or procedures, and (3) abandoning tasks that are not necessary to achieve the current goals of your company. This may even mean unloading duties that don't count much, even though you do them incredibly well. If you are feeling overloaded in your work situation, we invite you to do this overview and determine what you can reasonably delete. Of course, you do need to also assess what your organization and/or boss will allow you to discard.

6. Believing That It Is Usually Unwise to Take Risks

Many people adopt the strategy of "when in doubt, do nothing." Change often requires that decisions be made. Many people wait indefinitely until all the facts are in to move in a chosen direction. But the reality is that **all decisions are made on the basis of insufficient information,** for none of us are soothsayers who can accurately predict what the future will bring. Doing nothing is merely a decision not to decide. This does not mean that you should make impulsive decisions without carefully weighing alternatives, but if you wait around until all the data are in, it may be too late!

We are reminded of the story of a friend who worked in a professional capacity for a large mental health care practice. The owners decided to sell the practice to an interested buyer. Clearly, the shift in management was going to result in massive internal changes in the organization. Our friend was given an opportunity to buy into the practice and become one of the owner/partners, and he was offered a financial arrangement that was well within his means. Taking advantage of this opportunity would have greatly increased his authority, status, and earning potential, but would also have increased his responsibilities and therefore his level of stress. Fearful of taking on new duties, he balked. He decided to wait and "play it safe" to see how things shook out with the new owners. Within six months the new owners fired him, viewing him as "too cautious" to be a viable part of their organization. The irony here is that by playing it safe, he lost in a big way. He ended up without a job or an equity position. Had he bought into the business, he could have at least sold his shares later on, had he found out that he did not want to work with the new owners.

7. Expecting That You Can Control Everything If You Try Hard Enough

Many people make the mistake of expending lots of energy and effort trying to control that which is uncontrollable. They resist the inevitable and try to undo that which cannot be undone. This leads to frustration and chronic stress because they are fighting a battle that can never be won. This is more likely to occur in rapidly changing environments, where people fear uncertainty and loss of control and try to take charge to maintain equilibrium. They forget that sometimes you can gain control by going with the flow rather than resisting it.

Consider the following analogy, which we mentioned in Chapter 5: When white-water rafting, one of the dangers is that you could fall out of the raft and be carried downstream past large boulders and swirling rapids. Clearly, if this should occur, it would be frightening (that is, stressful) and potentially dangerous. How does one cope if this should happen? Conventional wisdom would have you swim with all your might against the current, toward the raft. Actually, what is recommended is to allow yourself to go with the current and not fight it. Go feet first, arms at your sides, and allow the current to carry you to the shallows. Surrender to the current, which, if you do not fight, will navigate you safely through the rapids into calm water, where your fellow rafters can then retrieve you.

So assess whether a struggle makes any sense or will it just be a waste of time. Some people maximize their stress level by picking the wrong battles and waging war on too many fronts. Often these individuals oppose almost every change their organization makes, sometimes even fighting for things that would not be in their best interests even if they got their way. This strategy is bound to fail and put them at odds with their boss, supervisor, or colleagues. The result is that they often alienate others whom they need as allies. Picking the wrong battles can eventually lead to burnout.

Remember the advice of Jonathon Kozol: "Pick battles big enough to matter but small enough to win." Likewise, avoid the trap of pursuing issues that are a lost cause. Recognize what decisions are irreversible and learn to accept that which cannot be changed. Channel your energies toward issues where you have a chance of making a real dent. Acceptance of the inevitable will greatly lower your stress.

8. Believing That It Is Okay to Psychologically Unplug from Your Job If It Gets Too Stressful

It can be difficult to maintain a high level of commitment to your job in the face of high-velocity change. If you are concerned with job security, or just feeling overworked from long hours or underappreciated from not enough pay or recognition for your work, it is easy to get fed up with the situation. You may be tempted to emotionally disconnect from your work as a way of coping.

A common method of unplugging is to avoid new assignments or unfamiliar duties. The assumption here is that it will be less stressful to stick with what you already know. When motivation is low and you adopt an "I don't care" attitude, it is easy to shy away from new demands. But that is a very shortsighted strategy for managing your stress. You are buying comfort today at the expense of tomorrow. Avoidance and delay tactics may end up making you a target for dismissal at worst, or guarantee that you are overlooked for promotion at best. Your confidence and self-esteem will certainly be a casualty of this approach.

We would like to encourage you to be wary of the desire to unplug. Recognize that a bad case of the blahs is a common side effect of workplace stress. It is easy to understand how you might fall prey to becoming disconnected, but recognize that this will only do further harm to your emotional well-being. When you lose passion for your work, when your commitment wanes, part of your life loses meaning. As a result, job pressures weigh heavier and your vulnerability to workplace stress increases. You cannot afford to stop caring, no matter how attractive that might seem.

High job commitment is an excellent antidote to stress; there is something magical about commitment that gives us emotional strength. Remember the three C's. When we are committed we are happier, more resilient, and more satisfied and secure, even about our jobs. And commitment shows. It is like a light that glows from within that your colleagues and boss cannot help but perceive. Sometimes a high level of commitment can end up saving your job. In times of downsizing, employers are often faced with tough choices about whom to keep and whom to let go. How they perceive your level of commitment may very well determine whether you get the ax.

We advise you to plunge in and accept new or tough assignments as a way of broadening your experience base and heightening your commitment. This may temporarily increase your stress at the outset, but over time it is likely to improve your job skills, making you more valuable to your employer or on the job market. You are stretching yourself today in order to be in better shape tomorrow. One of the best stress-prevention techniques is to keep updating your skills. Over time, this will make your current job easier to handle and guarantee that you will be highly employable if your job does not work out. Also, do not assume that it will be less stressful to ease in to a new situation. Instead of taking time to build up your nerve before tackling something new, build your nerve by doing it. Once you plunge in, you will often discover that your fears were unsubstantiated. The sooner you face your fears and go through them, the sooner your level of stress will diminish.

Find a way to fall back in love with your job. Don't let the stress of change drive a wedge between you and your work. It is true that your employer will benefit from your commitment, but you will reap far greater rewards.

9. Assuming That "Caring Management" Should Always Strive to Keep You Comfortable

In our so-called enlightened age where we have done away with sweatshops and other forms of employee oppression, we consider it an inalienable right that our employers "treat us well." We believe we are entitled to "caring management." But over and above that, we believe that caring for us is in the best interest of the employees and the business itself. But what does that really mean? You need to be careful about what evidence you look at in determining to what extent your organization cares about its workers.

You may make the mistake of assuming that "caring" always means keeping employees comfortable—that management would always put employees first and strive to make things easier for workers. Therefore "caring management" would be about lowering workplace stress and not about making things harder. This would amount to greater job security (no downsizing), ample pay raises, improved work conditions, and a slower rate of change. In an ideal world this scenario would be possible and highly desirable. But the business world of today is hardly a utopian environment. While minimizing job stress might sound like a caring move on the part of management, in this day and age it could be a cruel option. Why? Because first and foremost, management can show it cares for you by making sure the business stays in business, by doing what works so the company does not go under. Remember that management also must care about customers and even stockholders. Employees are not the only people the organization must cater to if it is to succeed. Your employers must ask you and your colleagues to do what needs to be done in order to survive in this age of instability. And that usually means hard work and stress.

Thus, the best definition of caring management in the business world of today needs to be defined by the end result. The organization must do what works so that it can meet its payroll and provide you with your job. What good would it do you if your company treated you like royalty, kowtowing to your every whim and need, but then inevitably went under, leaving you jobless and hopelessly spoiled?

A stressful work environment and steady work demands are often the best proof that your company is on the right track and will remain viable. Management definitely has your best interests in mind when it is concerned with keeping your job secure and your paycheck intact. Without that, what good are all the frills? If management always bent over backward to keep you comfortable, it could be the most heartless thing they could possibly do, for then you could easily end up on the unemployment line. So if you find yourself bemoaning the fact that your company is not making life easier for you, use this viewpoint as a helpful reframe for conceptualizing the situation. Once again, how you view the situation will determine in great part how you feel and how you respond.

Many larger businesses or corporations do attempt to provide support for employees, not necessarily by lowering stress levels or workloads, but by offering employee assistance programs (EAPs), which can offer short-term counseling, referral services, alcohol and drug intervention programs, and so on. If you are experiencing difficulties and your company offers EAP benefits, it may be worth taking advantage of those services.

10. Believing That the Future Is to Be Feared

Worries about the future have reached epidemic proportions. The acceleration in the rate of change has led to marked uncertainty and job instability. You might be worried about how you will be affected by changes in your field or in your workplace. Do you ever find yourself obsessing about whether you will be downsized, or if self-employed, whether your business will survive? If you have a high tolerance for ambiguity or uncertainty, then perhaps you are not concerned. But if you have difficulty coping with change and confusion, then you probably wish you could bring some order and certainty to your situation. You might find, however, that attempts to eliminate uncertainty and instability might backfire.

An environment of rapid change is by nature unstable and uncertain. Stability by definition implies that things stay the same. In contrast, today's world is very fluid and transitional. The ability to improvise, to roll with the punches, has become an essential skill. Instead of futilely working to stabilize the situation, learn how to exploit instability and take advantage of the opportunities inherent in a changing atmosphere. So if you attempt to settle things you might be setting yourself up to fail. In our rapidly changing business world, rigidity sounds the death knell for you and your career. Therefore, although it may appear that you would experience less stress if you could stabilize the situation, the reality is that you could not succeed in doing so and therefore would only end up heightening your stress.

It is in your best interest to increase your tolerance for constant change and midcourse corrections. Begin to welcome confusion into your life and allow yourself at times to "wing it." Learn to flex to the demands of the immediate situation rather than always trying to make your job conform to your preset expectations.

Learning to live with uncertainty will help quell your fears of the future. Expending large amounts of energy catastrophizing about the future depletes the energy left to invest in your work. Instead of worrying about all the things that might go wrong, put your energies into creating the kind of future that you want. To quote Price Pritchett, "The best insurance policy for tomorrow is to make the most productive use of today."

Chapter Summary

Workplace stress is increasing dramatically due to the acceleration in the rate of change worldwide. This ever-increasing speed of change is caused by population growth, the information explosion, and technological advances. Business and workers must constantly shift and adapt to stay competitive, and you must continually upgrade your skills and knowledge to remain competent. Workplace stress is also caused by maintaining faulty assumptions about what could and should happen on your job. Many of these assumptions revolve around unrealistic expectations about change. Fighting change is almost always a losing battle. Learn to pace yourself effectively at work to lower your stress level. Take a few moments to stretch at work to release pent-up muscular tension.

Chapter Questions

1. State whether each assumption is true or false.

_____ Your boss should be responsible for lowering your stress level.

_____ It is always possible to resist change.

_____ If you are not succeeding at work, just try harder.

_____ You won't always benefit from a low-stress work environment.

_____ If you try hard enough, you should be able to control everything.

_____ Sometimes it is actually safer to take a risk.

_____ Lowering your commitment to your job when the stress gets too high is essential to your well-being.

_____ Management that is truly caring will always strive to make you, the employee, comfortable.

_____ Learning to live with uncertainty will help you deal with your fears of the future.

_____ Victims are powerful because they get rescued and taken care of by others.

2. What three factors are causing workplace stress to multiply?

3. What factors contribute to job burnout?

Time Management

What You Will Learn in this Chapter

- To explain how procrastination increases your stress level.

- To follow the six steps for combating procrastination.

- To lower your stress level through effective management of time.

- To describe Covey's system for managing your time, including the role of importance and urgency.

- To use Covey's system to lower stress and heighten your effectiveness.

- To write your own personal mission statement for facilitating short- and long-term decision making and coping with stress.

Maintaining faulty assumptions is not the only factor creating stress on the job. Sometimes we create stress for ourselves as a result of procrastination. If you are one of the rare individuals who is very self-disciplined and motivated, tackling all duties in a timely fashion no matter how hard, aversive, or overwhelming, then we applaud you. But if you are like the rest of us, you may at times add to your stress by putting things off. And for some people procrastination is a chronic problem that feeds on itself.

Another common source of on-the-job stress is deadlines and time pressures. Continual fight-or-flight activation can be triggered by constant time demands. Study the following tips, suggestions, and guidelines for handling these contributing factors.

Procrastination

"Never do today what you can put off until tomorrow." That is the motto of the procrastinator. We all procrastinate to one degree or another. It becomes a major problem in your work life when important tasks or responsibilities are left undone or are completed in a slipshod manner because inadequate time was left to complete the task properly. Procrastination lowers anxiety in the short run due to the relief we feel from task avoidance. But it greatly increases our stress in the long run as tasks pile up or time runs short.

The main and most direct cause for procrastination is low frustration tolerance (Ellis & Knaus, 1977). You need to accept the fact that to receive future rewards, you often need to undertake present discomfort. Low frustration tolerance is based on the irrational notion that present pain or discomfort is "too hard to bear." This belief that you cannot stand present pain for future gain invites and practically commands you to continue your delay tactics. This can be a very debilitating cycle.

Again, everything hinges upon what you tell yourself about the onerous task. To overcome a tendency to procrastinate, you need to begin by learning to identify your irrational thoughts (Ellis & Knaus, 1977) and then replacing them with thoughts that promote productivity. If your frustration tolerance is adequate, you will take the temporary discomfort in stride and conclude that, indeed, the task may be aversive, boring, or anxiety-provoking, but so what? Where was it decreed that you have to like everything you do? After all, the task will not go on forever, particularly if you start now. If you tell yourself that it may be unpleasant, but so are many things that you easily survive, it will help you to persevere. If you remind yourself that there actually may be aspects of the task that will even intrigue you or benefit you, it can give you the wherewithal to get started.

For example, if you are avoiding beginning or completing a certain project at work or school, it is likely that you are thinking (on either a conscious or unconscious level) one or more of the following irrational and ridiculous thoughts: (1) that you will be totally miserable the whole time you are working on this task; (2) that you cannot possibly bear the torture of this duty; (3) that it is entirely unfair and sadistic for your boss or your teacher to foist such a terrible assignment upon you; (4) that you cannot possibly enjoy any part of this project; (5) that you are destined to fail horribly at this task; or (6) that if you rebel you will get a hero's acclaim down the road. In place of these self-sabotaging statements, you can choose to substitute the following: (1) that you can choose not to be miserable; (2) that you certainly won't die from working on this task, so of course you *can* stand it (no doubt you have endured much worse); (3) your boss's goal is not to ruin your life but to make the business succeed, and your teacher's goal is to ensure that you learn; (4) perhaps some aspect of the work will prove reasonably interesting; (5) there is no guarantee you will fail, and, in the event that you do, it is not the end of the world if you don't succeed in everything; and (6) the one you hurt the most by delaying is yourself.

Many people believe that if they wait until they *feel* more like doing the avoided task, then they will be able to finally get moving. But actually, often the reverse is more true and certainly more efficient. That is, if you wait around for your feelings to change, you could wait forever. But if you change your behavior, your feelings will change to match your new actions. This follows the tenet that "attitude change follows behavior change." When you behave differently you will tend to feel different, as emotions tend to shift to fall in line with your actions. Therefore, acting in a timely, efficient, and productive manner (even when you don't feel like it) actually creates the motivation to continue working and, in some cases, may even lead to increased task enjoyment. At the very least, you can enjoy the fact that you have completed the task and it no longer hangs over you.

Six Steps to Overcoming Procrastination

1. Use the Bits-and-Pieces Approach
One of the best antidotes to procrastination is to break tasks or projects down into doable chunks. Are you prone to letting tasks pile up until you feel overwhelmed and/or indecisive as to where to begin or how to prioritize the tasks? You might feel as though you need to accomplish an entire task once you get started, and this can become an overwhelming prospect. Giving yourself permission to do just one small piece can get you started and provide the necessary momentum for completion of the whole project in time. By using the bits-and-pieces approach, you can whittle down unfinished tasks and finish parts of projects (and eventually the whole project). Once you start a small part of a task and get into the swing of it, you might discover that you feel like finishing the whole thing, especially if it goes faster or smoother than you had anticipated. Or you can use your energy to switch over to another avoided task, which may prove to be easier once you have built up positive momentum from the former, especially if the tasks are related.

2. Get Organized
Lack of organization contributes to procrastination; when you approach your work in a disorganized fashion, tasks feel more overwhelming and generally take longer to accomplish. Experiment with the following tips for improving your organization.

- *Things-to-do lists.* Making a list of things to do on a daily or weekly basis is an excellent way of getting yourself organized and helping to remember small items or tasks that are easily forgotten unless you take the time to do a daily inventory. Post your list in a prominent place where you will be likely to see it often, or keep it in your appointment book if you refer to it regularly. Scratching items off your list once they are finished becomes quite rewarding, leading to a sense of relief and accomplishment each time an item is crossed off.

- *Create a realistic schedule.* Things-to-do lists are very useful, but they have their limits. In particular, avoid getting caught in the trap of spending all your time accomplishing unimportant items and scratching those off your list, while ignoring important, more difficult and time-consuming tasks. Without some sort of schedule, you can create stress by wasting time, working inefficiently, and missing opportunities because you didn't plan ahead. But over-scheduling yourself is stressful as well. There is an art to creating a workable daily, weekly, and monthly schedule. Start by compiling a list of all you want and need to accomplish over a certain time period, say a month. Begin your daily schedule by arranging time for any appointments or meetings scheduled for that day. Then block out chunks of at least an hour for high-priority projects that require sustained work over time. The earlier in the day you can get to these, the better you will feel. Next, build in time for medium-priority items. Then complete your schedule with routine, quick, or easy tasks that need to be completed that day.

- Make your schedule flexible. Build in time for interruptions, unexpected events, problem solving, and travel time, as well as for breaks and relaxation. If you can't finish everything (and this may occur often), postpone the lowest-priority items. Following a schedule will not guarantee that you always get everything done that day, but if you have made progress on your high-priority goals you will feel more in control. That feeling of control will lower your level of stress. Engaging in this type of planning may seem time-consuming at first, but it will actually increase your time in the long run. (We provide more tips on scheduling later in this chapter, in the section on time management.)

- *Do it when you think of it.* Often just the sheer volume of tasks makes you want to delay. By doing the task immediately, if possible, you can avoid the inefficiency involved in relocating the necessary materials, which saves time and effort. You also prevent yourself from forgetting to handle it.

- *Modify your work environment.* Your work environment can be conducive to getting down to business, or it can promote procrastination, depending on how you arrange your workspace. Remove as many distractions as possible from your work sphere. Take an hour to clean up your desk or workspace. Throw out all unnecessary papers or paraphernalia.

- *Block off escape routes.* Unplug the telephone, close your door, and turn off the TV. Arrange your work station so you have all the materials you need to get started. That way you avoid getting up, and possibly getting distracted, to get various items.

3. Use the Five-Minute Method

This technique can start a wave of positive momentum. Pick that task or project that you have been delaying starting and then agree to start and work on it for just five minutes. At the end of the five minutes, you can stop or you can ask yourself whether you are willing to invest another five minutes. Do this as a nondemand procedure and follow your sincere inclinations. You do not have to work beyond the first interval, but if you are like most people, once you have gotten past the first five minutes (getting started is often the hardest part), you will probably find that you can easily continue. So you work for another five minutes, and perhaps another, and before long you are working steadily. Many people find that once they get started, the task is far less onerous or aversive than they anticipated. Once a significant amount has been done, the drive for completion kicks in as you desire to get the task finished and behind you. Likewise, when you begin or complete one task it is often easier to switch over to other long-postponed activities (particularly if related to the first task), due to the buildup of positive momentum.

4. Don't Wait for Inspiration

Thomas Edison said, "Genius is 1 percent inspiration and 99 percent perspiration." People who procrastinate when faced with a creative endeavor at work or school often delay in order to wait for that moment of "inspiration" to overtake them before they begin. Instead of putting off your project, use probability theory to help you begin. When you begin a project, with or without any particular inspiration, you stand a good chance of perhaps stumbling into a streak of spontaneous brilliance and producing extremely good work. At the very least, you greatly increase your chances of getting some very good ideas for that task or for future projects. The more you produce, the greater the probability that some of it will be very good.

But what if your work or creation fails to live up to your standards? It is perfectly okay if some of what you turn out is not very good. Do you really think that every canvas turned out by Picasso was ready to hang in the Louvre? And do you honestly believe that Mozart never wrote a sour note, or that your favorite author doesn't have a wastebasket filled with crumpled, rejected pages? As consumers of artwork or books, we see only the finished products, which usually have been refined countless times. Successful artists and writers thrive by giving themselves permission to make mistakes and produce a certain amount of garbage in the process of doing good work.

Playing the probabilities also gives you the opportunity to hone your skills through experience and practice. If your work requires creative projects or writing, or if you are an artist, musician, or writer who is not currently inspired, forcing yourself to work at the very least will improve your level of expertise. So when inspiration does come, you will be far better prepared to perform.

5. Reward Yourself

All human behavior is motivated by reward or by the expectation of reward in the future. A reward is anything that feels good, be it money, praise, awards, a new car, a vacation, a back rub, and so on. Humans can often sustain unrewarded behaviors for long periods of time as long as there is some hope for reward down the line. Procrastination persists because it is reinforced by the immediate reward of relief from task avoidance. Tasks that you dread and delay may often have rewards associated with them, but typically they are in the future or you need to wade through discomfort first to get those rewards. Even though procrastination carries with it many long-term punishments (including increasing your stress level), the short-term rewards motivate you to keep delaying. To counterbalance the rewarding aspects of procrastination, it is important to find ways to make the dreaded task also rewarding in the short run. Peruse the following suggestions for ways to reinforce yourself and see which ones appeal to you. Try them out the next time you put something off.

- **The Premack principle.** One way to build in rewards for getting it done is to use the *Premack Principle*, postulated by David Premack, which states that if two behaviors differ in their likelihood of occurrence (that is, you are more likely to do one rather than the other), the less likely behavior can be reinforced by using the more likely behavior as a reward (Premack, 1965). In everyday terms, this strategy capitalizes on the fact that any activity you find enjoyable can be used as a reward or incentive for working on a task you tend to put off. You give yourself permission to engage in rewarding activities contingent upon doing tasks you tend to put off (for example, schedule a massage for yourself after finally completing that report or watch that movie after finishing your reading).

- **The profit-penalty system.** Rewarding yourself works when you make the rewards meaningful and present them only upon completion of the desired task (or chunk, if you are using the bits-and-pieces approach). In general, punishment is a very ineffective way of inspiring change. You have already been exposed to the negative consequences of procrastination many times, and if that worked you wouldn't continue to delay! Punishment as a way of modifying behavior can be useful, however, when it is done strategically and in combination with a reward system.

- In the *profit-penalty system*, you use both a reward and penalty in tandem. You start by breaking a project into doable chunks and set up a reward contingent upon successful completion of the piece. At the same time you can also penalize yourself for noncompletion. In the **double profit-penalty system,** you create a no-lose situation for yourself. You make a contract with yourself where noncompletion of one specified task is linked with the need to complete another avoided task. With such a plan you cannot lose, for whenever you delay, you must compensate by being productive in another area. Therefore, you "win if you do and win if you don't."

6. View Mistakes as Feedback

Perhaps you procrastinate for fear of making a mistake or doing something poorly. However, it is quite irrational to think that leaving yourself even less time to complete something will make you less likely to make mistakes. And where is it written that it is catastrophic or even necessarily bad to make a mistake? Mistakes are feedback, nothing more and nothing less. Both forms of feedback, correct and incorrect, are equally vital for the learning process. Without both, we learn more slowly.

Research reveals a strong link between procrastination and perfectionism (Flett et al., 1992). Perfectionism goes hand in hand with fear of failure. If you maintain a perfectionistic attitude, you will be more prone to stall until you can "do it right," or you avoid the task because you fear that you can never do it right. So what if you do it and part of it is wrong? Is the world going to come to an end? If you delay, that is the equivalent of doing it wrong anyhow. At least if you go ahead and complete it, you stand a chance of getting part or all of it right. We have no quarrel with striving for excellence, but that is not the same as holding out for perfection.

You cannot achieve excellence without making mistakes along the way or risking making other errors. In short, making mistakes is an essential part of improving yourself. What is necessary is to adopt a healthy attitude about being in error. It means learning to laugh at yourself and not taking yourself so seriously all the time. Often, what endears you to others are memories of those times when you made a funny mistake. We recognize that not all mistakes are funny, but the vast majority of errors are harmless and ultimately can be humorous or neutral if viewed from the proper perspective—that is, reframed appropriately.

Time Management

Most people find time pressures and deadlines at work very stressful. While you cannot always control the demands of your work environment, how you arrange your use of time can help promote efficiency and prevent problems, therefore lessening your time pressures and concomitantly lowering your stress level. While an exhaustive summary of time-management methods is beyond the scope of this book, we can offer you useful guidelines for managing your time effectively. Time-management strategies have evolved along with the demands of the workplace. The first generation consisted of notes and checklists. The second wave involved appointment books, recognizing the need for future planning and allowing for better scheduling methods. The third level included the important ideas of prioritization, goal setting, and planning. But some people chafed at systems that scheduled them, feeling they were restricted and lacked flexibility. Therefore, an emerging fourth generation emphasizes not the managing of time per se, but rather managing yourself in time more effectively.

Thus, there are many methods for time management that all have some useful aspects. But we would like to introduce to you one fourth-generation system, namely that put forth by Stephen Covey in his landmark books, *The Seven Habits of Highly Effective People* (1989) and *First Things First* (1994). Covey takes a somewhat different approach to time management than traditional systems. He emphasizes organizing your schedule around priorities rather than prioritizing your schedule. He recommends that you divide your work tasks and projects into four categories or *quadrants*, as illustrated in Figure 12.1.

Importance and Urgency

The two aspects that define any activity are its urgency and its importance. Things that are urgent, such as a ringing phone, demand to be attended to immediately, or at least very soon. Urgent matters are often popular or important to others, but they may or may not be important for you. Covey further recommends that you define

Figure 12.1 Stephen Covey's Time-Management Matrix

Quadrant I: Urgent and Important	Quadrant II: Not Urgent, but Important
Crises Pressing problems Projects with deadlines	Proactive activities Long-range planning Networking Relationship building Prevention and Maintenance
Quadrant III: Urgent, but Not Important	Quadrant IV: Neither Urgent nor Important
Interruptions Some phone calls Some meetings Some reports Some mail	Busywork, trivia Some phone calls Some mail Pleasant activities

Source: Covey, Stephen R. (1989). *The Seven Habits of Highly Effective People.* New York: Simon & Schuster.

importance based on how closely an activity is tied to your goals and desired results, as well as to your overall mission in life. Urgent activities call for a quick reaction. Tasks that are important, but not urgent, typically require more initiative and pro-activity. If you have not defined your goals and therefore are unclear as to what is important to you, it is very easy to be swallowed up by urgency.

Quadrant I tasks, both urgent and important, typically take the form of crises or problems that require immediate attention. Although we all have some Quadrant I activities in our work lives, many people are consumed with Quadrant I work and are beset with problems all day long. While the demands of any quadrant could potentially be stressful, clearly Quadrant I activities contain the greatest potential for raising your stress level. The more time you spend in Quadrant I, the more it appears to expand, because you are not taking the time to be proactive and prevent future problems. When you are overly immersed in Quadrant I work, you tend to escape to the more mindless, easy Quadrant IV activities. While that might provide a temporary breather, it does little to set the stage for a meaningful decrease in Quadrant I and its inherent stress.

When people spend a lot of time in Quadrant III activities, urgent but not important, it is usually because they assume that these tasks are really important and lie in Quadrant I. This is based on being influenced by the expectations of others, because the matter is urgent or important for them. That does not necessarily mean that it need be urgent or important for you unless it fits with your workplace goals.

Quadrant IV activities, often termed busywork, are often pleasant and offer an opportunity to take a break. Be wary of spending the majority of your time in Quadrant III or Quadrant IV, for that leads to irresponsibility. Successful, effective people minimize time spent in Quadrant III or Quadrant IV, saving that work for mini-breaks (see the section on pacing in Chapter 11) because, urgent or not, those tasks not important.

The key to effective time management is to maximize time spent on Quadrant II activities, which are important but not urgent. This involves work that is proactive and preventive, such as long-term planning, networking and building business relationships, establishing a business plan and personal mission statement, preventive maintenance and preparation (along with maintaining your health and personal relationships), and so on. These are all things we want to do, and know we should do, but tend to put off because they are not deadline-driven. But only by engaging in Quadrant II activities can you shrink the stressful Quadrant I, by preventing crises and problems in the first place, thereby lowering your stress level.

Initially, the only way to spend more time on Quadrant II activities is to subtract time from Quadrants III and IV. Obviously you cannot ignore Quadrant I, but it will begin to diminish once you increase your Quadrant II proactivity. In order to lessen time spent in Quadrants III and IV, you have to learn to say no to some activities (even if they are important or urgent to others) or to delegate.

A ringing phone is a typical example of a Quadrant III situation. It urgently demands that you interrupt your work to answer and respond, but often the calls are only important to the caller. The perfect example of this is telephone solicitation. We have lost count of how many times our work has been interrupted by someone trying to sell us something they think we desperately need, be it a new long-distance phone service, a new credit card, computer supplies, and so on. These salespeople are fast-talking and know every trick in the book to keep us on the phone. We are amazed by how many of our colleagues patiently sit through sales pitches and then list all the reasons why they are not interested. Meanwhile, five to ten minutes was wasted. Our method for handling such calls is short and sweet. We nicely and diplomatically state, "Sorry, we don't accept telephone solicitation," and then hang up immediately without waiting for a response. Over the years we have probably saved weeks of valuable time by ducking such time wasters.

Your Personal Mission Statement

Stephen Covey strongly recommends that each person develop his or her own personal mission statement or philosophy that can help determine priorities, and, therefore, assist managing time more effectively. This mission statement needs to focus on the kind of person you want to be (your character) and what you want to contribute or accomplish, along with the values and principles upon which you desire to base and guide your life. This philosophy is akin to your own personal constitution and can function as the basis for making major life decisions as well as everyday decisions. It can empower you with a guiding set of values in the midst of change or stress. Your mission statement needs to reflect your uniqueness as a person.

Covey reminds us that one important key to coping with change (and therefore stress) is to have a *changeless core*, or sense of who you are, what you are about, and what you value. This enables you to flow more easily with change and to determine what directions you should take and what is important. Having a sense of mission creates a linchpin of your own proactivity. It gives you the vision and values from which to guide your life and helps you to set your short- and long-term goals. As previously indicated, developing your mission statement is definitely a Quadrant II activity, but perhaps one of the most important ones you can ever do.

Additional Tips for Managing Your Time

1. Use the 80/20 rule. Eighty percent of the benefit comes from doing 20 percent of the work. Figure out the most important and beneficial 20 percent and make that your priority to tackle first. Completing the important 20 percent first often expedites or simplifies completion of the remaining 80 percent of the work.

2. Focus on one task at a time. People with problems managing their time often flit from one project to another or try to do several things simultaneously. The result is often delays, mistakes, and disorganization, which wastes rather than saves time. Uninterrupted concentration on a task, when possible, produces a better product in less time. Arrange your work space to minimize distractions.

3. Don't try to do things perfectly; just focus on doing them well. Striving for perfection leads to fear of failure, procrastination, and having to do things at the last minute, all of which adds up to a potent recipe for stress.

4. Pay attention to your body rhythms. Schedule difficult, challenging tasks for the times you are most alert and energetic. If you are a morning person, do the difficult, energy-consuming tasks early in the day. If you are a night person, save the challenging projects for the evening. Save the easy, routine tasks for times when your energy is at low ebb (midafternoon for many people).

5. Use small chunks of time to complete quick, routine tasks. While waiting at the doctor's office, use that fifteen or twenty minutes to pay bills, read your mail, or balance your checkbook. If waiting in line, pull out a sheet of paper and make necessary lists (Scott, 1980).

6. Learn to say no to low-priority items or requests, which only distract you from completing the work that is really important. Delegate if possible.

7. Take short breaks to refresh and revitalize, particularly if you notice your concentration faltering. Sometimes engaging in a *power nap*, shutting your eyes for five to ten minutes and reclining in your chair, is all you need to perk up. Or take a five-minute walk around your workplace and step outside for some fresh air.

8. All work and no play is a sure way to maximize stress. Make time for relaxing activities and fun. Don't be afraid to occasionally take a day off to recharge and revitalize yourself. We refer to this as a "mental health day," taking a day off so as to prevent yourself from getting sick. Your energy for your work will increase as a result and you will therefore make much better use of time allotted for work.

9. Deal with each piece of paper only once if possible. Each time you handle a piece of paper, do something to move it along. When in doubt, throw it out! Don't write when a phone call (typically quicker and cheaper) will do.

Chapter Summary

Procrastination and poor time-management skills can contribute to your level of workplace stress. Procrastination is fueled by low frustration tolerance and irrational thoughts. You can overcome procrastination by recognizing and replacing irrational beliefs, remembering that attitude change follows behavior change, and breaking tasks into doable chunks. Time management can be enhanced by following Covey's system of scheduling your priorities rather than prioritizing your schedule. Divide work tasks based on urgency and importance. Increase the time you spend in proactive undertakings, thereby preventing and minimizing problems and crises, which will help lower your stress level. To facilitate your ability to determine what is really important and therefore worthy of high priority, spend time thinking about and composing your personal mission statement to help guide your decisions regarding how to best use your time. Using your time well will go a long way toward lowering your stress level.

Chapter Questions

1. What kinds of irrational beliefs contribute to procrastination?
2. Describe the five-minute method for combating procrastination.
3. Which of the six techniques described for overcoming procrastination would you use if you found yourself delaying unnecessarily on something?
4. According to Stephen Covey, what kinds of tasks (in terms of their relative importance and urgency) help us to be proactive?
5. Define the 80/20 rule.

Assertiveness

What You Will Learn in this Chapter

- To define what constitutes assertiveness.

- To distinguish between passivity, aggressiveness, and passive-aggressiveness.

- To explain the consequences of passivity and aggression.

- To list the benefits you can accrue by being assertive in your personal and occupational spheres.

- To describe how assertiveness relates to stress reduction.

- To explain why many people fail to behave assertively.

- To practice using the four-step framework for assertiveness at work or in your personal life.

- To practice refining this framework by using empathic assertion or escalating assertion.

- To elucidate the role of congruent nonverbal behavior in bolstering the assertive response.

- To explain how the use of timing and tact facilitate being persuasive.

For many people the main source of workplace stress is not the work or workload itself, but strained relationships with co-workers, supervisors, subordinates, bosses, or customers. The hardest tasks we face are often about giving or receiving negative feedback. Learning to be appropriately assertive goes a long way toward easing such situations and significantly decreasing your stress level.

Consider the following scenarios, which may resemble situations that you or someone you know has had to face. These scenes were derived from stressful work situations presented by participants in our Stress Mastery workshops.

- Scenario 1: You are a school administrator in charge of supervising a number of office personnel who have direct contact with students. You notice that one of your subordinates has been rather sarcastic, impatient, and inconsiderate toward several students. You are hesitant to fire her, knowing she needs the job desperately, so you decide to give her feedback and hope she will improve. You meet with her, give her feedback, and assume her attitude will improve. Several days later you observe her engaging in the same old behaviors. Meanwhile the parent of a student calls you to complain that her son was mistreated by that office worker.

- Scenario 2: You have developed a reputation at your company for being an excellent worker. As a result of your competence your boss keeps adding to your responsibilities. Although your workload has increased significantly, your boss has not offered you a raise. In order to keep up with your rising workload you have to work overtime several times a week. Since you are a salaried employee, you do not get paid for overtime. You are growing increasingly resentful and stressed out. You worry constantly about keeping up with your work, but you are afraid to turn down new assignments and disappoint your boss.

- Scenario 3: You work in the clerical division of a large company. One co-worker and friend is having a lot of personal problems, and as a result she is often absent from work or too distressed to be productive when at work. At first you offer to help her with some of her work as a way of easing her load. Also, you fear she will be fired if she continues on this path. You expect that she will pull it together and function normally again soon, so you pitch in and help in the interim. Unfortunately, she does not pull her act together and she begins to expect and regularly ask you to do her work or help her. You are falling increasingly behind in your own work, and you are starting to resent her. The friendship is suffering.

- Scenario 4: You are a legal secretary working for a high-powered attorney in a large law firm. Your boss, Mr. Reynolds, has a habit of strolling into work late in the morning and wasting time until the afternoon, when he goes into high gear and is quite productive. But because of his chronic lateness in getting down to work, paperwork that needs to be finished and filed that day is often not completed at the end of the workday at 5:00 P.M. You routinely work overtime for up to one full hour on almost a daily basis in order to complete paperwork that must be filed that day. Although it is inconvenient for you to stay late, the extra money you earn from overtime pay comes in handy and makes it worth your while. One day the firm's top managers announce that due to dwindling profits, all overtime work and pay will be indefinitely suspended. Your boss is not in agreement with this new policy, but has no power to change the mandate. You are very worried that you will be put in the uncomfortable position of having to work overtime for free in order to complete necessary tasks.

- Scenario 5: You are a woman who has just been promoted to a management position in a large corporation that has only recently allowed women to rise in the ranks. You are confident in your knowledge base and managerial skills; in fact, you feel that your expertise actually exceeds that of many of your male superiors, who appear somewhat threatened by you. You notice that at meetings your comments often seem to be disregarded and dismissed with some teasing remarks. Although you are not being sexually harassed as such, it is obvious to you that if you were male your contributions would be taken more seriously. You are then put in charge of a big project along with another male manager, who is in a position parallel to yours. You discover that your colleague is consistently undermining your decisions and taking over aspects of the project that you had thought were assigned to you.

Assertiveness Defined

The scenarios described represent the kinds of stressful situations that we all confront each workday. What these situations have in common is that they call for an assertive response. Whether you are a boss, manager, new employee on the bottom rung of the ladder, factory worker, salesclerk, restaurant server, CEO, university professor, administrator, government worker, police officer, doctor, or beautician, situations will arise where you will need to assert yourself in order to deal with the situation and lower your stress level. Assertion involves standing up for your personal rights and expressing ideas, needs, feelings, and beliefs in direct, honest, and appropriate ways without violating the rights of other people (Lange & Jakubowski, 1976). When you are assertive you can accept compliments and take criticisms. You can negotiate for what you need, disagree with another, and ask for clarification when you don't understand. You can set limits when necessary, and you are able to say no (Fensterheim & Baer, 1975).

The basic message you are communicating when you are assertive is: This is what I think. This is what I feel. This is how I view the situation. This message expresses who you are and is said without dominating, humiliating, or degrading the other person. Assertion involves respect for others, but not deference. Deference is acting in a subservient manner, as though other people are right or better simply because they are older, more powerful, more experienced, more knowledgeable, or in an authority position over you. When you express yourself in ways that are self-effacing, appeasing, or overly apologetic you are showing deference. Two types of respect are intimately involved in assertion: (1) respect for yourself—that is, expressing your needs and defending your rights, and (2) respect for the rights and needs of the other person.

Assertive self-expression is the hallmark of effective communication skills. It is a prerequisite for satisfying interpersonal relationships. Being assertive will not give you an ironclad guarantee of having things go your way, but you maximize your chances of success while minimizing the chance of alienating others. Research suggests that assertive individuals are more resistant to the deleterious effects of stress (Honzak, Veselkova, & Poslusny, 1989). Assertiveness leads to higher self-esteem, less stress, and more satisfying interpersonal relationships (Davis, Eshelman, & McKay, 1988).

Differentiating Assertiveness from Passivity and Aggression

Nonassertion, also called *passivity*, involves violating your own rights by failing to express honest feelings, needs, thoughts, and beliefs and consequently permitting others to potentially take advantage of you. It also involves expressing your thoughts and feelings in such an apologetic, diffident, or self-effacing manner that others can easily disregard you and your message. Nonassertion shows a lack of respect for your own needs. It can also imply a subtle lack of respect for the other person's ability to handle disappointments, to shoulder some responsibility, to handle his or her own problems, and so on. The goal of passivity is to appease others and to avoid conflict at any cost. And often there is a high price to pay for routinely avoiding conflict.

Aggression involves directly standing up for your personal rights and expressing thoughts, feelings, needs, and beliefs in ways that can be dishonest, are usually inappropriate or intimidating, and always violate the rights of other people. The usual goal of aggression is domination and winning by intimidation, forcing the other person to lose—or at the very least, to lose face. Winning is assured by humiliating, degrading, belittling, or overpowering others so they become weaker and less able to express and defend their needs and rights. You need not get physical in order to be aggressive.

We can think of assertiveness, passivity, and aggression as being on a continuum, with assertiveness representing the effective middle ground between aggression and nonassertion. It represents a balance of respecting the rights of others while also respecting your own rights. It represents the effective middle ground of diplomacy between the deference and self-effacement characteristic of passivity, and the intimidation and bullying characteristic of aggressiveness. Put simply, when you are assertive you can set up a win/win situation. When passive, you create a lose/win scenario and, obviously, when you are aggressive you produce a win/lose situation.

There is another ineffective option to assertiveness: *passive-aggression*, which may sound like a contradiction in terms, but represents a form of behavior that we have all demonstrated at one time or another. Passive-aggressiveness is an indirect form of aggressiveness where we literally get back at someone, not by what we directly do or say, but by what we fail to do or say. For example, a formerly dedicated employee who feels that his boss is too demanding may eventually adopt an "I don't care" attitude, deliberately working slowly and finding excuses to take time off work. The classic example is giving someone the silent treatment.

Negative Consequences of Nonassertion

Failure to handle situations in an assertive fashion can have very negative consequences for you and for your business and personal relationships. In the short run, a passive stance helps you avoid anxiety-producing conflicts. However, in the long run, if you are frequently passive you will feel a growing loss of self-esteem and an increasing sense of resentment or anger. This increases your stress level, which can lead to anxiety, depression, and psychosomatic difficulties (headaches, ulcers, hypertension, and so on). On the other hand, handling situations in an aggressive manner also works in the short run because you may achieve a temporary emotional release and get your needs met through intimidation. But in the long run, the negative consequences of aggressiveness are obvious. Highly aggressive behavior at work may ultimately cost you promotions or even your job. Bullying your employees (if you are the boss), subordinates, or co-workers leads to poor interpersonal relationships and literally invites passive-aggressive retaliation by your colleagues. For example, a tyrannical boss may find that her subordinates react to her aggressive, authoritarian stance with work slowdowns, deliberate mistakes, property damage, theft, backbiting, and so on. In your personal life, aggression can lead to failed relationships, high blood pressure, fights, and even potentially trouble with the law. People who are frequently aggressive eventually feel deeply misunderstood, unloved, and unlovable because they fail to recognize the impact of their behavior on others and how such alienation is inevitable.

Benefits of Assertion

Being assertive maximizes the likelihood that your needs and the needs of others will be met. It will certainly lower your personal level of stress and help ward off illness. Perhaps the greatest benefit of assertiveness is that it will definitely increase your self-respect and self-confidence, as well as garner respect from others.

Why People Fail to Behave Assertively

There are many reasons why people do not behave assertively, and not all of them will apply to you. Ponder those reasons that are relevant for you and be aware of the misconceptions that often underlie your line of reasoning.

- Fearing loss of approval from others or of getting an angry response.
- Failing to distinguish between assertiveness and aggression—that is, mistaking assertiveness for aggression. This is a particular problem for women in our culture, who are given so many double messages. For example, they are encouraged to be strong and outspoken and then vilified for being bitchy or masculine (Phelps & Austin, 1987).
- Mistaking nonassertion for politeness or consideration. How can you learn to differentiate nonassertion from graciousness or politeness? A good rule of thumb is to listen to your body. Certain body signals will cue you when your

response changes from politeness to nonassertion. Tension and discomfort will arise that typically are not present when you are being polite. If you are confused as to whether to assert yourself or whether to keep quiet and "be polite," you need to ask yourself the following questions:

Am I likely to bring this up later?

Will my relationship with this person suffer or change if I keep silent?

Is a hidden expectation present?

Will I feel used because I have unexpressed expectations about reciprocity that may go unfulfilled?

- Mistaking passivity for being helpful because agreeing to do things you really don't want to do might help another person. In genuine helping, you eventually make yourself obsolete. In rescuing, you end up in the victim role with feelings of being used or taken advantage of by someone with an expectation that you will always be there to bail him or her out.

- Behaving aggressively as an outgrowth of feelings of powerlessness, when you believe that you will be controlled too easily by others unless you behave aggressively. Here you tend to behave aggressively as an overreaction to past emotional experiences.

- Believing that aggression is justified and that the only way to get through to other people can also fuel aggressive behavior.

- Acting aggressively on feelings of anger or hurt that have built up to a boiling point, leading to an explosion. If the situation had been dealt with assertively in the first place, the aggressive episode could have been prevented.

- Failing to accept your personal rights. It is hard to be assertive if you do not believe you have the right to express your reactions, take care of your needs, and stand up for yourself. Some people not only feel they shouldn't express their needs, but think they should not even have them in the first place (Smith, 1975).

The foundation of improving your assertive skills involves understanding and believing that you have certain rights as an individual and that it is not only okay, but healthy and useful to yourself and others to stand up for your rights (Alberti & Emmons, 1974). Individuals who are appropriately assertive and self-confident have internalized the following tenets.

The Assertive Bill of Rights

1. I have the right as a human being to have needs, and my needs are as important as the needs of others. I have the right to ask (not demand) that other people respond to my needs.

2. I have the right as a human being to have feelings and form opinions. Furthermore, I have the right to express these in ways that respect the feelings and opinions of others.

3. I have the right to expect respect from other people. It is incumbent upon me to also show the same respect for others. Respecting others does not mean that I allow them to take advantage of me or disregard my needs.

4. I have the right to choose whether, in a particular situation, I want to or can reasonably meet other people's needs or expectations.

5. I have the right to say no.

6. If I frequently compromise my needs or sacrifice my rights, I am teaching others to take advantage of me.

7. If I live my life in such a way as to always avoid conflict or the possibility of hurting someone under any circumstances, I will end up hurting myself and others in the long run. It is only through the honest (and timely) expression of needs, feelings, reactions, and thoughts that I can ultimately develop satisfying interpersonal relationships. When I am assertive, everyone will benefit in the long run.

8. If I stand up for myself while simultaneously showing respect for others, I will gain self-respect as well as the respect of others.

9. By being assertive with others and explaining how their behavior affects me, I am giving them the opportunity to change their behavior and respecting their right to know where they stand with me.

10. I do not have the right to demean, intimidate, or manipulate other people into meeting my needs. I do have the right to ask, however, and to attempt to persuade while respecting their right to refuse.

A Useful Framework for Assertive Behavior

Assertiveness training has been found to be a very effective stress-management technique for a wide variety of populations (Brehm, 1998). When learning to become more assertive or polishing your assertive skills, it can be very useful to have a framework or steps to follow in order to know how to construct a potentially effective assertive response. This applies on the job or in your personal life. You should find the following four-step framework helpful, especially at those times when you may be tongue-tied, for you can always fall back on these steps. This framework is not the gospel; you don't always have to follow this format, and this is not the only effective way to proceed. But nonetheless, it is still a very useful summary of how to construct an assertive response.

• **Step One: The Problem Behavior.** The first step is to identify the problem behavior. It is important to keep your language to specific discussions of observable behaviors; do not address personality characteristics. For example, it is much more effective to say, "I am aware that you have not completed several reports that were due," rather than, "Lately you have been so lazy!" The first sentence is merely a description of behavior (or lack of behavior) you observed, whereas the second sentence includes value judgments. If you make value judgments or comment on personality characteristics, particularly in a derogatory fashion, you are just likely to anger the other person, even if your description is totally accurate. You stand a greater chance of resolving the issue and getting the other person to listen to you if you limit your descriptions to observable behavior. If you merely tell someone he or she is "an idiot," it only demeans the person and gives absolutely no information about what he or she did or did not do behaviorally to have merited that insult. Whenever possible, your language should include "I-statements."

- **Step Two: Effects.** Next, identify what effects the problem behavior has on you. There are two types of effects. The first is the difficulties or inconvenience that the problem behavior causes for you or your organization, and the second is how you feel about the problem behavior (angry, confused, hurt, disappointed, and so on). In some cases only difficulties are involved, in others only feelings, and in some instances both. In some cases where both are involved, you may opt only to mention the difficulties and keep the feelings to yourself, such as in situations where you are dealing with strangers or peripheral acquaintances. This can often apply in a business situation as well, where it might be far more appropriate to deal with the problem behavior at hand than to express personal feelings.

- **Step Three: Consequences.** It is very important to note that this step is optional. Here you identify the consequences of the problem behavior if it persists. Basically, you are saying what will happen if the person does not stop the problem behavior. It is not always appropriate or possible to specify consequences, and that is why this step is optional. Sometimes the situation only calls for you to express how you feel about something, and specifying consequences would be overkill. At other times it may be more strategic to wait to specify consequences and determine whether there is a need for escalation later on if the person refuses to change or acknowledge that there is a problem. Never specify a consequence that you are not thoroughly willing or able to follow through with, for then you run the risk that the other person will call your bluff and your credibility and clout will be damaged. If there are no consequences you can readily state and follow up on, then skip this step entirely.

- **Step Four: Alternatives.** The last step involves specifying alternatives to the problem behavior. What is it that you would like the other person to do instead of or in addition to the problem behavior? You may think that this should be obvious and you don't need to spell it out, but many times, just because it is obvious to you what the person ought to be doing, it may not be obvious to him or her. Other people are not mind readers. If you are going to give feedback, give it fully and let others know clearly and diplomatically what your expectations are. Once you have elucidated your expectations and have some inclination from the other person that he or she is receptive, you need to ask for a commitment for change. Do not be afraid to ask people to commit themselves to behaving differently. If they verbally agree to change, they are more likely to follow through.

Fine-Tuning the Assertive Steps

When asserting yourself it is often very helpful to incorporate a style known as *empathic assertion*. Here you convey sensitivity to the other person over and above expressing your feelings or needs. When it is possible to proceed in this fashion, empathic assertion is often highly effective because it helps to establish rapport and minimize defensiveness on the part of the other. It involves making a statement, usually in Step One, that conveys recognition of the other person's situation or feelings followed by another statement where you stand up for your rights and suggest other alternatives. It requires that you put yourself in the shoes of the other person and let him or her know that you have at least some understanding of his or her situation or feelings, but you still have your own needs to take into consideration.

Likewise, there are times when your initial efforts to be assertive are discounted and you will need to escalate. *Escalating assertiveness* describes a situation in which you start with a minimal assertive response and, for whatever reason, it does not work. At this point you do not back down, but rather become increasingly firm and escalate without becoming aggressive. Here you may opt to include Step Three (consequences), because the other person has not responded appropriately to less firm statements on your part. Here you can gradually increase from a request to a demand—or when someone is asking something of you, increase from stating a preference of "no" to an outright refusal. Escalating assertiveness could also mean switching from an empathic assertive approach to a more firm, cut-and-dried approach.

When you assert yourself, others will often use a variety of tactics to derail you before you get your point across. The most common tactic involves the other person interrupting you to tell their side of the story. Do not allow this. Firmly speak up and say, "Excuse me, I'd like to finish what I am saying." If they persist with interruptions, escalate and say, "Please stop interrupting me. I will give you plenty of time to reply, but now I would appreciate it if you would let me finish." Another side-tracking tactic is deflecting. Here a person responds to your assertion by bringing up things from the past, often irrelevant, that you have done to aggravate him or her. The best way to handle this is not to take the bait. Refuse to let the conversation be drawn in another direction, even if the complaint is valid. If it is valid, you should promise to deal with it after your issue is resolved or thoroughly discussed. For example, you could say, "That is not relevant. If you want, we can discuss that after we get through this."

Using the Four-Step Framework

If we return to the scenarios at the beginning of this chapter, we can construct assertive responses using the four-step framework. Study the following examples.

Scenario 1
- *Step One.* "I thought you had made a commitment to being more considerate toward students in our last evaluation meeting. Yet today I noticed that when two students asked for information you said that you had better things to do than be a babysitter. And you need to know that yesterday a parent called and complained that you made very sarcastic comments to her son."

- *Step Two.* "I am very disappointed that you did not take my feedback in our previous meeting more seriously. And I am also very concerned that your attitude toward students is hurting the ability of this office to help our students."

- *Step Three.* "If you do not heed this warning I will be forced to terminate your employment here at Any Town Middle School. This is your final warning."

- *Step Four.* "You need to develop more patience and consideration toward students. You need to be more diplomatic and tactful when dealing with them. And you need to realize that part of your job does require that you meet students' needs. I want to meet with you weekly to discuss how to handle sticky situations so we can prepare you to deal effectively with the student body. Are you willing to make a commitment to change your attitude?"

Scenario 2

- *Step One.* "I have been with this company for four years now and I am very pleased that you are happy with the quality of my work. Several times over the last few months I have, at your request, taken on increasing volumes of work. In order to finish I have to work overtime and/or bring work home, for which I do not get paid because I am salaried. And I have not gotten a salary raise in two years."

- *Step Two.* "Given all the extra work I have taken on, I am easily doing the work of two employees. Although I have been willing to do the extra work out of loyalty to the company, I do not feel I am being adequately compensated for the work I am doing."

- *Step Four.* "I truly feel I deserve at least a 10 percent raise. My taking on extra work, over and above my job description, saves you from hiring someone else full or part time. I deserve to get some of that savings back in terms of increasing my salary. Can I receive a raise at this time?"

Note: If this should fail and the boss refuses then escalate and include Step Three.

- *Step Three (option 1).* "If you cannot see clear to raise my salary at this time, then I have no choice but to refuse to take on any more extra work. My job description does not indicate that I am responsible for those tasks."

- *Step Three (option 2). This option is designed to use your leverage (the fact that you are a highly valued worker) to persuade your boss to give you a raise.* "If you cannot see clear to raise my salary at this time, then I may have to begin searching for a new job. If I am going to be doing work at this level, then I deserve to be paid for my efforts. I know I can make significantly more money at other companies. My preference would be to stay here, but I may have no choice if you cannot raise my salary. Can I count on you for a good reference? By the way, keep in mind that if I have to leave, you may need to hire two people to handle the load that I have worked. So I believe it is in everyone's best interest for you to give me a raise."

Scenario 3

- *Step One. (empathic assertion)* "I know you have been going through a really rough time, and that it has been very hard for you to keep up with your work. You know that I really feel for you and have tried to help in many ways. But the fact is that for the last three months you have relied on me to finish many things for you. Lately you seem to expect that I will stay overtime to finish your work while you leave early to take care of your situation."

- *Step Two.* "Now I am falling behind in my work because I am spending so much time doing your work. And I'm starting to feel as though you are taking advantage of me, as if you just expect I will be there forever to pick up the slack for you. I do not want to feel resentment and have that hurt our friendship."

- *Step Four.* "I can no longer continue to help you with your work at this level. It was one thing to fill in for a few days or even a week or two, but this has gone on for months. I need for you to phase back into your job full time. I know you may not be able to do that overnight. I suggest we have a meeting and work out a schedule where you gradually resume doing all your work, perhaps over a two-week period. I would appreciate it if you could agree to that. I know you can do it, particularly if we do it in steps."

Scenario 4

- *Step One.* "Mr. Reynolds, it is very important that we discuss the new rule about working overtime. *(empathic assertion)* I know that you had nothing to do with the new ruling. I do not blame you in the least. But this is creating a problem for both of us. Your work habits are such that you come to the office late and don't really begin getting down to business until the afternoon. As a result, I have had to stay overtime on almost a daily basis in order to get all the paperwork finished and filed on time."

- *Step Two.* "If I do not stay late, then important papers may not be filed on time. Our clients and your reputation will suffer and I will feel as though I am not doing a good job. I am now concerned that I will be put in the difficult position of having to work overtime for free, which I feel is unfair to me. Working overtime takes away from my time with my children and makes it hard for me to keep up with responsibilities at home. I was willing to do it when I could earn a significant amount of extra money."

- *Step Three.* "I am not willing to work overtime on a regular basis unless I am compensated for my time. I may have to leave without completing important papers."

- *Step Four.* "But I have some ideas about how we can resolve our mutual dilemma. First of all, you could agree to pay me out of your own pocket for overtime work, and then I will be glad to continue as before. If that is not acceptable to you, then we need to work together on time management. You need to come to the office by 9:00 A.M. and use your morning time more productively. If you are able to get the paperwork to me earlier in the day, then I will have no difficulty in completing and filing all necessary papers by 5:00 P.M. I am willing to meet with you early each morning to help you organize your morning time more productively. We have to do something different because clearly we cannot continue functioning the same way. Which of these alternatives would you prefer?" *When asserting yourself with individuals in authority over you, it can be very effective to offer several options and ask them to pick one. That way they retain the illusion of being in control (that is, they get to choose) and will often admire your ingenuity in developing solutions.*

Scenario 5

It is best to approach this from an empathic-assertive perspective. The female manager needs to build collegial relationships and establish rapport with her colleagues, as well as educate them about the ramifications of chauvinistic attitudes. She should begin by asking the other manager to meet privately with her in her office.

- *Step One.* "Mitchell, I thought it was important for us to meet in order to coordinate our activities as co-directors of this project. I am having difficulty working with you on this project, and I wanted to explain why so we could hopefully get past this and develop a good working relationship. *(empathic assertion)* I know that having a woman working in this position is new for this company and perhaps a bit uncomfortable for you. I can understand that. But I do bring knowledge and expertise that this project really needs. There are a number of things you have done that are creating problems for our team and for me. I have frequently observed that you are counteracting directives I have given to other team members. Lastly, although we agreed I would be in charge of purchasing, you have taken steps to purchase equipment without consulting me first."

- *Step Two.* "If we work at cross-purposes to one another, the project will suffer and we will both come out looking bad. It will also take twice as long to finish if I tell our team to do one thing and then you send them out to do something else. Not to mention how that affects our working relationship."

- *Step Three.* "You know full well I could get you in a lot of trouble if I went to the company president and told him about how you were undermining me on the project. If we are unable to forge a more satisfactory working relationship, I will not hesitate to take this step."

- *Step Four.* "But what I would really prefer would be for us to work well as a team. That means we meet regularly and work off the same agenda with the same steps. I expect you to respect my directives and orders, and I will respect yours. We need to create a division of labor and then stay out of each other's way. If you disagree with me, please come to me first and discuss it and I will gladly listen to your feedback, before you negate my decision or orders. This project will certainly fail if we can't learn to work together as a team. Can I have a commitment from you to build a better working relationship with me?"

Nonverbal Aspects of Assertiveness

How you say what you say is just as important as what you say—that is, the body language you display has a profound effect on how your words will be interpreted and on the responses you will get. No matter how well-crafted your assertive response may be or how appropriate your words, if your nonverbal behaviors are not congruent with your verbal communication you can totally sabotage your message and greatly reduce the likelihood of getting the reaction you seek. If your nonverbal behaviors reflect passivity, deference, self-effacement, timidity, or lack of confidence, you will undermine your message and invite others to discount your words. On the other hand, if your words are assertive and appropriate but your demeanor is intimidating or aggressive it will also detract from your message. Other people will respond with fear or resentment rather than accommodation.

Basically, you want to present a demeanor that is consistent with assertiveness. It is neither timid nor aggressive, but rather forthright, confident, and matter-of-fact. One of the most effective ways to present a confident demeanor is to maintain eye contact. When you look directly at someone's eyes while talking to him or her it conveys confidence, self-assurance, and that you mean what you say. A passive stance usually involves minimal eye contact or looking down, which conveys lack of confidence or uncertainty about your position. An aggressive stance often involves staring a person down, which is not what we mean when we suggest making eye contact. Sometimes it is hard to maintain eye contact, particularly if you have trouble being assertive, because it may make you uncomfortable. Despite this, we encourage you to force yourself to do so for several reasons: (1) it will make your assertive responses more effective, and (2) keeping eye contact gets a lot easier once you practice doing it.

Posture is also important when delivering an assertive response. You can maximize your effectiveness if you stand up straight, face the person squarely, and lean forward slightly. This conveys a sense of confidence. Likewise, if you are sitting down it is useful to lean forward slightly. Leaning back conveys fear or lack of confidence. People tend to lean back and look down when they are unsure of themselves or afraid. Obviously, getting too close to someone or getting in his or her face is an aggressive posture that you want to avoid. It is always wise to respect the personal space of other people.

What you do with your arms reveals a lot about your internal state. For example, have you ever seen two people sitting across from each other in a restaurant, both with their arms folded across their body? Even though you might not overhear the content of their conversation you can usually tell, just from their arm postures, that they are either arguing or annoyed with each other. How do you know this? Arms crossed over the body is referred to as a "body armoring" response, an unconscious way to protect or hug yourself when feeling threatened. When threatened, most people immediately adopt this posture unconsciously. Thus, it is very important not to cross your arms over your body or you will convey that you feel intimidated by the encounter. Rather, make a point to leave your arms open. Open arms communicates that you are confident and comfortable and that you mean what you say. Incidentally, when on the receiving end of feedback at work (from a boss, supervisor, or colleague) it is useful to maintain the open arm posture. In this way you will come across as nondefensive and open to feedback, qualities that are respected in the workplace.

Also, allow yourself to gesture freely while asserting yourself. People tend to gesture and use their arms when they are comfortable. When you gesture you communicate comfort and confidence, and people are much more likely to take you seriously. But there is one gesture we recommend that you definitely avoid: pointing at someone. People hate it when you point at them like a scolding parent or an angry schoolteacher. They will tune you out and resist you if you resort to finger pointing.

Perhaps the most important nonverbal aspect of assertiveness is tone of voice. So much is conveyed by the volume, pitch, and rhythm of your voice. Avoid shouting, which is perceived as aggressive. Also avoid being so soft-spoken that you come off as timid. It is best to speak in a firm, consistent voice tone where you pause for emphasis, and also emphasize key words by slowing down your voice tempo and increasing your volume slightly. Do not talk fast or swallow your words when asserting yourself. It may be useful to talk a little slower, particularly if you are a fast talker, and a little louder than usual for emphasis. Table 13.1 summarizes the differences between passive, assertive, and aggressive communication styles.

Asserting Yourself with Aggressive People

One big source of stress, whether at your workplace or in your personal life, is having to deal with aggressive, unreasonable, or nasty individuals. When dealing with such people, it is common to feel as if you have no control and to become angry and aggressive yourself. The following pointers should prove useful for handling encounters with aggressive people.

- *Make ample use of empathic assertion.* Try paraphrasing what you have heard the person say or commenting on the feelings that are being expressed in their demeanor. For example, simple comments such as, "You sound like you are feeling very angry," or, "This is obviously very upsetting for you," can help an angry person feel understood, and in some cases can help defuse his or her anger. It is also helpful to ask questions to get the person to clarify the problem and work toward a solution.

- *Keep your focus.* Aggressive interactions, particularly with people you know well, often get sidetracked from the original issue with laundry lists of everything else that is a problem. Work to bring the focus back to the issue at hand. Use phrases such as, "We've gotten off the subject. You were talking to me about . . . ."

- *Postpone the discussion until cooler heads prevail.* If you and/or the other person are enraged, and it does not look as though either of you will cool off soon, it may be wise to suggest discussing the matter later when both of you have calmed down. If the other person refuses to delay, explain that you need time to think about the issue, and make a definite appointment to discuss it as soon as possible.

- *Try the broken-record technique.* In an ordinary situation calling for an assertive response, the broken-record technique could come off as obnoxious. But when dealing with an aggressive person who refuses to listen to your

Table 13.1   Differentiating Communication Styles

	Passive	Assertive	Aggressive

Verbal Behaviors	Apologetic
	Indirect statements
	Rambling
	Not saying what
	  you really mean
	Giving up easily
		Direct statements
		Honest expression
		  of feelings
		Describing objective
		  behavior
		I-statements
		Straightforward
		Good listener
		Talking slowly
		Emphasize key
		  words
			Accusations, threats
			Insults, put-downs
			Blaming
			You-statements
			Sarcasm
			Failure to listen
			Manipulative comments

Nonverbal Behaviors	Incongruencies Poor eye contact Soft, timid voice Looking down Fidgeting Leaning back Slumped posture	Actions congruent with words Good eye contact Firm, calm voice Assured manner Gesturing Leaning forward Erect posture Open arms Face person squarely	Staring Yelling, shouting Loud, hostile voice tone Arms crossed over body Finger pointing Getting too close Clenched fists Breaking things
You Are	Scared, anxious Helpless Manipulated Ignored Resentful	Confident Effective Respectful Valued Relieved	Angry, full of rage Indignant Misunderstood Controlling Guilty
Others Feel	Frustrated Puzzled Unsure of your needs	Respected Valued	Intimidated Alienated Angry, resentful Humiliated, hurt Defensive

Results	Stress
	Depression
	Low self-esteem
	Helplessness
	Failure to solve
	  problems
	Resentment
	Lost opportunities
	Health problems
		Problem solving
		High self-esteem
		Self-respect
		Respect of others
		Satisfaction
		Good relationships
		Less stress
		Improved health
			Interpersonal stress
			Guilt, remorse
			Low self-esteem
			Loss of self-respect
			Loss of respect from
			  others
			Passive-aggressive
			  responses
			Frustration
			Failure to solve problems
			Broken relationships
			Loneliness
			Hostility from others

assertive response, and who fails to respond to your efforts at escalation, this technique can come in handy to reinforce your request. Basically it involves repeating your request over and over, like a broken record, even if the other person is arguing, or ranting and raving. You just calmly continue to state your request, even during his or her protestations. It often involves being willing to interrupt. All parents have had to rely on this method at times when dealing with resistance or disobedience from children.

Dealing with the Impossible Boss

It is important to note that before asserting yourself in the workplace with your boss, you need to make a rational assessment of any risks involved. If possible, get feedback from colleagues (particularly those who have known your boss for a long time) about whether asserting yourself is too risky. There are those occasional bosses who will not tolerate any attempt at assertiveness from employees, and who misinterpret even diplomatic feedback or requests as insubordination. If you are unlucky enough to work for a boss like this, then the risks of assertion (losing your job or being demoted) may outweigh the potential gains. If the risk is too great and the issue too important to ignore, looking for a new job may be your best alternative. That too represents an assertive way of handling a situation that you realistically have no power to change.

Assertiveness and Persuasion

Often, as part of a large organization or even a small business, you will be required to participate in business or planning meetings. Many people are concerned about how to ensure that their voice will be heard, that their ideas and input will be taken seriously by the group, the boss, supervisors, or subordinates. Getting lost in the shuffle can be stressful and contributes to feelings of loss of control. It is important to learn how to be influential in groups, at work and in your personal life, and how to maximize your impact without being perceived as aggressive or overbearing. Basically this is about being persuasive, which is related to your assertive skills. Two principles can maximize your ability to persuade others when giving your opinion at work, in meetings, on committees, and so on: how to use *timing* and *tact* when expressing honest opinions.

Timing involves several issues. First of all, you have to decide where your priorities lie. Otherwise you run the risk of being assertive just for the sake of being assertive, and talking too much and too long. The result could be that others would view you as being on an ego trip and tune you out. You want to save your assertive efforts for those points that are really important to you. Observations of groups indicate that it is usually more effective to express an opinion after one-third to one-half of the group participants or committee members have already voiced their positions. By that point the members have a good sense of the group's general position and can address themselves to the points being raised, but this timing reduces the chance that group members will have already made up their minds before you speak up.

To be maximally persuasive when expressing an opinion, you need to state your thoughts clearly, concisely, and without self-deprecating remarks. For example, saying, "I just don't understand. Maybe there is something wrong with me but this proposal doesn't feel right to me," implies that you are inadequate, that there is something wrong with you. It is generally more persuasive to express yourself as a capable person. It is more effective to say, "The way I see it, there seems to be a flaw in this proposal that is hard to pin down. Does anyone else sense that too?" Needless to say, the nonverbal behaviors accompanying opinions are extremely important in determining how that opinion will be received.

Tact is also very important when taking a position that is in opposition to the rest of the group or a powerful group member such as your boss or supervisor. Here it is often most effective to use empathic assertion in order to "stroke" or warm up the group to your opinion. This does not mean using flattery or making ingratiating comments, but rather finding something that is genuinely good about the group consensus or another person's point of view. For example, "Susan, your point is really well taken. But despite the obstacles we face, I believe we need to take action rather than do nothing."

In summary, we urge you to practice using the four-step framework the next time you find yourself in a situation that calls for an assertive response, whether this happens on the job or in your personal life. These principles apply to all situations calling for effective assertiveness. Your next opportunity to practice may present itself in your personal life before a work dilemma develops. That is just fine, for it will allow you to fine-tune your skills before you need to use them in a business context. In any event, pay careful attention to how you feel after you assert yourself. Although you might experience some fight-or-flight activation as you initially engage in assertive behavior, the resulting relief and surge in self-confidence you are likely to feel afterward will go a long way toward lowering your level of stress and boosting your self-esteem.

Chapter Summary

Situations that call for an assertive response, at work or at home, can be quite stressful. It will be useful for you to assimilate a framework that you can use to help you develop assertive behavior. Assertiveness represents the effective middle ground between passivity and aggression. It involves expressing yourself in a diplomatic, straightforward fashion while respecting both your own needs and the needs of others. An effective guideline for constructing an assertive response involves using four basic steps: (1) identify the problem behavior; (2) specify the effects (including feelings); (3) specify consequences (optional); and (4) offer alternatives. It is also important for you to adopt and practice assertive nonverbal behaviors so there is congruence between your words and actions. You can become more persuasive, particularly in a work context, by paying careful attention to timing and tact in expressing your opinions. Behaving assertively will maximize your personal effectiveness and increase your self-respect and confidence, all of which help diminish stress.

Chapter Questions

1. How does assertiveness differ from passivity and aggression?
2. What is passive-aggression?
3. What benefits are possible as a result of assertive behavior?
4. Identify the four steps for assertive communication. Why is Step Three optional?
5. Explain empathic assertion.
6. Why is your nonverbal behavior so important when you are delivering an assertive response?
7. What are three important nonverbal aspects of assertiveness?
8. At what point in a meeting should you express your opinion in order to maximize the impact of your input?

Section 6

Conclusion

Chapter 14: The Big Picture
The Master Strategy Revisited

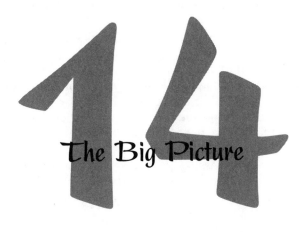

The Big Picture

What You Will Learn in this Chapter

- To employ a cohesive spiritual perspective to help guide you in mastering stress.

- To develop balance in your life to contribute to the process of managing stress.

- To explain the reasons why we must learn to accept uncertainty.

To include a chapter on a spiritual perspective in a book about stress mastery may impress some as painfully obvious, and others as patently unscientific and unnecessary. After all, we, the authors, are scientists and as such are obligated to attempt to cite evidence to substantiate our point of view. Traditionally, spiritual matters have been outside the realm of the scientific and relegated to the corridors of faith and speculation, or, at worst, merely the superstitions of those with an unsophisticated grasp of probability theory, placebo effects, and psychopathology. Yet the vast majority of people on our planet hold to some kind of belief system that affects their day-to-day quality of life. These beliefs, unscientific or not, can be sources of great pain, guilt, feelings of inadequacy, hopelessness, confusion, and fear. But they can also be a source of love, compassion, joy, vitality, and a peace that surpasses understanding. A complete treatise on this subject is well beyond the scope of this text, but to leave it unaddressed is to abandon our charge of presenting you with a wide buffet of ideas regarding the mastery of stress.

But what if you are scientifically minded? Then you are in great company because many of the leading scientific minds of our time and the past century realize that, in fact, the most advanced representations and speculations about the nature of reality do not preclude the possibility of a spiritual reality. Furthermore, they do not suggest a reality that is capricious and unlawful. They simply suggest that our most sophisticated attempts at measurement, in the scientific sense, have led us to the realization that consciousness, the activities of our minds, directly affects the "reality" around us. This is indeed a slippery slope for science, because it implies that the results of experiments may vary solely due to the intentions of the researchers. This is a variable that is seldom controlled, and frankly, in most situations, was thought to be something that did not need to be controlled, outside of placebo studies.

While much of modern Western psychology has been based on extrapolations of work with animals to create models for human experience and treatments for problems, there is no shortage of theories regarding the interface between psychology and spirituality. These various models are groped under the rubric of what has come to be known as *transpersonal psychology*. That is, these models speak to the belief that humans are much more than a bag of skin and bones with a very sophisticated computer animating the machinery. Carl Jung's most important work began after he broke with Freud over Freud's unwillingness to see humans as anything more than advanced, complicated animals driven by sex, aggression, and pleasure seeking. Jung took a larger view of humankind and explored the possibilities of spiritual experience with concepts such as the *collective unconscious*, a storehouse of experience to which all of us are connected.

Currently, theoreticians such as Stanislov Grof, Ken Wilbur, and Jean Houston are actively pursuing ideas such as the reality of the soul, reincarnation, and the whole realm of paranormal phenomena. There is even a division of transpersonal psychology within the American Psychological Association and a journal dealing with transpersonal issues. As we proceed through the remainder of the chapter we will cite references, when appropriate, to current theoretical models that bridge what appears to be the gap between the spiritual and the scientific.

We do not know what anything is. The summarization of
our existence is Mystery, absolute, unqualified confrontation
with what we cannot know.
And no matter how sophisticated we become by experience,
this will always be true of us.

Da Free John

The Larger Conceptual Framework

We began this book with a tale of tasting mangoes—our simple premise being that it is one thing to know about mangoes intellectually and quite another to truly taste a mango, savor the experience, and be fully alive in that moment. After all, when we cut through all of the words and rationalizations about stress and its mastery, what we are after is a sense that we are really alive and living an existence that is meaningful to us. Some might refer to this as a spiritual quest. This chapter, too, is full of words and ideas and questions, but if you do not taste them, chew on them, and mull them over then you will have missed the point. Words, while they are wonderful tools, always reduce experience. They aren't the experiences themselves. Joseph Campbell once related in a lecture that the best things in life cannot be told because they are beyond thought. The next best things are misunderstood, and the next best are those things about which we talk. Consider the words written here as only fingers pointing at the moon. As the ancient expression goes, "Focus too much on the fingers and you miss the heavenly splendor above." If you get caught up in the rightness or wrongness of these words you will fall into the trap of being right that we discussed in Chapter 6, and miss the opportunity to choose happiness. Paraphrasing the words of the mystic Rumi, out there beyond ideas of rightdoing and wrongdoing there is a field. We would like to meet you there. We'll bring the mangoes.

This chapter is about coming to terms with what we believe are fundamental human concerns that we all must confront if we are to truly become masters of stress and ultimately masters of living our lives joyfully and effectively. Something that is fundamentally stressful to humans is the experience of having an inadequate map for a territory that they are exploring. Unfortunately or fortunately, depending on your perspective, life lived well will present you with the unexpected, and you will be scrambling to find directions and maps to guide you. We would like to humbly offer some landmarks that we hope will help you find your way, or at least help you learn to enjoy being lost. Remember, maps are never the territory that they represent. You do not eat the menu when you go to a restaurant. We hope these maps are useful. Some may even be true!

This chapter is also about how you face the inevitable choices and decisions that you must make throughout the course of your life. If you avoid making these choices, ultimately they will be made for you. To minimize stress by enhancing your sense of control, you need to again consider the maps on which you base your decisions. You must determine what is important to you, or your life will not be your own and surely stress will master you.

What follows are simply guideposts, ideas worth considering. When you find yourself struggling to get your bearings, attempting to make some sense out of life and your place in it, remember these things.

Life Is a Mystery

For one of the authors, who was educated largely in Catholic schools, a very frustrating memory of childhood was being told that the answer to his inquiries about God and life was "It's a mystery." Now, he appreciates the essential truth of that assertion. No matter how many books we read, how much knowledge we acquire, how many experiments we conduct, there will always remain that which is elusive, mysterious. Consider building a fire on a moonless night deep in the woods. The larger the fire, the more trees we illuminate. However, the amount of darkness that we become aware of expands in direct relationship to the areas of light. Of this you can be sure: nobody knows what's really going on here. Life is ultimately a mystery that won't ever be solved no matter how big you build your bonfires. But you can develop a relationship with life. That relationship begins by humbly acknowledging the depth of the mystery and then setting out to seek answers anyway.

Action step: Begin building a relationship with the mystery (or God, Goddess, the Fates, or whatever you choose to name it). In the privacy of your own mind, begin to have a conversation with God. Say the things you've always wanted to say. Ask the questions you've always wanted to ask. Now, as in most conversations, the real key to success is *listening*. In this game, listening means quietly focusing your attention so as not to be drawn into the meandering of your own mind. It means to be open to signs and synchronicities (meaningful coincidences). Answers may appear in many forms. For example, you may turn on the radio or TV and the next words you hear may seem to be the perfect reply to your inquiry. Or you may meet a stranger standing in a line who just happens to say something particularly meaningful to you at that moment. Unexpected feelings of contentment or joy may flow through you without warning. It is possible to hear "the still small voice" that is spoken of in metaphysical literature. Meditation is one key skill in quieting the mind.

Some suggested readings in this area would be the following:

The Search for the Beloved by Jean Houston, Ph.D.

Journey of Awakening by Ram Dass

The Meditative Mind by Daniel Goleman

Therefore, Life Is Uncertain

Things change. Get used to it. Be thankful for it. This is the one thing you can be certain of: that things will change. This is true not only in the world of work (as elucidated in Chapter 11), but in all aspects of your life. You may ask yourself, "Will my life ever calm down, become stable and predictable? Will I ever get caught up?" The answer is yes, and then things will change. When things are going badly, things will change. When things are going well, things will change. Peace seems to lie in realizing and accepting this fact. It is about reassuring yourself that *when times are bad, this too shall pass.* Repeating that phrase to yourself is one of the most effective stress reducers. You can be grateful for the changes you know will carry you out of difficult times and be appreciative for the good times, because all good things will ultimately change or come to an end.

Action step: Cultivate an attitude of gratitude. One of the authors did a yearlong internship on a spinal cord injury ward. The most important thing that he drew from that experience was a constant appreciation for having an intact body and being able to walk, something that we regularly take for granted. We recommend that whenever you feel particularly mistreated by life, you should consider the ramifications of losing one of your senses, or the function of some part of your body. Remember the last time you were ill or had a toothache or headache, and appreciate just how wonderful normal is.

Everything Is Connected

One of the most profound illusions of our being is the essential solidity of the objects around us. Science, particularly physics, assures us that in spite of appearances, things are more empty space than solid matter. What appears to be solid is really a vibrating group of particles, most of which have no mass. These particles seem to be influenced by the people who try to study them (this is the Heisenberg Uncertainty Principle), and they retain a relationship with one another over astronomical distances. Furthermore, all beings constantly exchange particles with one another. The science of ecology demonstrates that change in one part of a system necessarily provokes change across the system. Chaos theorists have demonstrated that profound changes can be induced by minor perturbations in a system, as minor as a butterfly flapping its wings. We are ultimately not separate from anything. Therefore, be careful and consider the actions you take on every level, including your thoughts. Whatever you do, you do it to yourself. Do not burn your own house down. This fundamental truth underlies the various versions of the Golden Rule. It makes sense to treat others how you would like to be treated. After all, they are you!

Action step: Reinforce this belief by reading about cutting-edge discoveries in science. Paradigms for understanding the mystical/spiritual view of life are becoming more and more accepted and are supported by experimental data.

Some reading to whet your appetite includes the following:

The Holographic Universe by Michael Talbot

Recovering the Soul by Larry Dossey, M.D.

A New Science of Life by Rupert Sheldrake

Life Is Trouble

To again quote Zorba the Greek, "Life is trouble. Only death is not. To be alive is to undo your belt and go looking for trouble." Now before you seek out a barroom brawl, let us suggest that it is the attitude that is important here. Life very often involves dealing with problems. We have a choice. We can whine about them or we can deal with them. We have tried whining. Sometimes, even very dedicated whining! It doesn't help. We recommend taking the challenge, jumping into the fray and solving problems.

Action step: You really don't have to worry about an action step here. Trouble simply cannot be avoided. Those who have tried to elude it report that it comes looking for you!

Death Is a Great Therapist

"I don't believe in life after death, but I am bringing a change of underwear."

Woody Allen

Whatever comes after this life, the apparent rule is that we will all get the opportunity to find out (that is, everybody dies). This is your shot at *this* lifetime. Scanning the literature and lore on death and dying, you will probably find very few people who on their deathbed said, "I wish I had spent more time at the office." Death has a remarkable ability to clarify our thinking about what is important.

Action step: Suggested readings include the following:

Tuesdays with Morrie by Mitch Albom

Journey to Ixtlan by Carlos Castaneda

When faced with difficult choices, when you find yourself resistant and unwilling to take a risk, try having a conversation with Death. When you find that Death has no guarantees to offer other than, "I'll be back," you may discover a new intensity permeating your actions in any moment. After all, this may be the last time you make love, sip some tea, hug your children, go to a class, and so on. Give yourself fully to those moments because . . .

Here and Now Is Better Than There and Then

The single best antidote for stress is to place yourself fully in the moment. Lost in thoughts of what has happened and what will happen is a fine way to create anxiety and depression. These don't seem to exist in the fully experienced moment.

Action step: Any activity that carries you into a profound awareness of the present moment is a worthy practice. The writings and recordings of Thich Nhat tHanh on mindfulness are very inspirational. Any meditation discipline is a fine approach, but so are pottery, poetry, painting, or playing at anything in which you lose track of time and become fully involved in the moment. As to what will fully involve you, you need to consider the next section.

Are You Getting What You Really Want or What You Are Supposed to Want?

"Thinking at its highest level is asking the right relevant question."

Walter Pauk

"Follow your bliss."

Joseph Campbell

The questions you ask go a long way toward shaping the possible answers you will find. Questions like "What should I do with my life?" contain an inherent appeal to look outside yourself for answers, validation, and reassurances that you are doing the right thing. Yet all wisdom traditions suggest that knowing and trusting yourself, and looking inside of yourself, leads to the best and most fulfilling answers.

The Sufi mystic Rumi once said, "Start a large and foolish project, like Noah. It makes absolutely no difference what people think of you." If you don't take the time to seek answers, if you don't make the effort to really get to know yourself and what really moves your heart, you risk living somebody else's life. Yes, life is difficult, full of choices, seemingly unfair at times. But life is also beautiful, effortless, and involving when you do the things you love, the things that come easily to you. When you find ways to serve others while doing what you love, success is virtually inevitable.

Action step: You need to spend more time with your dreams and fantasies. Take quiet time to remember times that have made you smile, warmed your heart, filled you with compassion, excited you, put you at peace. While you are feeling any of these feelings, follow the flight of your thoughts. Your heart is a compass that will point to your path.

Seek Balance

The universe is a perfectly balanced ballet of opposites: light and dark, cold and heat, pain and pleasure, chaos and order, and so on. The perception of any form necessarily involves the presence of a background. Ultimately, we are physical, mental, and spiritual creations, and our well-being depends on balancing the needs of all these different aspects of ourselves. Often when people question what they want in their search for fulfillment, they neglect to consider this vital issue from a balanced perspective. One way to remedy this situation is for you to consider the multiple roles you fill in your daily life. Besides being an individual you may also be a mother, father, son, daughter, brother, sister, student, teacher, employee, employer, professional, friend, and so on and so forth. Thus, as you explore the path toward which your heart steers you, seek to set goals for all the roles of your life. To totally ignore or shortchange any role is to invite regret to haunt you later.

Action steps: (1) Imagine attending your own funeral. Consider what you would want those in attendance to say about you. Choose to listen in on people from many areas of your life and imagine how you would like to be eulogized. (2) Learn to juggle. This deceptively challenging task teaches you to gracefully and playfully keep many things in the air at once. It requires physical and mental balancing that can give you an intense involvement in the here and now. Whose life hasn't felt like a juggling routine from time to time?

When In Doubt, Do Something Different

Doing the same things you've always done and expecting to get different results is a kind of madness. A more useful madness is to be willing to break out of the rut of established routines that are not working for you. It can be as simple as driving home in a new way, or trying the dish on the menu that you've never tasted. It can be as daring as returning to school after years in the workforce or taking time off to go on a spiritual retreat. The same old thing gets you the same old things. Someone once said, "You can either have what you want in this lifetime or have all the excuses why you didn't get it."

Action step: Try something different. Go on . . . *DO IT!*

Get Comfortable with Confusion

Understanding occurs when we discern a pattern in our experience of the world. Confusion is what happens just before we begin to understand. Getting upset over your confusion simply doesn't help. Better to breathe, relax, pay attention, and wait until understanding comes around. Relaxing facilitates understanding, for it makes it far easier for you to access your intuitive wisdom. What you need to attend to is right in front of you. If you take your attention away from it, you will simply take that much longer to come to an understanding. Also, remember our first premise: *life is a mystery.* Some confusion is part of the tour package. We suggest that breath and attention can transform confusion into wonder in the same way they transform fear into excitement.

Love Yourself While You Discover That Love Is the Answer

> "You might as well like yourself. Just think of all the time you're going to have to spend with you."
>
> Jerry Lewis in *The Nutty Professor*

The wisest teachers throughout history assure us that life at its core is found to be an ocean of love of which we are all a part. We are never really separate from this love, even though the trials and tribulations of life seem at times to be anything but loving. We choose to believe this premise simply because it seems to work for us. To us it means that we are all as good at our center as the best of us. Be patient and loving with yourself along the way. Trust the intuitions of your own heart. Have fun! Learn to forgive yourself, again and again and again.

Chapter Summary

Life is ultimately a mystery; therefore, life is uncertain. Everything is connected, so how you treat others will ultimately be reflected back toward you; "what goes around, comes around." Life is trouble. You can whine about it or deal with it. The shadow of Death has a remarkable ability to clarify what is important. Live each day as if it could be your last. This involves learning to really be in the here and now, which, by the way, is the single best antidote to stress. Learn to discriminate what you really want from what you think you should want. Look within yourself for answers. Seek balance in your life. Remember to honor all of the roles you play in your daily life. When in doubt, do something different. When what you are doing isn't working, don't just try harder, try doing it differently. Learn to get comfortable with confusion; it is the state that immediately precedes understanding. Learn to really love yourself and, above all, to laugh at yourself and at the world. Love and humor are the great healers.

The Master Strategy Revisited

As soon as you are aware that you are under stress, remember to do the following:

1. Breathe.
2. Relax.
3. Assume a peaceful stance (it helps to smile).
4. Be aware; observe your experience.
5. Ask yourself, "Is there another way of looking at this?"
6. *Choose* your response.

To better enable yourself to follow the preceding six Master Strategy steps, practice the following techniques, strategies, and suggestions.

- Breathe from your diaphragm, slowly, deeply, and rhythmically.
- Practice active relaxation techniques; use progressive relaxation, and stretch your muscles daily if possible.
- Adopt the witnessing stance to facilitate your awareness.
- Cultivate the stress hardiness attitudes of control, commitment, and challenge.
- Approach life as a peaceful warrior.
- Use reframing strategies to shift your perceptions and/or work through anger.
- Identify, challenge, and replace irrational beliefs.
- Give yourself permission to be an optimist.
- Practice giving up the need to always be right. Learn to step into the shoes of the other person to assist you in this process.
- Learn to forgive, especially yourself.
- Eat a balanced diet.
- Get plenty of regular exercise.
- Experiment with high-tech relaxation tools.
- Assert yourself. Use the four-step framework to guide you in this process.
- Identify your unrealistic expectations about your workplace and challenge them. Learn to embrace change and make it your friend.

- Follow the six steps to thwart procrastination.
- Schedule your priorities rather than prioritize your schedule. Managing your time will then be a far easier process.
- When what you are doing isn't working, don't just try harder; do something different.
- Love yourself. Have fun, play, and laugh at yourself and the world around you.

Appendix

In 1988 we co-developed MindWorks, International, Inc., a combination stress-management center and private practice of clinical psychology. Our center offers a variety of Stress Mastery Training seminars, as well as a full line of supporting materials to assist you in your practice of stress mastery and relaxation skills.

Brainwave Synchronizers

If you are interested in obtaining a light and sound machine for your personal use, MindWorks carries three models produced by Comptronics Ltd.: (1) the David Paradise; (2) the David Paradise XL; and (3) the David Jr. These models are the most effective ones on the market for creating the relaxation response, and they vary in price. They all offer the same profound relaxation experience, but differ in the number of preset programs and special applications offered.

The Core Relaxation Program Tape Series

We developed and produced this three-tape set to assist you in your relaxation practice. Tape 1 contains instructions for diaphragmatic breathing along with guided breathing exercises. Tape 2 promotes the development of the body wisdom of the peaceful warrior along with guided exercises for progressive relaxation. Tape 3 facilitates generalization of relaxation skills to your daily life via a double-induction hypnotic format. These tapes can also be used in conjunction with light and sound equipment.

Double-Induction Hypnotic Tapes

MindWorks carries a full line of Ericksonian hypnotic tapes and tape sets designed to facilitate relaxation, promote stress mastery, and achieve various self-help goals. Titles include:

Quick Stress Busters	Self-Hypnosis
Stress Management	Assertiveness
Natural Self-Confidence	Rapid Pain Control
Deep Sleep, Sweet Dreams	Weight Loss
Overcoming Procrastination	Getting Past Smoking

Changing Emotions—Overcoming Anxiety and Depression
Personal Ecology—the Complete Self-Esteem Program
Feeling Better—The Mind/Body Connections and Healing

If you are interested in getting more information or ordering any of these products, please call (305)232-MIND (6463) or write:

MindWorks, International, Inc.
15321 S. Dixie Hwy.
Suite 202
Miami, FL 33157

References

Alberti, R., Emmons, M. (1974). *Your Perfect Right*. San Luis Obispo, Calif.: Impact Press.

Allred, K. D., & Smith, T. W. (1989). "The Hardy Personality: Cognitive and Physiological Responses to Evaluative Threat." *Journal of Personality and Social Psychology* 56: 257–266.

Beck, A. T. (1970). "Cognitive Therapy: Nature and Relation to Behavior Therapy." *Behavior Therapy* 1: 84–200.

Benson, H. (1976). *The Relaxation Response*. New York: Avon Books.

Benson, H. (1985). *Beyond the Relaxation Response*. Berkeley, Calif.: Berkeley Books.

Bonner, R. L., & Rich, A. R. (1991). "Predicting Vulnerability to Hopelessness: A Longitudinal Analysis." *Journal of Nervous and Mental Disease* 179: 129–132.

Bourne, E. J. (1990). *The Anxiety and Phobia Workbook*. Oakland, Calif.: New Harbinger.

Bray, G. A. (1969). "Effects of Caloric Restriction on Energy Expenditure in Obese Patients." *Lancet* 2: 391–397.

Brehm, B. (1998). *Stress Management: Increasing Your Stress Resistance*. New York: Longman.

Brown, J. P. (1991). "Staying Fit and Staying Well: Physical Fitness as a Moderator of Life Stress." *Journal of Personality and Social Psychology* 60: 555–561.

Brownell, K. B., Marlatt, G. A., Lichtenstein, E., & Wilson, G. (1986). "Understanding and Preventing Relapse." *American Psychologist*, 41:765–782.

Brucato, L., & Abascal, J. (1990). *The Effects of Multiple Afferent Sensory Stimulation Enhanced Relaxation*. Unpublished manuscript.

Brucato, L., & Abascal, J. (1991). *Effects of M.A.S.S. Induced Relaxation as Related to Baseline Arousal Levels*. Unpublished manuscript.

Budzynski, T. (1991). *The Science of Light and Sound*. Unpublished manuscript.

Carpi, J. (1996). "Stress . . . It's Worse Than You Think." *Psychology Today* (January/February): 34–41, 74, 76.

Castaneda, C. (1998). *The Teachings of Don Juan: A Yaqui Way of Knowledge*. Berkeley: University of California Press.

Castaneda, C. (1991). *Journey to Ixtlan: The Lessons of Don Juan*. New York: Simon & Schuster.

Cohen, S., & Edwards, J. R. (1989). "Personality Characteristics as Moderators of the Relationship Between Stress and Disorder." In Neufeld, R. (Ed.), *Advances in the Investigation of Psychological Stress*. New York: Wiley.

Contrada, R. (1989). "Type A Behaviors, Personality Hardiness, and Cardiovascular Responses to Stress." *Journal of Personality and Social Psychology* 57: 895–903.

Cousins, N. (1981). *Anatomy of an Illness.* New York: Bantam Books.

Covey, S. (1989). *The Seven Habits of Highly Effective People.* New York: Simon & Schuster.

Covey, S., Merrill, A., & Merrill, R. (1994). *First Things First.* New York: Simon & Schuster.

Davis, A. (1965). *Let's Get Well.* New York: Harcourt, Brace & World.

Davis, M., Eshelman, E. R., & McKay, M. (1988). *The Relaxation and Stress Reduction Workbook.* Oakland, Calif.: New Harbinger.

deVries, H. A., Wiswell, R. A., Bulbulian, R., & Moritani, T. (1981). "Tranquilizer Effects of Exercise." *American Journal of Physical Medicine* 60: 57–66.

Ellis, A. (1975). *A New Guide to Rational Living.* North Hollywood, Calif.: Wilshire Books.

Ellis, A., & Harper, R. (1961). *A Guide to Rational Living.* North Hollywood, Calif.: Wilshire Books.

Ellis, A., & Knaus, W. J. (1977). *Overcoming Procrastination.* New York: Signet, New American Library.

Fensterheim, H., & Baer, J. (1975). *Don't Say Yes When You Want to Say No.* New York: David McKay.

Fixx, J. (1977). *The Complete Book of Running.* New York: Random House.

Flett, T. K., Blankstein, K. R., Hewitt, P. L., & Koledin, S. (1992). "Components of Perfectionism and Procrastination in College Students." *Social Behavior and Personality* 20: 85–94.

Freedberg, S. (1996). "Mounting Cost of White Collar Stress." *Miami Herald* (November 17), 1B.

Friedman, M., & Rosenman, R. H. (1974). *Type A Behavior and Your Heart.* New York: Knopf.

Goodman, D. (1974). *Emotional Well-Being through Rational Behavior Training.* Springfield, Ill.: Charles C. Thomas.

Gorman, M. O. (1999). "Handle Stress Like an Expert." *Readers Digest*, May: 98–102.

Gortmaker, S. L., Must, A., Perrin, J. M., Sobol, A. M., & Dietz, W. H. (1993). "Social and Economic Consequences of Overweight in Adolescence and Young Adulthood." *New England Journal of Medicine* 329: 1008–1012.

Holmes, D. S., & Roth, D. L. (1988). "Effects of Aerobic Exercise Training and Relaxation Training on Cardiovascular Activity during Psychological Stress." *Journal of Psychosomatic Research* 32: 469–474.

Holmes, T. H., & Rahe, R. H. (1967). "The Social Readjustment Rating Scale." *Journal of Psychosomatic Research* 11: 213–218.

Holt, P., Fine, M. J., & Tollefson, N. (1987). "Mediating Stress: Survival of the Hardy." *Psychology in the Schools* 24: 51–58.

Honzak, R. A., Veselkova, A., & Poslusny, Z. (1989). "Personality Traits and Neurohumoral Stress Response in Healthy Young Sportsmen." *Activitas Nervosa Superior* 31: 100–102.

Hutchinson, M. (1984). *The Book of Floating: Exploring the Private Sea.* New York: Morrow.

Hutchinson, M. (1986, 1991). *MegaBrain.* New York: Ballantine Books.

Hutchinson, M. (1994). *MegaBrain Power.* New York: Hyperion.

Jacobson, E. (1929, 1974). *Progressive Relaxation.* Chicago: University of Chicago Press, Midway Reprint.

Kobasa, S. C. (1979). "Stressful Life Events, Personality, and Health: An Inquiry into Hardiness." *Journal of Personality and Social Psychology* 37: 1–11.

Kobasa, S. C. (1982). "Commitment and Coping in Stress Resistance among Lawyers." *Journal of Personality and Social Psychology* 42: 707–717.

Kobasa, S. C. (1984). "How Much Stress Can You Survive?" *American Health* (September): 64–71.

Kobasa, S. C., Maddi, S. R., & Puccetti, M. C. (1982). "Personality and Exercise as Buffers in the Stress-Illness Relationship." *Journal of Behavioral Medicine* 5: 391–404.

Kramsch, D. M. (1981). "Reduction of Coronary Artherosclerosis by Moderate Conditioning Exercise in Monkeys on an Atherogenic Diet." *New England Journal of Medicine* 305: 1483–1489.

Lange, A., & Jakubowski, P. (1976). *Responsible Assertive Behavior.* Champaign, Ill.: Research Press.

Lawler, K. A., & Schmied, L. A. (1987). "The Relationship of Stress, Type A Behavior, and Powerlessness to Physiological Responses in Female Clerical Workers." *Journal of Psychosomatic Research* 31: 555–563.

Leveille, G. (1985). *The Setpoint Diet.* New York: Random House.

Lick, J. R., & Heffler, D. (1977). "Relaxation Training and Attention Placebo in the Treatment of Severe Insomnia." *Journal of Consulting and Clinical Psychology* 45: 153–161.

Loehr, J. E., & Migdow, J. A. (1986). *Take a Deep Breath.* New York: Villard Books.

Long, B. C. (1984) "Aerobic Conditioning and Stress Inoculation: A Comparison of Stress Management Interventions." *Cognitive Therapy and Research* 8: 517–542.

Manning, M. R., Williams, R. F., & Wolfe, D. M. (1988). "Hardiness and the Relationship between Stressors and Outcomes." *Work and Stress* 2: 205–216.

Marshall, V. R. (1999). "Stress at Work Is Risky Business." *AFSCME: Public Employee* (May): 6–9.

McCann, I. L., & Holmes, D. S. (1984). "Influence of Aerobic Exercise on Depression." *Journal of Personality and Social Psychology* 46: 1142–1147.

McGilley, B. M., & Holmes, D. S. "Aerobic Fitness Response to Psychological Stress." *Journal of Research on Personality* 22: 129–139.

McGuigan, F. L. (1984). "Progressive Relaxation: Origins, Principles and Clinical Applications." In Woolfolk, R. L., & Lehrer, P. M. (Eds.), *Principles and Practices of Stress Management.* New York: Guilford Press.

McKay, M., Davis, M., & Fanning, P. (1981). *Thoughts and Feelings: The Art of Cognitive Stress Intervention.* Oakland, Calif.: New Harbinger.

Miller, A. (1988). "Stress on the Job." *Newsweek* (April): 40–45.

Miller, N. E. (1985). "Rx: Biofeedback." *Psychology Today* (February): 54–59.

Milman, D. (1991). *Sacred Journey of the Peaceful Warrior.* Tiburn, Calif.: H. J. Kramer.

Morris, (1953). "Coronary Heart Disease and Physical Activity at Work." *Lancet* 2: 1053–1057, 1111–1120.

Nowack, K. M. (1989). "Coping Style, Cognitive Hardiness, and Health Status." *Journal of Behavioral Medicine* 12: 145–158.

Osterkamp, L., & Press, A. (1988). *Stress? Find Your Balance.* Lawrence, Kans.: Preventive Measures.

Paffenbarger, R. S., Hyde, R. T., Wing, A. L., & Hsieh, C. C. (1986). "Physical Activity, All Cause Mortality, and Longevity of College Alumni." *New England Journal of Medicine* 314: 605–612.

Phelps, S., & Austin, N. (1987). *The Assertive Woman.* Calif.: Impact Press.

Premack, D. (1965). "Reinforcement Theory." In Levine, D. (Ed.) *Nebraska Symposium on Motivation.* Lincoln, Neb.: University of Nebraska Press.

Pritchett, P., & Pound, R. (1996). *A Survival Guide to the Stress of Organizational Change.* Dallas, Tex.: Pritchett & Associates.

Rhodewalt, F., & Zone, J. B. (1989). "Appraisal of Life Change, Depression, and Illness in Hardy and Non-Hardy Women." *Journal of Personality and Social Psychology* 56: 81–88.

Rossi, E. (1986). *The Psychobiology of Mind-Body Healing.* New York: Norton.

Roth, D. L., & Holmes, D. S. (1987). "Influences of Aerobic Exercise Training and Relaxation Training on Physical and Psychological Health Following Stressful Life Events." *Psychosomatic Medicine* 49: 355–365.

Roth, D. L., Weibe, D. J., Fillingian, R. B., & Shay, K. A. (1989). "Life Events, Fitness, Hardiness, and Health: A Simultaneous Analysis of Proposed Stress-Resistance Effects." *Journal of Personality and Social Psychology* 57: 136–142.

Rotter, J. (1966). "Generalized Expectancies for Internal vs. External Locus of Control of Reinforcement." *Psychological Monographs: General and Applied* 80 (Whole No. 609).

Schultz, S. (1999). "Why We're Fat." *U.S. News & World Report* (November): 82–85.

Scott, D. (1980). *How to Put More Time in Your Life.* New York: Rawson, Wade.

Seaward, B. L. (1997). *Managing Stress.* Boston: Jones & Bartlett.

Seligman, M. (1991). *Learned Optimism.* New York: Knopf.

Selye, H. (1956). *The Stress of Life.* New York: McGraw-Hill.

Selye, H. (1974). *Stress without Distress.* New York: Dutton.

Selye, H. (1982). "History and Present Status of the Stress Concept." In Goldberg, L. & Breznitz, S. (Eds.), *Handbook of Stress: Theoretical and Clinical Aspects.* New York: Free Press.

Shapiro, L. (1997). "Is Fat That Bad?" *Newsweek* (April): 58–64.

Sheppard, J. A., & Kashani, J. H. (1991). "The Relationship of Hardiness, Gender, and Stress to Health Outcomes in Adolescents." *Journal of Personality* 59: 747–768.

Smith, M. (1975). *When I Say No, I Feel Guilty.* New York: Dial Press.

Sonstroem, R.. J. (1984). "Exercise and Self-Esteem." *Exercise and Sport Sciences Review* 12: 123–155.

Stamford, B. (1995). "The Role of Exercise in Fighting Depression." *Physician and Sports Medicine* 23: 79–80.

Taylor, T. E. (1983). *Learning Studies for Higher Cognitive Levels in a Short-Term Sensory Isolation Environment.* Paper delivered at first International Conference on REST and Self Regulation, Denver, Colorado.

Thayer, R. E. (1987). "Energy, Tiredness, and Tension Effects of a Sugar Snack vs. Moderate Exercise." *Journal of Personality and Social Psychology* 52: 119–125.

Underwood. A., & Kalb, C. (1999). "Stress." *Newsweek* (June): 56–63.

Weil, A. (1995). *Spontaneous Healing.* New York: Knopf.

Yerkes, R. M., & Dodson, J. D. (1998). "The Relation of Strength of Stimulus to Rapidity of Habit Formation." *Journal of Comparative and Neurological Psychology* 18: 459–482.

Index